WOMEN AT WAR

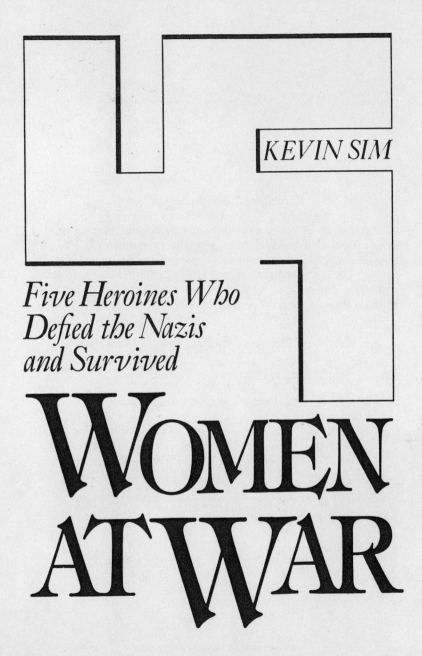

KEVIN SIM

*Five Heroines Who
Defied the Nazis
and Survived*

WOMEN AT WAR

William Morrow and Company, Inc.   New York   1982

Library of Congress Cataloging in Publication Data

Sim, Kevin.
    Women at war.

    Based on the British television series, Women
of courage.
    1. World War, 1939-1945—Women. 2. World War,
1939-1945—Prisoners and prisons, German. 3. World
War, 1939-1945—Biography. 4. Women—Europe—
Biography. I. Women of courage (Television program)
II. Title.
D810.W7S53   1982   940.53'15'042   82-8092
ISBN 0-688-01324-4   AACR2

Printed in the United States of America

First Edition

1 2 3 4 5 6 7 8 9 10

BOOK DESIGN BY PATTY LOWY

To Jill, Hannah, and Sam

Acknowledgments

This book would not have been possible without the help of literally hundreds of people from more than a dozen countries in Europe and North America. For many of them, it involved reopening the most difficult and painful areas of the past, and I should like to thank them all for their patience and kindness.

To my colleagues in Yorkshire Television, I owe a great debt of gratitude—especially to Barbara Twigg whose researches took her from Norway to Jerusalem and the Caucasus to California. The project was conceived in the offices of John Fairley and benefited throughout from his support and encouragement as well as that of Michael Deakin. My co-producer, Peter Morley, brought to the series his many years of experience directing documentary films for British television, and the camera team of Frank Pocklington, Alan Wilson, Mike Donnelly, Kevin Quirk and Jane Stewart added, along with expertise and great commitment, a sense of fun to the whole enterprise. The manuscript was deciphered and typed by Carole Sedler and Kate Rutter.

To my wife, Jill, there must be special thanks. Her criticisms were always helpful and often essential. Her

7

warm support throughout my long, private war with the typewriter was indispensable.

Finally, to Kitty Hart, Hiltgunt Zassenhaus, Maria Rutkiewicz, Mary Lindell and Sigrid Lund no thanks can be great enough. This book, I hope, will be testimony to my admiration for them and for the people of the Resistance. I have tried to serve them well. The stories in the book are theirs. The errors and omissions are mine alone.

—KEVIN SIM

WOMEN AT WAR

Prologue

Wer die Wahl hat, hat die Qual.
He who has choice, has torment.

—GERMAN PROVERB

Today in Paris, Mary Lindell takes her dog, Tommy, for his daily walk in the Bois de Boulogne. It is sixty-three years since the *Daily Mail* announced that she had been killed on the Western Front during the First World War. It is thirty-eight years since the announcement that she had been shot by the Nazis in the Second World War. In Oslo, Sigrid Lund visits her son and his family. In Warsaw, Maria Rutkiewicz goes to the Palace of Culture and Science to see a new play designed by her daughter. In Baltimore, Hiltgunt Zassenhaus works her way through another waiting room full of patients, and in Birmingham, Kitty Hart does her exercises in the garden shed.

In 1943 it would not have been possible for one person to have discovered what was happening to these women.

Mary Lindell had been shot in the neck and the skull by SS guards as she tried to escape from the express taking her to execution in Paris.

Sigi Lund and her family were marching across the icy lakes of southern Norway to escape over the border into Sweden.

Maria Rutkiewicz had given birth to her twins in the

9

Gestapo headquarters in Warsaw and had been told she would be shot within a week.

Hiltgunt Zassenhaus was in Hamburg, caught in the world's first firestorm.

And Kitty Hart, aged sixteen, was on her way to Auschwitz.

People who began the Second World War as young men and women are already starting to die of old age. Children are being born whose grandparents are too young to have known anything of the war.

It has become history, like any other war. Yet in a curious way the Second War demands attention different in kind from that given to most other historical events. Kaiser Wilhelm, Von Hindenburg, Ludendorff —these are historical personalities. For the man in the street their masks are hardened and well set; for historians the enigmas of their motives and behaviour are the proper material of academic debate. Hitler, Himmler, Heydrich, Goebbels, Goering, Eichmann, Bormann, Frank, Ribbentrop, Hess—this is not a roll call of historical personalities at all. These are creatures of demonology and myth.

The Second World War has always been seen as something different. Different, that is, from a conflict like the Great War, which, awful and tragic though it was, had by 1939 already come to be seen as a traditional slogging match among rival European nations whose industrial experience over the previous century had enabled them to contemplate destruction on an unprecedented scale. Hitler's war, by contrast, was seen as the first confrontation between radically different values since ancient times.

The Nazis were ruthless, but they were not hypocritical. This made them very difficult to deal with. People with different sets of values from one's own are frighten-

ing, and they become more frightening the more different their values and beliefs are. In the case of the Nazis,
the difficulty was compounded because it was hard to tell
where their differences began or to distinguish between
the admirable and the intimidating. It was easier and
certainly more reassuring to believe that behind the
ideological posturing they were really just like everybody else, that their extraordinary claims and demands
were made on behalf of ordinary political goals. After all,
they were, as we were, heirs to a great Christian and
humanitarian tradition, and not savages. The ambiguity
surrounding their intentions was a great asset. It meant
that not only did the Big Lie work because people
wanted to believe it; but that the Big Truth also worked
because no one wanted to believe it. So the Nazis told the
world about their territorial ambitions; and they told the
world about what they were going to do to the Jews and
nobody believed them.

And if Hitler's explicit international aims, and the
Nazis' overt eagerness for, and glorification of, war led
to the rapid rearmament of the thirties and eventually to
war; the equally explicit demands of their racist ideology
led to something far more sinister—systematic terror.

The war itself—that is to say, the fighting between
soldiers—makes easy history. It can be looked at and
analyzed in the same way as other wars. Rommel at
Alamein drew up his battle lines in a manner that would
have been familiar to any general on the Western Front
in the First World War; the Germans' blitzkrieg tactics,
the use of their highly mobile panzer divisions emanated
from the work of B. H. Liddell-Hart and J. F. C. Fuller,
British veterans of the First World War. In other words,
although in military terms the conflict may have been
innovatory, it was also a conventional struggle between
armies marshalled in ways familiar to both sides. The
German Army was a subculture within the Nazi state

which by and large stuck to the internationally accepted rules of the game. When soldiers were taken prisoner they went to prisoner-of-war camps, not concentration camps. At least this was the experience of the Western Allies.

But the Nazi terror was different, and does not sleep easily in history. It is awake all over Europe wherever the Nazis have been, and, even more startlingly, where they were excluded. There is a component of this terror which is independent of time or space or the numberless cruelties of which it is comprised. It horrifies and fascinates at the same time.

What is the Second World War? It is the modern invention of terror. The Allies destroyed the Nazi armies but they did not—could not—eradicate the *idea* of terror. This was the Nazis' lasting achievement: They demonstrated that all we had imagined standing between us and bestiality—our laws, our humanity, our civilization and our basic decency—could not be trusted if the issue was forced to the point. They mobilized each man's worst fears of what could happen to him and his family —fears which had hitherto served as the inspiration only for apocalyptic visions of purgatory and hell—and exploited them as a tool for social control. In doing so, they swept away forever the curtain between hell and everyday life.

Hitler, Himmler, Heydrich . . . there exists in the recitation of their names a living element of terror. Auschwitz, Dachau, Buchenwald, Treblinka, Gestapo, SS . . . the chill we feel is a reflection of this terror, a reminder of what it made possible.

German military strength was directed against enemy armies. Terror was a weapon against individuals. Its purpose was to eliminate not only individual action and criticism against the state but also any anti-Nazi thoughts or consciousness. From the first, Nazi leaders were clear and open about this. "There is no longer to be any private life in Germany," said Himmler. "The only private life for a person is when he is asleep."

Reinhard Heydrich, arguing for greater powers for the secret police as opposed to the ordinary branch, wrote in a memo: "Undoubtedly, however, the total and permanent police coverage of all men within the Reich and the resulting possibility of keeping check on the situation of each individual must be with that police authority responsible not only for executive security measures but also for security in relation to ideological and other aspects of life."*

Even a man like Hans Frank, willing to sign away the lives of thousands of Polish intellectuals for *raisons d'état*, was concerned at the direction in which Nazi arbitrary and ruthless power was heading. He wrote (on August 28, 1942):

> Unfortunately, the view appears to be growing, even among leading National Socialists, that the greater the uncertainty regarding the legal position of ordinary citizens, the more secure is the position of the authorities. Arbitrary use of police power is now so general that it is not too much to say that the individual citizen has lost all rights in law.... As things are today, when any citizen can be consigned to a concentration camp for any length of time without any possibility of redress, when there is no longer any security of life, freedom, honour or honestly earned possessions, it is my firm conviction that any ethical relationship between the leadership of the state and its citizens is being totally destroyed.†

---

*Quoted from "The SS—Instrument of Domination" by Hans Buccheim in *The Anatomy of the SS State*, eds. Helmut Krausnick, Hans Buccheim, Martin Broszat and Hans-Adolf Jacobsen (Collins, 1968).

†Buccheim et al. op. cit.

If this was the perception of "the Butcher of Poland," a man who at another time had mused, "Humanity is a word that one doesn't often dare to use, as though it has become a foreign word," what then could have been the interpretation of the "ordinary citizen"? And if this was the truth for Germans, what was the situation of those in other countries who found themselves under German control and for whom no "ethical relationship" was deemed necessary or desirable?

At least in Germany the Nazi rulers depended ultimately upon some ultimate consent from the people. The Führer and the Party were after all acting *in the name of the German people* or *as executors of the will of the German people*. If Germans no longer had "any security of life, freedom, honour," what of those people whom the Nazis held to be of as little consequence as lice and vermin? Here terror replaced every form of social attachment. It was not merely a substitute for a legal and ethical relationship between the state and its citizens, but permeated the space among individuals themselves.

The machinery of terror operated in different ways in different places. Nazi rule was seldom subtle, but it was understood that there was one way to behave in, say, Denmark, a country destined to become part of a racially pure "Great Germanic Empire," and Poland, whose population was earmarked as "a people of leaderless slave labourers." In such circumstances even terror knows discretion.

There were other considerations too. In some occupied countries there were Quisling governments willing —sometimes eager—to work with the Nazis. Not all the inhabitants of western Europe found themselves in the position of the Jews, or the Gypsies, or, after 1941, the Communists, towards whom the Nazi terror had a limited and generally fatal range of response. In general, people were offered a choice: collaboration (or at least acquiescence) or terror; and although many, maybe most, could go a long way without actually having to make the choice, the experience of most countries seems to show that as the war went on, people of conscience had to make their minds up one way or the other.

The importance of this choice is that it was demanded of so many people, and that once the nature of the question was apparent, *there was no way to avoid answering it.* Not to answer meant, in effect, acquiescence and passivity in the face of the destruction of all one's values. This, of course, is exactly what the Nazis wanted, for if the object of propaganda is to confuse the issue, to allow a little more scope for the conquerors' arguments, the object of terror is to paralyze with fear the ability to think at all.

Intimidation, a sense of menace, was experienced in different ways. Sometimes indirectly, as in the case of Dr. Carl Stromberger, who helped Hiltgunt Zassenhaus in her work for Scandinavian prisoners. He felt anxiety at the sheer pervasiveness of the regime.

"I think it is very difficult for anyone who does not know this feeling to imagine it. This feeling of oppression and fear—it is important to have felt it, not just to have heard the words, to understand what it means for a man. It began when you stepped out of the house and it ceased only when you had closed the door behind you. . . .

"You lived always under suspicion, and had the feeling that anyone who didn't like you could do you harm.

"I will give you a little example of how such a common feeling was spread. We lost—we had to lose—the personal greeting in the morning, or even in letters, and instead this funny thing 'Heil Hitler' was introduced and replaced the greetings between people. And this name, Hitler, came into the mind every day, everyone had to say 'Heil Hitler,' so this name was always in the brain; it was very difficult to think. This diabolic sort of greeting and the loss of freedom were connected, the minds of people deteriorated and so almost every decision to act, to do something was paralyzed. This was the background against which all other things developed."

In other cases terror was far more straightforward. Kitty Hart was twelve years old when she saw German troops for the first time on the streets of Lublin in Poland.

"At first I thought they were tremendous, with their smart uniforms and their polished boots all the way up to the knees. I would go down to the center of the city to see them marching.

"Then one day I was with my friend, a boy of about fourteen. We saw two German officers walking towards us on the pavement. Now there was this rule that when you met Germans you had to get off the pavement. And somehow, I got this idea of danger, so I stepped off the pavement. But my friend didn't. And one of these soldiers got out his pistol and shot him straight through the head, and he just fell down dead.

"And that was the first time I realized that they were out to get people like me. . . ."

The difference between these two perceptions lies in the fact that the first originates in Germany and the second in Poland. Nazi terror was dispensed as required, except when directed against those "alien races that are no longer needed." In answer to a newspaper correspondent who had asked him about the difference between the Nazi rule in Bohemia and Moravia and that in Poland, Hans Frank replied: "I can tell you a graphic difference. In Prague, for example, big red posters were put up on which could be read that seven Czechs had been shot today. I said to myself: If I put up a poster for every seven Poles shot, the forests of Poland would not be sufficient to manufacture the paper for such posters."

The inhumanities of the Nazis were reflexive. Their

impact can be judged by the effect on the perpetrators themselves. One of the reasons given for the experiment of gas chambers was the effect the mass shootings were having on the ranks of the specially composed *Einsatzgruppen*. Nazi leaders recognized that the pitilessness, cruelty and sheer scale of their excesses could not be carried out or even witnessed without a quite unusual degree of hardness, and the inculcation of this "hardness" became a keynote in the training of SS recruits. In an infamous speech made to the SS leaders at Poznan, Himmler declared: "Most of you know what it means to have seen a hundred corpses lying together, five hundred or a thousand. To have gone through this and yet—apart from a few exceptions, examples of human weakness—to have remained decent, this has made us hard. . . ."

The *Kommandant* of the Ravensbrück concentration camp showed a visitor to the camp the scarred leg of one of the women used for medical experiments. It was, he said, *schrecklich*—horrifying.

It was not that the Nazis themselves had no conception of compassion or humanity but that these "weaknesses" were put aside in deference to some higher objective reality.

Of Reinhard Heydrich, Joachim Fest has written, in *The Face of the Third Reich:*

> His pessimistic and thwarted outlook on life was at the bottom of his idea that men were base, worldly and selfish but also easily deceived. He seemed curiously incapable of understanding unselfish attitudes, and his deep-seated conviction of the total impotence of morality persuaded him that power could only be achieved by understanding and exploiting the meaner side of human nature.*

---

*Joachim Fest, *The Face of the Third Reich* (Weidenfeld and Nicholson, 1970).

This Nazi reality had little time for the scruples of legal or moral codes. The old humanitarian standards were sham values easily exposed by the application of force. Individual conscience had little relevance in a society which believed that the basic unit of consciousness was the State or Race or *Volk*. Individuals' perception of fear was more profound than the perception of right or wrong, the Nazis argued. It was an article of faith that idealists or intellectuals would not have the spunk to fight.

In 1941, when the Germans had successfully conquered all of continental Europe, and the Russian armies were rolling back before the onslaught of Operation Barbarossa, there must have been tremendous force in these arguments. And yet all over Europe the women whose stories make up this book had already taken the decision to step out of the crowd and into active resistance. Already each one of them had appreciated the true nature of the terror. They all knew what the consequences of their choice would be for themselves and their families.

Most books about the Second World War have been written by people actually involved in some aspects of the fighting. For them the question, Why fight the Nazis? might appear curious—even naïve. But the television series upon which this book is based was made largely by a team which was too young to have had any experience of the war itself. We grew up in its shadow with impressions that swung from legend to nightmare: from the Battle of Britain to the Gestapo. During this period the war became a new quarry of mythical material as rich in heroes, monsters and epic adventure as classical mythology. It became a paradigm of the struggle between good and evil, which is why from the African bush to Palestinian refugee camps you can hear guerrillas justifying their struggle in terms of "our finest hour" or of "standing alone." But the great difference between the modern and ancient myths is that many of those who fought in the cosmic struggle of the twentieth century are still around. Another important distinction is that the protagonists in ancient conflicts have a noticeable tendency towards the godlike. It is an uncomfortable characteristic of modern war that it confronts ordinary mortals with epic experience. When the war finished, these people, those of them who survived, the protagonists and eyewitnesses of the modern *Iliads, Odysseys* and Descents into the Underworld, returned to their anonymous and ordinary lives in the cities and countrysides of Europe and America. And that is where, if you like, you can go and speak to them.

Our first thought was to find women from different countries who had had "an interesting war" and who could throw different perspectives on the course of the war in their homelands. We wanted to know how the reality matched up with the myth; what life was really like under the Occupation; what it felt like when you were waiting to be interrogated by the Gestapo.

There were two main limitations to our choice, both dictated by the filming but both in the circumstances severe enough: Our women should be alive and they should be able to speak English.

Many we spoke to, many remarkable women, could not communicate well in English. They testify to the thousands whose incredible experiences remain unrecorded. Some were old and ill—it is, after all, forty years since the events took place. Others, among them very, very brave women, were too diffident to appear on film or were afraid that their stories would be somehow traduced: They feared most of all being presented as heroines.

Those we chose came from different countries and different classes. They differed in their beliefs and

ideologies. One or two were very old, the others in vigorous middle life. Some were celebrated, others unrecog-
nized. Some had helped escaping airmen, others had
assassinated Gestapo generals. Many had been imprisoned, tortured and sent to concentration camps; others
had escaped.

What they had in common was this: Given the choice,
they had all made the decision to resist. It had been a
clear choice. Throughout occupied Europe people
planned for the future; life-insurance agents continued
to collect weekly premiums. On a more or less depleted
level life went on—and to a greater or lesser extent from
country to country that is what people opted for.

In France they even had a word for it—*attentisme:*
waiting to see what happens and surviving in the meantime. For the majority, for most of the war, the answer
to the question, Why fight the Nazis? was, Why indeed!

Those who, as the women in this book did, chose to do
something, did so for all kinds of reasons. But wherever
and however that decision was taken, up until 1941 there
was a common thread: It was a choice made completely
against the logic of events.

So we return to the question, Why?

Why did they turn down the chance of a quiet life?

Why were they prepared to sacrifice themselves and
their families in the service of a cause whose victory was
by no means certain?

What was the nature of their convictions that made
them immune to either the blandishments of Nazi propaganda or the menaces of Nazi terror?

What gave them the strength to endure as their children were taken away by the Gestapo, or as they themselves were faced with interrogations or concentration
camps?

The responses to these questions came not so much as
answers but as revelations. We had grown up with the

idea that Nazism had bankrupted European civilization, that when faced by the barbarism and inhumanity of the Nazis, our culture had somehow complied. ". . . A fair proportion of the intelligentsia and of the institutions of European civilisation," writes George Steiner in *In Bluebeard's Castle*, "letters, the academy, the performing arts —met inhumanity with varying degrees of welcome. Nothing in the next-door world of Dachau impinged on the great winter cycle of Beethoven chamber music played in Munich. No canvases came off the museum walls as the butchers strolled past, guide-books in hand."*

We live, Professor Steiner argues, in a "post-culture": The damage done to our civilization is irreparable. If this is true, then the Nazi view of "the total impotence or morality" has prevailed, and the questions posed by terror, as an instrument of this view, have remained unanswered.

And yet, in Paris, Warsaw, Hamburg, Birmingham and Baltimore, the women whose stories make up this book offer a testimony that confounds pessimism. They all had different reasons for doing what they did, but across the curtain of darkness that the Nazis threw over our century their voices provide a continuity with decent, simple, humane values that had appeared to have been lost. If Nazism has widened our perception of the depravity of which mankind is capable, these women expand our understanding of what individuals—even in the worst and most oppressed circumstances—can aspire to and endure.

---

*George Steiner, *In Bluebeard's Castle* (Faber & Faber, 1971).

Mary Lindell

The spring of 1940. From London events on the Continent are too bewildering and sad to contemplate. Poland has been defeated; Denmark, Norway, Holland and Belgium overrun; France is about to fall. Late on the fine and sunny afternoon of June 4, an English journalist and politician whom Hitler calls "the vilest agitator of them all" prepares to address the House of Commons. Around him are MPs from both the major parties who until quite recently would have endorsed the view of the German Führer. As recently as January his speeches have been criticized, by one of his friends, as "too rhetorical . . . too belligerent for this pacifist age," reminding people "of a heroism they do not feel." Just over a month ago the gossips in Whitehall were whispering that his "drive and initiative have been undermined by his legend of recklessness." But now that seems in the distant past, before the real war started, before Hitler's armies had struck west into the heart of France. Now as he raises his familiar huddled and circular figure to its feet, his fellow MPs cannot fail to be aware of the transformation in his stature. Beside him the former Prime Minister, Neville Chamberlain, appears "timid and fragile." Fierce and indomitable, he begins one of the most famous speeches in parliamentary history: ". . . we shall fight on the beaches, we shall fight on the landing grounds, we shall fight in the fields and in the streets, we shall fight in the hills; we shall never surrender. . . ."

Harold Nicolson wrote afterwards in his diary that it was the finest speech he had ever heard. "The House was deeply moved." Several Labour members cried. Winston Churchill had discovered his hour at last. One or two of those present could not help noticing that he appeared to be enjoying it. "There is always the quite inescapable suspicion that he loves war," wrote Sir Henry (Chips) Channon a few days later, "war which broke Neville Chamberlain's better heart!"

"There are those who, inhibited by the furniture of the ordinary world, come to life only when they feel themselves actors on a stage," wrote Isaiah Berlin in *Mr. Churchill in 1940.* The cataclysm of the beautiful June days of 1940 offered that opportunity to many besides Churchill. A few—like him—had been waiting for it for a long time.

From her apartment near the Bois de Boulogne in the smart XVIème Arrondissement in Paris, Mary Lindell, an Englishwoman married to a French count, followed the collapse of the great French army without attempting to hide her feelings. Many years in France had sharpened her sense of her own Englishness to the point of eccentricity, and she watched the growing panic in Paris with haughty and open contempt. The four years she had spent in the Great War nursing French soldiers on the Western Front had left her with a Croix de Guerre for gallantry and a lingering taste for adventure. Peacetime had been a disappointment. Being young, rich, beautiful and something of a heroine, she had had little difficulty in marrying the Comte de Milleville. In the twenties and thirties they brought up their children and threw themselves into society, where Mary lost no opportunity to remind the French that in any biological scale of values they occupied a place considerably below the English. Among the *gens du monde* of Paris, where patriotism had become simply *démodé*, she was considered *un peu chauvine*. By the end of the 1930s, she had long realized that marriage alone could not satisfy her. When Britain declared war on Germany on September 3, 1939, it was just what she had been waiting for. "Well, Mother," her children had joked, after listening to Chamberlain's broadcast on the radio, "now you can go to war."

In the beginning the war too was a disappointment. She had volunteered immediately for the French Red Cross and had been turned down. Instead of being on active service, she had been forced to spend the phony war—or the *drôle de guerre*, as the French called the first winter of curious inaction—at home, frustrated, reading in her newspaper how her well-intentioned friends from Parisian society had formed a committee to send roses to brighten up the Maginot Line.

By June 1940 the Maginot Line had proved about as useful as the roses.

France was in panic. The Army had been broken. The British had been lucky to escape at Dunkirk. There was nothing left to save Paris from the Germans. The roads swelled with refugees. Whole populations of villages, towns and cities had just taken to their heels. Many had no food, no transport, no shelter and nowhere to go. Their condition was pitiful. In Paris there were disgraceful scenes as people were trampled to death at railway stations; and bicycles, wagons and petrol changed hands at ludicrous prices. Everywhere streets emptied, shutters went up. "I have the feeling that what we are seeing here in Paris is the complete breakdown of French society," reported William Shirer, the CBS correspondent. "It is almost too tremendous to contemplate." A six-year-old boy from Trouville remembered it another way: "Forty million Frenchmen were shitting in their pants at the same time."

June 13. Mary waited in Paris. An oily black cloud from the burning petrol refineries outside the city rolled over the deserted streets and shut out the sun. The first Germans were only hours away. For Mary running away was unthinkable. Since Dunkirk she had known there was a job to do in Paris which would begin only when the Germans had arrived. Edith Cavell had done it in the First War. Now it was her turn. It was as though she had heard another, less well-known part of Churchill's great speech on June 4, in which he had spoken of those Englishmen who hadn't got away from Dunkirk: "We have had a large number of wounded come home safely to this country, but I would say about the missing that there may be very many reported missing who will come back home, some day, in one way or another."

On June 15, Hitler arrived in Paris to savour his victory. Within a month there was a high-ranking officer of the Welsh Guards hiding in Mary's flat: Already she was smuggling stranded British servicemen out of occupied France.

For twenty years, like Churchill, she had been "too belligerent for this pacifist age." As he had, she had reminded people of a heroism they preferred to forget. The single, organizing principle which ruled her life was simple, uncomplicated and unfashionable: a patriotism so strong and so biting that it could be felt by all who came near her. It was what she lived for, fought for, was arrested and interrogated for, was sent to a concentration camp for, and what to the very end she was prepared to die for. In the polite and knowing Parisian society in which she moved it could not have been taken very seriously. But for the time being polite society had been swept away like the rest of France. Only Mary remained, and she—with the country she loved—would fight alone. Her hour too had come at last, and she was determined to enjoy it.

In 1895, when Mary Lindell was born, Great Britain was the most powerful nation on earth. The Union Jack flew over one fifth of the world's surface and almost a quarter of the world's population found themselves under British rule. It was the height of empire, and Mary was born into a family rich enough to enjoy all the benefits of empire. The family, says Mary, was simply stinking with money. Her father had money; her mother had money; and from the age of fifteen, when her grandfather died, Mary had a nice little lot of money too. "I suppose that is why I've become arrogant and independent—because from the age of fifteen I never knew what money was, it was just there."

It was a commonplace of the imperial age that if privilege had its rewards, it also had its duties.

Mary discovered hers in August 1914. In London, Paris and Berlin cheering crowds were celebrating the outbreak of war as a victory for the human spirit, a triumph over the dull mediocrity and routine of peace. The Germans were promised *ein frisch und fröhlicher Krieg;* the French were told that the new German bullets didn't really hurt; and the English that God had blessed them with this hour. The old world, the golden age of Edwardian England, marched off to war without a care. Mary at nineteen was a spirited young woman used to having her own way. She was not going to miss it.

She volunteered to join the V.A.D.s, the Voluntary Aid Detachment. It was not the happiest start to the war. But Mary's own account does not attempt to conceal the fact that she was not the easiest recruit to deal with.

"The matron didn't like me. She was quite right—I didn't like her either. She put me to lighting the fires and of course I didn't have the remotest idea of lighting a fire, and so the soldiers used to jump out of bed and say, 'Get out of the way, miss, we'll do it,' and they used to light the fire. So they put me into emptying the pots—which I didn't like. She hated me! So then she gave me the bedpans and I put them to wash under the bath water, which was much easier. Then she came in and said, 'Do you think that's washing a bedpan?'

"So I got the old brush and said, 'No, but you'll learn what it is to wash your old face!' And I gave her a good old smudge with the brush.

"And of course I was put in prison for that—hitting a superior officer."

Thus ended a short and undistinguished career with the V.A.D.s. But Mary was determined to reach the Western Front and her family had the means and the connections to indulge her. Strings were pulled in Paris; the family funded a ward of forty beds at a French army field station, and Mary was permitted to join the Secours aux Blessés Militaires. By late 1914 she was on the Western Front. She remained there for the next four years, known to the injured French soldiers as the Bébé Anglaise. Her 1918 citation for the Croix de Guerre reads: ". . . for days and nights without number she helped to save the lives of hundreds of wounded in the face of constant bombardment. . . ." It goes on to describe how she evacuated a field station under fire, dodging the shelling and enemy fire in no-man's-land. By the time she was reunited with her unit, she had been reported missing.

The *Daily Mail* in London went further—it reported her dead.

What had started so unpromisingly had ended splendidly. Mary had had a "good war." Even today, over sixty years later, she recalls these incidents with undiminished relish. They represent the Lindell style: the English V.A.D.—stubborn, quick-tempered, with scant regard for authority; and the French nurse—capable, caring, resolute and absolutely fearless. A curious very English mixture of bloody-mindedness and integrity, designed not so much to please as to impress. It was a style that represented true substance; a style which could not hope to find full expression in the twenty years that followed the armistice of 1918, but which reemerged in 1940 as intact and effective as ever.

Mary was forty-five when she began her Second World War. By then she was the Comtesse de Milleville, a mother of three teen-age children, who preserved only a distant, sparring relationship with her husband, the Comte de Milleville. She had a flat in Paris, a motorcar, contacts throughout France and immense self-confidence. With these, and no other resources, she began to organize her escape line.

From the beginning, Mary's approach was unconventional. It is a sensible and generally observed rule of underground activity that leaders should be inconspicuous, that individual members should be as little known to one another as possible, and that security is always an overriding consideration; in other words, that discretion is the better part of valour. Nobody ever doubted Mary's valour, but many worried about her discretion.

"My mother," remembers Maurice de Milleville, "is a fairly outspoken person. She's terrifically plucky but in some ways her courage is sometimes dangerous. She'd go out into the street and order people around. Get into this car, Get this, Do this, Do that—speaking in English when it was fairly obvious that any German going by would hear you speaking English and wonder." Mary considered such behaviour as confidence-inspiring propaganda. All the same, flamboyance was a rare trademark in the Resistance.

In the early days Mary had no time for the painstaking safeguards of more carefully organized clandestine operations. Stragglers from Dunkirk were arriving every day, wandering aimlessly around Paris with nowhere to go. Something had to be done at once, and Mary improvised her escape line from what was closest to hand—her children and their friends. The security arrangements were of necessity rough-and-ready.

"I really had a very special ceremony in the flat because I didn't want the wrong people to get over to England. I had to be sure that (a) they really wanted to go over to fight, and (b) there wasn't some clever Alec coming in to give you a trip.

"I had a tray of earth which they had to swear on. It was British earth which I'd got from the embassy garden. (Although it was occupied and closed by the Germans, I'd managed to get in—you can always get in with a little money!) Everybody had to put their hand on this earth and swear—I forget what it was they had to swear, I think we brought God into it—that they wanted to go to England and fight.

"If they didn't, well, they were just shoved out and that was the end of it.

"I was lucky, I never got anybody who didn't want to go. There were French—I sent a tremendous lot of French over, and, of course, the British. . . ."

Such an organization could survive in the early days, while the Gestapo were still finding their way around the Métro. But nothing about it inspired confidence in a long future.

The armistice between France and Germany was concluded on June 22. Its terms were hard and the circumstances humiliating. Hitler had insisted that the signing take place at Compiègne to the north of Paris in the same railway compartment in which Germany had capitulated in 1918. France was to be divided. In the north and along the Atlantic coast, the Germans would rule as the occupying power. In central and southern France, a

French government, under Marshal Pétain, would govern a truncated nation with limited autonomy. In addition, the French were to pay the cost of the army which was occupying their own soil. The document was signed at ten to seven in the evening. Shortly afterwards it began to rain.

The first German soldier arrived in Paris on a motorcycle. It was not long before he was followed by what Churchill called "the dull brute mass of the ordinary German army." The Parisians—at first conspicuous by their absence—had expected looters and rapists. Instead they discovered tourists and pleasure seekers. The Germans were very polite, they stood up for old ladies on the Métro, and they patted young children on the head. They were difficult to hate.

At first there was very little resistance. The French were stunned by defeat and confused by the government at Vichy. Pétain, "the hero of Verdun," was a national figure who carried weight. Many were prepared to believe that what was good enough for the Marshal was good enough for everyone. By contrast, De Gaulle was little known and his first broadcast from London was heard by very few. There were not many willing to stick their necks out for Great Britain. In the immediate aftermath of defeat there was a feeling of revulsion against the former ally and a widespread belief that where France had succumbed, Britain was sure to fail. The French felt they had been betrayed at Dunkirk. Beside the German propaganda that "the English will fight to the last Frenchman," Churchill's claim that Britain would continue the fight on France's behalf looked dubious and feeble. The voice of collaboration seemed no more than the voice of realism: Defeat had been so swift and so complete that France had no alternative but to seek partnership with a dominant Germany in a new European order. A few, of course, as Mary did, refused to accept defeat and resisted from the beginning. But these *résistants de la première heure* knew that they could count on the active support of very few of their fellow countrymen and had to expect the hostility of many.

Jean-Paul Sartre wrote of the Occupation years:

> If the wife or the mother of a vanished man had been present at his arrest, she would tell you that he had been taken away by very polite Germans, like those who asked you the way in the street. And when she went to ask for news of her husband at the offices in the Avenue Foch or the rue des Saussaies she would be very graciously received and might be given comforting reassurances. And yet all day and late into the night screams of pain and terror could be heard coming from the buildings in the Avenue Foch and the rue des Saussaies.*

The true nature of Nazi rule revealed itself only gradually. The first to resist were the first to learn.

Mary's small, inexperienced group had a limited aim. Escapers had to be smuggled out of the German Occupied Zone across the demarcation line into so-called Free France. From there they were expected to make their own way back to England via Spain or by boat from Marseilles or one of the other ports on the southern coast. Vichy France was, of course, hostile territory, and the Spanish went out of their way to make things difficult, but the principal obstacle was the German-patrolled border between the two zones of France. Mary's first crossing place was at a farm which straddled the border at Sauveterre-de-Béarn, a village just some forty kilometers east of Bayonne and Biarritz. It be-

---

*Quoted from "Paris Under the Occupation" by Jean-Paul Sartre in *French Writing on English Soil*, ed. and trans. J. G. Weightman (Sylvan Press, 1945).

longed to the governess of Michèle Cambards, one of Maurice's schoolfriends, and quickly became the center of a busy escape route. In the first six months of the Occupation, Michèle remembers helping about fifty men across, half of whom were English. Sometimes they were driven the 350 kilometers from Paris in Mary's Peugeot, but as petrol was scarce, they travelled more frequently by train. Michèle and Maurice often made the journey two or three times a week. They thought it was exciting and fun and they made a little pocket money on the side by smuggling contraband.

There was no shortage of escapers. They turned up in Paris from the north usually in poor shape, occasionally wounded, and always with little idea of how to get much farther. Maurice and Oky, Mary's second son, sometimes picked them up off the street and brought them back to the flat in the rue Erlanger. At other times, they would be forwarded to Mary unofficially by contacts in the American Embassy. They were sheltered either in Mary's apartment or in a nearby flat, until it was safe for them to be taken across the border. The pace was breathless, and the atmosphere unrealistic. The Germans had put up posters all over Paris threatening to shoot anyone who rendered assistance to Allied personnel. But this hardly entered their heads.

Maurice de Milleville says, "We were aware of the fact that it was dangerous because it was posted all over the walls. But we were unconscious of the fact that we could be caught. When you're really taken in by a job, and you're doing it, you have no time to think of the danger around the corner. The work just keeps on cropping up and we just felt that we wouldn't be caught."

The most significant of the escapers during this time was James Windsor-Lewis, a captain in the Welsh Guards. His story is important not only for what it reveals of the reemergent Lindell style, but also because it was Windsor-Lewis's report to secret service chiefs in London which first alerted them to the activities of an extraordinary—and otherwise possibly incredible—Englishwoman operating a free-lance escape line from her flat in Paris.

Windsor-Lewis had been captured at Boulogne in May 1940 with a serious leg wound. He escaped soon afterwards from a hospital in Liège, and after passing through Brussels, arrived in Paris in mid-July disguised rather unconvincingly as a Belgian workman. The American Embassy was not persuaded by his claim to be an American citizen, but a friendly contact there passed him on to Mary. He arrived at her flat on July 15, one month to the day after Hitler had come to Paris to savour the first hours of the German victory. He was handsome, charming, very English and quite clearly important. Mary decided at once that she herself would supervise his escape. It was her manner of doing so that raised eyebrows in London on Windsor-Lewis's return.

From the first moments of the Occupation, petrol was strictly rationed to five liters per car per month—just over a gallon. For all practical purposes this meant immobility. For Windsor-Lewis's escape, however, Mary found a novel solution to the petrol problem: She asked the Germans for it.

In the last frenzied weeks before the fall of France, Mary had organized Red Cross help for refugees streaming through Paris from the north. Now, wearing her smartest Red Cross uniform, she went to Count von Bismarck, the great-grandson of the Prussian Iron Chancellor, with a story of how she was compelled to cross the demarcation line to bring a young child back to its mother in Paris. Von Bismarck, who ran the *Ausweise* office in the rue Faubourg St. Honoré, issued her with permits for herself and her mechanic and vouchers for the necessary gasoline for so long a journey. He was, he told her, happy to oblige the Comtesse de Milleville on her errand of mercy.

On the journey itself, Mary astonished Windsor-Lewis by stopping to pick up a German pilot who was hitching a lift. Returning from a bombing sortie over England, he and his crew had bailed out after his airplane had been hit by Spitfires. The conversation took place in English. Windsor-Lewis sat nervously in the back seat of the Peugeot as the German told Mary that her mechanic did not look very intelligent, and Mary agreed. She drove the pilot to his station at Châteaudun, where his commanding officer was so impressed by Mary's kindness that he would not let her leave without presenting her with more petrol coupons.

Mary drove on across the demarcation line to Limoges, where she put Windsor-Lewis on a train to Marseilles. The mission had been a complete success. But by the time, a few months later, that Windsor-Lewis had arrived safely in London and was writing his report, Mary herself was in deep trouble.

Late in 1940, Mary's daughter, Barbé, who had contacts among high-ranking German officers in Paris, warned her mother that she was on a list of people suspected of anti-German activities. Mary's reaction was predictable. "First," says Maurice de Milleville, "she didn't believe it, and secondly she considered that as long as she could do it, she was going to get as many men out as possible. She considered that her job was not to think about herself, she didn't even think about us at that time, she was so busy. Her heart was really in getting those people out. I mean there was no other thing. She wasn't my mother anymore, she was an officer doing a job which had to be done."

On February 3, 1941, Mary warned Michèle Cambards that something was wrong and that she should disappear for a while. It was the last time they saw each other for the rest of the war. A few days afterwards, late in the afternoon, Mary heard the doorbell ring at the first-floor flat in the rue Erlanger. Outside stood two very polite Germans. "I am very sorry," said one of them, "but I'm afraid we've come to arrest you."

There were two different Nazi secret police forces, both of which were popularly known as the Gestapo. The Sicherheitsdienst (SD) was a section of the SS and operated as an organ of the Nazi Party itself. The men who arrested Mary were from the Abwehr, the military intelligence and security police. They took Mary to the Cherche-Midi, a military prison in the heart of Paris, to await her trial by a military tribunal. Her account of the proceedings has the by-now-familiar stamp of a Lindell adventure.

The trial took place on March 3. The lawyer for the defense had visited Mary in prison and told her to expect anything from eleven years to death and had received clear, if daunting, instructions from his client: "You just put in for death—because I shouldn't like eleven years."

In the event it was probably best that he was held up on the Métro and didn't arrive until the tribunal had already begun.

"By the time he got in he found that I was defending myself better than he could do it.

"They said, 'You've had English officers up at your flat!'

"And I said, 'Did I? I hope they were handsome.'

"And they said, 'Of course they were.'

" 'Well,' I said, 'in that case I'm sorry I didn't see them.'

"And that was that—and I got away with it.

"Then they said that I'd insulted the German Army. I told them to stop talking nonsense.

" 'Yes,' they said, 'our agent says you said, "These swine have arrested me!" '

" 'Oh,' I replied, 'he didn't understand. In English swine doesn't mean pig, it means ferocious, brave, wild boar!' The general opposite me nearly burst out laughing.

" 'So,' I said, 'it was no insult to the German Army.'

"Then my lawyer produced my citation for the Croix de Guerre and gave it to the president, who didn't like me, and he gave it to the interpreter, and the interpreter interpreted it into German, and the whole lot of these clots stood up and saluted me. Of course, I felt a perfect fool.

"Then they all went out and when they came back they gave me nine months.

" 'Marvellous!' I said. 'Just time to have a baby with Adolf!' "

Mary's lawyer did not wait for the interpreter to translate her last remark. In the circumstances, he told the court, his client thought the sentence fair.

As Mary was driven off to serve her nine months' solitary confinement she passed few on the streets of Paris who would have given her cause—England's cause—any chance at all. On the contrary, the Nazis were about to tighten their grip on Europe. In the first three months of her imprisonment, German troops overran Yugoslavia, Greece and Crete and Rommel's Afrika Korps advanced over the deserts of North Africa. In London, on the eve of Mary's sentence, Harold Nicolson, a key figure in the Ministry of Information responsible for propaganda and morale, agonized in his diary over the difficulty of the job:

> If only we could show people some glimmer of light at the end of the tunnel, we could count upon their enduring any ordeal. But the danger is that there is no light beyond the light of faith. I have that light. I know in the marrow of my bones that we shall win in the

end. But I get depressed when I realise how difficult it is to convey that faith to the public, since it is not based, as far as I can see, on reason or calculation.*

A cause with no reasonable grounds for hope. Such was the view of one of those most directly responsible for inspiring the British people with the will to go on. It was small wonder that most people on the Continent were still fainthearted.

Mary was sent to the prison at Fresnes, just outside Paris. By now she considered herself a British officer and was determined to act like one.

"They came in the morning and threw a broom at me and said, 'Sweep it up!'

"And I said, 'No, British officers don't sweep out. I'm your visitor and you can do the sweeping!'

" 'We'll fetch the commandant.'

"And I said, 'You can fetch God Almighty, it won't worry me.'

"And of course the commandant came down and he said that the orders were that I should sweep out my cell.

"So I said, 'Why the heck aren't they written out and hung up on the wall? You've made a mistake and you can pay for it. As to sweeping out your cell—absolutely nothing doing. No. No. That's the end of the story.'

"And I never swept it . . . and I never swept it in any prison. Would you?"

Not long afterwards, in July 1941, Mary's son and chief lieutenant Maurice was also picked up by the Gestapo. He had been betrayed by a frightened French youth to whom he had given a pistol. Maurice was sent to Fresnes for a year.

For the time being, Mary's unlikely escape line suspended operations. The De Millevilles had been lucky.

---

*Harold Nicolson: Diaries and Letters 1939–1945, ed. Nigel Nicolson (Collins, 1967).

Their line had chalked up some successes in spite of its hair-raising amateurishness. The price they had paid was hardly severe by the standards of the time. In 1915 Edith Cavell had been shot, and many more inspired by her would lose their lives in the Second World War. They had also survived—without bruises—their first contacts with the Gestapo. As she lied about her role in organizing escapes, Mary had been proud, aristocratic and terribly British. As he lied about his role, Maurice had been humbler, apologetic, and had made out that it had all been done in a spirit of fun—like a game. "The Gestapo were not always as bad as people make out," he recalls today, "they only hit you if you were arrogant or working-class."

This time they got away with it lightly. They were not so lucky the second time.

On July 27, 1942, a telegram from Barcelona arrived at Room 900 in the War Office in London, advising that a woman dressed in full Red Cross uniform and wearing British medal ribbons had arrived from France with papers suggesting that she was a "stranded governess." The message continued to give details of a career that involved helping evaders from Dunkirk and a nine-month spell in Fresnes Prison. It added that she now wanted to come to London with a view to returning to France to start up a new escape line.

Room 900 was a tiny cheerless chamber on the second floor of the War Office. In peacetime it was little more than a large cupboard where the tea was made. In war it had become the nerve center of MI9, the top-secret unit which coordinated escapes from occupied Europe. It was run by two brave officers from smart English regiments who had themselves both made spectacular escapes. Capt. James Langley of the Coldstream Guards had found his own way back to England after being badly wounded and losing an arm at Dunkirk. His colleague, Airey Neave, had been the first Englishman to escape from Colditz (at the third attempt) and had returned to England only two months before. But neither their professional nor personal experience of escape lines in Europe had prepared them for anything quite like the arrival of Mary Lindell in wartime London.

The summer of 1942 found the British people tired, scruffy and fed up. In nearly three years of war there had been little to cheer them and a great deal of discouragement. The fall of Singapore and Tobruk had focused attention on a war effort that seemed to be leading nowhere. There was a pervading feeling that "the Germans and the Japanese have always been a march ahead of us," a mood that permeated the whole of the country. In the House of Commons, Winston Churchill faced a motion of no confidence. In the country, the people, in their third year of rationing, were fed up with seeing his face filled with a fat Havana cigar. In shopping queues everywhere there were vexed and ratty questions whenever anyone was served with what appeared to be more than a fair share. It was the summer when the Americans arrived to a friendly but dubious reception. They marched quietly. They did not tramp through the streets like British troops. They were smart, it was said, in spite of their rubber-soled boots. More than ever the streets were full of uniforms. But instead of the troops inspiring confidence there were more complaints about foul language and the alarming rise in venereal disease. When Mary eventually arrived in London on July 29, the atmosphere was not heroic: It was grumpy.

Mary, released from Fresnes in November 1941, had quickly realized that Paris was no place for an Englishwoman already known to the Gestapo. Her escape had been audacious and arduous, complicated by a bout of pneumonia which at one stage had threatened to kill her. She had crossed the demarcation line between occupied and unoccupied France near the small town of Ruffec in the Charente, and from there had moved through the

Iberian peninsula with the same swagger but in the op- posite direction of the Duke of Wellington's, astonishing a series of British diplomatic and consular officials with tales of her adventures, and her imperious way of dealing with bureaucracy.

"At Barcelona they liked to give anyone who escaped a present, and I was a bit tatty, my shirt was tatty. So when they said, 'What would you like, a gold cigarette case, or a watch?' I said, 'No, I don't want anything. Oh, yes, I'd like a couple of pair of pants, 'cause mine are getting a little bit elderly.'

"So they just burst out laughing and said, 'This lady just wants a couple of pair of pants!'

"So I said, 'Make it three: one on, one in the wash, and one hoping.' "

MI9's man in Barcelona cabled his impressions to Langley and Neave in London, who now waited for her with reservations at least as great as their sense of antici- pation. In his book *Saturday at MI9*, Airey Neave has left a vivid picture of Mary at the time of her arrival in England:

> She was standing in the sunshine, dressed in the royal blue uniform of the French Red Cross, with a row of French and British decorations. She was at this time about forty-five, but looked considerably younger. She had dark brown eyes and chestnut hair, and her face was finely proportioned. Her figure was slight and her uniform well-cut. She seemed very feminine, but in her expression there was an intensity, a stubbornness which somehow did not fit her smart appearance.
>
> As soon as she spoke, I understood why. She was very definitely English and used to getting her own way.*

---

*Airey Neave, *Saturday at MI9* (Hodder & Stoughton, 1969).

By this time Neave and Langley had read Windsor-Lewis's escape report and had some idea what to expect. Yet for Jimmy Langley, a man who controlled a great many brave and resourceful agents in the field, there is still a sharp edge to the memory of that first encounter with Mary in MI9's secret flat in St. James's Street. "From the word go we were perhaps not on the same wavelength. She's a very tough, brave and courageous woman but she likes to have her own way.

"I gave instructions that she was not to see Windsor-Lewis over here since she had volunteered to go back and we did not like people making contacts in England if they were going back into enemy-occupied territory. She instantly disobeyed that order and said she'd see who she liked and didn't care a damn what I felt about it. . . . She did get across people, there's no doubt about that, and a lot of high-ups in MI9—all those who did meet her —came away with an impression that she was all right in very small doses."

There were two sides to this story. Mary considered herself a free-lance operator with useful knowledge and experience of conditions in occupied France. She was impatient of deskbound men in London who thought they knew everything, but she realized that she relied upon them to get her back to France.

MI9's point of view was, naturally, a little more complicated. Mary clearly did not fit into any category of agent that a security-conscious secret service chief feels happy about sending into the field. Her casual disregard of instructions, which might be dismissed as merely vexing in London, could prove disastrous in France. Her manner attracted attention—worse, had already attracted the attention of the Gestapo, something which normally would have disqualified her from further underground work. Mary was brave enough, she had experience of escape lines, and boasted an enviable number of contacts throughout France, but the fact remains that had there been a choice she would not have been sent back. However, as Neave and Langley knew too well, there was not any choice. MI9 was the poor relation of the wartime secret services. Usually, promising candidates for clandestine operations overseas were enlisted by the more glamorous agencies, MI6 or the S.O.E. (Special Operations Executive). MI9 was desperately short of people, and whatever their reservations they could not afford to turn Mary down. "It was simply a case that she volunteered to go back and we trained her to send her in again, knowing the risks we were taking, or rather, let's be fair, the risks she was taking."

The risks were considerable. At first the Germans had been slow to realize how many airmen shot down over Europe were making their way back to Britain. But when Goering discovered that very often the larger part of the crew of a bomber remained unaccounted for, he reacted violently. The Gestapo were called in, and as Langley remembers "from that moment it was one long fight. We reckoned that if anybody worked on escape and evasion in enemy-occupied territory the maximum time they could do it without being caught was six months. After that it was very nearly inevitable that they would be caught. We would have pulled her out after six months whether she liked it or not. Very often agents wouldn't come out, in which case we had to shrug our shoulders—it was their lives. Not ours."

The night of October 20, 1942, was clear and moonlit. As Airey Neave drove Mary Lindell to the RAF station at Tangmere his mind was not free from doubt and misgivings. She had refused to work with the radio operator suggested by MI9, and as no other was available, she was being sent back to France alone. But at a deeper level he was troubled, as he always was when thinking of his women agents, about the treatment Mary could expect if she fell into the hands of the Gestapo. It was something, he wrote later, "which distressed many intelligence officers of my generation . . . an attitude which many of the women agents scorned as Victorian, and perhaps it was."

Mary, of course, was in no mood to be sentimental. Before takeoff there were certain things that had to be attended to.

"I'd hardly got in when there was a knock on the door. And I said, 'What the hell! I haven't finished . . . I want to do a wee-wee.'

"So they said, 'Well, there's the pilot, he wants to speak to you.'

"I was furious. I thought the pilot was going to say that everything was all right and it really wasn't dangerous. So I came out and there was this Canadian who said, 'I'm sorry to have pulled you out from where you were, but I want to thank you for what you're doing for all of us.'

"I said, 'Don't be silly—you're the hero.'

"He said, 'No. I'm going to put you down. I know where I'm going to sleep, you don't.'

"I thought it was really so priceless of this lad. It was the most thrilling thing that happened to me in the whole war."*

Mary crossed the tarmac to the shadowy outline of the waiting Lysander. There was an atmosphere about those still grassy aerodromes that made people reflective. So many men and machines flying out into the beautiful and hostile night, uncertain of return. In the ops room at Tangmere there was a young WAAF, a radio telepho-

---

*Quoted from the British Broadcasting Corporation's *Woman's Hour* program of September 15, 1969, in *The Long March of Everyman 1750–1960*, ed. Theo Barker (André Deutsch & BBC, 1975).

nist, who would later remember what it was like, night after night: "We used to see them out and then count them back, and then you'd wait, and there'd be some missing, then perhaps two or three would dribble back, and then you'd wait for some time and know that no more would be coming back. And then you'd get this awful sort of weeping in the various rooms at night, there was always, always, some weeping girl somewhere. It was just a sort of sound that always seemed to be behind the battle."

There were good military reasons for investing so much in bringing back shot-down airmen: Britain was short of trained pilots. There were good economic reasons: A bomber pilot cost £10,000 to train and a fighter pilot £15,000. But even had this not been so, the "sound that always seemed to be behind the battle" would have justified the risk. For whatever reason, Mary Lindell, her head full of Kipling and her heart full of England, now found herself following in the path of those who had not come back.

In occupied France, the mood had changed a great deal since the first days of defeat in 1940. The early resisters had mostly been highly individualistic, highly impractical and highly unpopular. The majority had persuaded themselves that the catastrophe was the reward of France's inner rottenness and the consequence of the perfidy of her major ally, Britain. The German victory had been a chastisement, and in Marshal Pétain the French saw a father figure who had not only salvaged something out of the wreck of defeat, but who promised to unify the nation and restore it to the path of true righteousness. To resist was a *refus absurde*, a refusal to accept the facts of life. The change was gradual. It occurred not only because of the rapacity and cruelty of the Nazis, but because people came to realize that Pétain and his Vichy regime could not be the guarantors of French

honour and French interests. While Frenchmen sub-
sisted on meager rations, they watched the Germans
milking the nation's industry and agriculture. They
watched too how Vichy implicated itself in the persecutions and deportations of Jews and how Pétain's puppet
government acquiesced in increasing Nazi control of
French life. Even the "Marseillaise" was rewritten. The
jour de gloire was replaced by a harmless "day of hope";
"work and harmony" were substituted for the traditional bloodcurdling lines with which—since the early
days of the Revolution—the French have threatened the
enemies of their nation.

There were clear indications of the change of attitude.
In August and September 1941 the first assassinations of
German soldiers took place in Paris and Bordeaux. At
first public reaction was not favourable. But there was
widespread repugnance when the Nazis shot hostages in
reprisal and a sense of shame when it became known that
Pétain himself had described the assassinations of the
Germans as "criminal acts," and his own government
had cooperated with the Nazis in the selection of hostages to be executed. By 1942, when the privations of the
Occupation had pushed up the death rate in Paris by a
quarter, and in Marseilles by over a half, it was becoming
more difficult for Vichy to persuade Frenchmen that
such acts of cooperation with the Nazis were helping to
preserve the French way of life. As the reputation of
Vichy tarnished, and its authority diminished, people
looked towards what was happening in the world outside France. Nine-fifteen in the evening became BBC
time. The news broadcasts from London were circulated
by a burgeoning underground press. There was a new
confidence among resisters, now no longer disorganized
and scattered, but becoming a coordinated force com-
prising of large groups of like-thinking men and women:
Communists, socialists, people who were outraged by

what was happening to the Jews. These strands and others from right across the social and political spectrum were being pulled together as the Resistance. At last a realistic alternative to the Nazi view of the war and the destiny of Europe was beginning to emerge.

In any case, to the ordinary Frenchman, the *attentiste* —hedging his bets, sitting on the fence—the Nazi view of the world was already crumbling. When Mary escaped to London, there had been little to inspire confidence in an Allied victory. But by the time she returned there had been an entire transformation in people's expectations. The Americans were arriving in England in huge numbers, turning "Perfidious Albion" into an armed camp poised for invasion. In Russia the German advance had been checked at Stalingrad. For the first time the Axis powers seemed to have lost the initiative. The defeat of Germany no longer appeared inconceivable. On October 23—two days after Mary Lindell touched down on French soil near Limoges—General Montgomery ordered the artillery barrage to begin at El Alamein. A little over a fortnight later, Winston Churchill's speech at the Lord Mayor's Day luncheon in the Mansion House, London, reflected the change in atmosphere: "I notice, my Lord Mayor, by your speech that you had reached the conclusion that the news from the various fronts has been somewhat better lately," he began. Only four months after he had faced a vote of no confidence in the Commons, he warmed to this theme with some personal satisfaction: "I have never promised anything but blood, tears, toil and sweat. Now, however, we have a new experience. We have victory—a remarkable and definite victory."

El Alamein was the Nazis' first major defeat of the war. The point was not lost on those hesitant Frenchmen balancing their sympathies with their long-term interests.

And it was to them that Mary now came as an apostle of a new creed: the creed of victory.

Ruffec is a small, grey and unremarkable town built along the main Paris-to-Bordeaux road and serving as a market for the farmers in the surrounding Charente countryside. Nothing about it now reveals the part played by the town in the Resistance, except an easily missed plaque plastered into the wall of the Hôtel de France, marking the death during the war of the previous owners. Yet because of its location just a few kilometers east of the demarcation line between occupied and unoccupied France, wartime Ruffec witnessed an unusual volume of clandestine activity. It was from a farm close to the town that Mary herself had crossed the border on her way to England, and it was here that she now returned to start up her new escape line: the Marie-Claire line. She arrived in the little town at the very moment of Montgomery's victory in the desert.

Thirty-five years later, in the Toque Blanche, an unpretentious little bistro on the main road, they still talk of the arrival in Ruffec of the Englishwoman in Red Cross uniform. The handful of middle-aged farmers and workers who once made up the Marie-Claire line recall a fearless, headstrong woman whose face and bearing were quite unlike that of a local girl. She had class and authority. To which M. Flaud, the village baker who was once the village Romeo, adds, "She was a pretty woman too—that was quite noticeable. It's a good job she wasn't younger."

It may seem strange that such men sharing all the inbred caution of the French countryside should risk their skins under the command of such a curious, and foreign, leader. But Mary's authority derived from two powerful sources. First, being able to prove that she had been sent direct from London made a tremendous impression in the middle of the war. And secondly, her own brand of unalloyed patriotism lent her leadership an irresistible charisma.

"My mother was outspoken and outspokenly patriotic," recalls Maurice. "She didn't know what fear was —at least she didn't express it at any time. Her heart was in the job one hundred percent—and she knew how to communicate it. That made a lot of people follow her, I mean blindfoldedly they used to follow her."

In Mary's mind the patriotism and the fearlessness were inextricably linked. "I tell you, I represented, in my tuppenny-ha'penny mind, I represented Great Britain, who was standing up against the world and fighting for it. And I wasn't going to let Great Britain down. It just didn't enter my head. And I wasn't frightened. I always say, if you're shot, well, you're shot—and there's an end to the story. And it wouldn't have worried me."

The new escape line was intended to be more ambitious than Mary's first endeavours in the immediately post-Dunkirk period. Fugitive Allied airmen were to be passed not just over the demarcation line dividing the two zones of France but also led across the Pyrénées into neutral Spain. The Marie-Claire line was "official" and could draw on essential reserves of cash smuggled into France from the British legations in Switzerland. Normally, such a line would have been in regular radio contact with London. But Mary had been sent in alone, having refused to work with the radio operator that MI9 had allocated to her, a man who later went on to work with distinction for another line. London had trained Mary in Morse code and in other underground skills, but from the beginning of the operations it was clear that the new Marie-Claire line would have more in common with Mary's first line than with the orthodoxies of Room 900. What little Neave and Langley were to hear of Mary's activities from brief reports of other lines, and from their agent Donald Darling in Lisbon, was hardly reassuring.

London was getting jittery in this period, and when Darling passed on a report from the Côte d'Azur that an Englishwoman in full Red Cross uniform had caused quite a stir walking down the Promenade des Anglais— a long way from Mary's official area—it only added to the growing alarm about her unconventional behaviour. MI9, recalled Airey Neave, was brought near to apoplexy. "Being young," he wrote in his memoirs of this period, "I was delighted with her unconventional ways, but they became increasingly difficult to defend with the establishment, and later I was sharply forbidden to send a radio operator to her." For Mary, of course, such rebuffs were exactly what could be expected from officialdom. Many others who had worked in the field found the grey bureaucracy of the War Office depressing rather than inspiring. Although she liked and respected Airey Neave, she had missed in London any real appreciation of the excitement and adventure of an underground game of cat and mouse with the Nazis, of what it was really like to be doing it. In short, she saw no reason to change her ways to please Whitehall. It worked in France—and that was enough.

Some idea of the impact of the Lindell style on the ground can be gained from the experiences of the Abbé Blanchebarbe in Foix, a small town just to the north of the Pyrénées. Today Blanchebarbe, at eighty-seven, is the canon of the cathedral at Metz, a large barrel of a man with the expressive gestures of a cleric equally at home at the supper table as at the altar, and with the spiritual ease of one who knows that he has served his country at least as well as he has served his God. During the war Blanchebarbe was one of the key figures in the impressive resistance organization of the Ariègeois, which because of its geographical location just to the north of the Spanish border was primarily concerned with *pasajes*— smuggling fugitives over the frontier. Marie-Claire was only one of many escape lines that he helped. He was shrewd and experienced and he evaluated the English-woman with a detachment which understood that lives depended on his judgment. This incident he describes with the kind of excited relish reserved for something which happened only yesterday, and it reveals Mary at the height of her powers:

"It was mid-1943, and the escapes were at their height. Our line was in danger of being discovered by the Germans, but at that moment Marie-Claire wanted to pass a very important group of squadron leaders. She had agreed with the driver of the train to slow down between Foix and Tarascon in a very isolated spot where there was no risk of being seen. There they were to jump down and be met by a guide, who was, we discovered later, a double agent.

"When the day arrived, I was warned that at the very place Marie-Claire was going to descend with her airmen there was a whole detachment of Gestapo ready to take them. It was then we took the decision to stop Marie-Claire at the station at Foix. Therefore, as I knew Marie-Claire, I was to stop her with a signal.

"It was not easy because all around us at the station were Gestapo men who didn't know why we were there —and we knew only too well why they were there.

"When the train arrived, I signalled to Marie-Claire. She got the airmen (disguised as a party of deafmutes) down onto the platform, followed me, and I told her why she could go no farther. She understood quickly and I went with her to the leader's house."

The airmen, thus rescued, were quickly spirited across the border into Spain. But there remained the problem of the double agent. He was stopped by customs officials friendly to the Resistance and brought to the Abbé Blanchebarbe's house in the rue del Cassé at Foix.

"There," continues Blanchebarbe, "he sat opposite us

—Marie-Claire and myself—and we lectured him and uttered dire threats if he ever let out anything to the Gestapo. He promised everything, but Marie-Claire, a very fierce woman, drew out of her pockets two Browning pistols (I didn't even know she was armed) and then, facing the agent threateningly, she said, 'See this? If you ever betray us, I shall shoot your head off. And if this one doesn't shut you up, I'll blow your guts out with this one.'

"I admired her. She managed her group with extraordinary energy and her arguments were irresistible. She was also very cool under pressure. In my life I've seen a lot of heroism, but she is certainly the bravest woman I've ever met: For a woman, she is a very great man."

Whatever Whitehall's reservations, all the flamboyance and audacity which had characterized Mary's early escape work in 1940 survived undiminished in the Marie-Claire line of 1943.

But it was also characterized by bad luck.

It struck almost at once. Just five weeks after Mary arrived back in France the British submarine, H.M.S. *Tuna*, surfaced in the Bay of Biscay a few miles off the French coast. It was seven-thirty in the evening. Into the icy December waters the submarine launched five small canoes, each manned by two black-faced commandos of the Royal Marine Boom Patrol Detachment. Their task was to paddle up the River Gironde and destroy the shipping in Bordeaux harbour. The official code name of the raid was Operation Frankton. The men were to become known as the Cockleshell Heroes. It was not expected that many of them—if any—would ever return.

In London the dangers of the raid had given rise to unusual concern. Lord Mountbatten, then chief of Combined Operations, had insisted that the commandos be given an escape route to get them out of France after the raid. Such a move was unprecedented. It went against one of the most fundamental security safeguards of MI9. Nevertheless, because of the special circumstances Neave and Langley in Room 900 complied. Reluctantly they instructed the commandos that after the raid they should make for Ruffec, where they would get in contact with the Marie-Claire line.

Unfortunately, at the time Marie-Claire was in no position to help anyone. Mary was in the hospital. Her ribs and shoulder bone had been shattered in a road accident near the demarcation line at Blois. Without radio contact she had no way of informing MI9 that she was out of action—and they had no way of telling her that she should expect some very important visitors.

On December 12, 1943, the first mine exploded in Bordeaux harbour. The explosions continued all morning, completely destroying one large cargo ship and leaving the others beyond repair for the rest of the war. The raid was a complete success. But the dangers had not been underestimated. Of the ten commandos who set out, only two survived. At least six of the others were caught by the Nazis and shot under Hitler's notorious commando law. Corp. Bill Sparks, one of the two survivors, now a bus inspector at the London transport garage at Barking, recalls: "Up to the time of the raid itself, the planning seemed almost perfect. They had it all thought out—everything worked like clockwork. But it was only after we'd done the job, it seemed that no one had really given much thought to how we were going to get out. That's when things began to go wrong."

Sparks and the other survivor, Major "Blondie" Hasler, made their way towards Ruffec as instructed. But once in the small town they discovered they had no way of knowing how to locate Mary's HQ. Tired, confused and hungry, they walked past Mary's headquarters at the Hôtel de France and entered instead the little Toque Blanche bistro, fifty meters down the road. It was a mistake that could have cost them their lives. Today the *patron* of the Toque Blanche remembers how he watched them arrive:

"That day, towards two P.M. two men came in, quite badly dressed and seeming very tired. They asked me for something to eat, and when we had served them and the time came to pay, I found in the notes a message on a small piece of paper: 'We are two escaped Englishmen—please help us.' We didn't know what to do. We couldn't be certain of their nationality and we hesitated between believing them English or German."

Hasler and Sparks were lucky: The *patron* gave them the benefit of the doubt. By sheer luck he was able to put them in touch with his friends who were in the Marie-Claire line. But because of her injuries, it would be a long time before the two commandos met Marie-Claire herself.

The old friends and neighbours who made up Mary's organization in Ruffec sprang into action. For a few hours the two fugitives were hidden in a room down the road from the Toque Blanche. Then M. Flaud, the baker, drove them to the demarcation line in his bread van. There was a whistle in the night, and Hasler ran across the lonely track which separated the two zones of France and off into the shadowy woods beyond. Another whistle, and Sparks followed. Eight hundred meters from the track they came to the farm of Armand Dubreuile. There, in a little room along the corridor from the kitchen, they waited for the next forty-one days for the next stage of their escape. It was the same room where, a year before, Mary herself had been hidden while she recovered from pneumonia on her escape to England.

Christmas passed. And New Year's. The two men of action grew restless and carved wood. They were accustomed to a tough training regime and felt cooped up and threatened. Patrols visited the farm, sometimes German but at other times the equally dangerous French police, the *Milice*. Dubreuile and his wife dealt with them coolly. They had been in the Resistance since the earliest days and had sheltered many men, both French and English, in their home. Living near the demarcation line, Dubreuile had also watched the convoys of Jews brought across the frontier by "professionals" working for profit. But Dubreuile worked for nothing and he worked discreetly. Not even his mother-in-law, who lived with them at the farm, knew that men were hidden there. Nevertheless, as weeks passed without news of the Marie-Claire line, even he began to feel anxious about the two commandos.

Eventually, early in February 1943, Maurice de Milleville arrived to escort Hasler and Sparks on the next leg of their journey—to Lyons. It was here that they came face to face with Marie-Claire for the first time. She made —as she usually did—a lasting impression.

"We knocked on the door and this is where we got our first look at Mary. Lovely little lady, small. It was very surprising to me that she was so small—and very heavily bandaged from her accident. Her arm was in a sling— but she was the master power, and seeing my commanding officer taking orders from a little lady was very humorous for me. But she left us in no doubt that she was the governor. . . ."

Sparks is speaking, thirty-five years later, in the reassuring comfort of a seedy suburban pub in London. There is no doubt about the effect that Mary had on him as a young corporal in the marines. He speaks of her as fondly as he cradles his pint of bitter.

"Apparently, the flats were under surveillance by the Gestapo. So Mary had to move us on. She came down herself, her one poor old sleeve tucked in her pocket, and her arm in a sling, and she said, 'Come on, lads, we've got a journey to make on a tram.' Well, in those days the trams were very, very full—and we didn't speak the language. We got on and were jostled about. And I found myself at one end of the tram and Mary at the other end. Well, when the time came for getting off, Mary in broad English shouted down the tram and said, 'I say, Bill, we get off here.' I shrank into my collar. I thought, She can't be talking to me, that's for sure, and I tried to slide off without anybody noticing. Everybody looked round, but this was our Mary. She cared for no one."

For the young commando, on the run in a foreign, occupied country, it was not the perils of the Marie-Claire line that made the strongest and most lasting impression: "The impression she gave me was one of safety. I felt safe when Mary was about. Even though she spoke English, and she had very funny ways—I don't think any other organization thought a lot of her ways—this girl really gave me confidence. She was afraid of no one and she passed this on to everyone. Anybody who had dealings with her felt the same way."

By the late spring of 1943, Hasler and Sparks were safely back in England. About six months had passed since Mary had landed in France, just about the average life expectancy of an agent in Nazi-occupied Europe.

In London the return of the Cockleshell Heroes was a rare and much-needed piece of good news. The period since Mary's arrival in France had been, in Airey Neave's phrase, "a winter of disaster." The Gestapo had at last begun to get the measure of the escape routes that crisscrossed their territory and were striking back with devastating effect. Informers and double agents were penetrating the lines and causing havoc. The two principal escape organizations in France and Belgium, both responsible for the escapes of hundreds of Allied servicemen, had been smashed and their leaders arrested. In Whitehall, Room 900 was struggling for survival in the face of fierce attacks from its secret service rivals who claimed that the escape lines were poorly organized and that they jeopardized the more important clandestine operations of sabotage and intelligence. As an answer to these critics, Mary's activities were a double-edged sword. On the one hand, the escape of the two commandos was a spectacular success. But the reports that filtered back of her eccentric *modus operandi* only confirmed the worst fears of MI9's security-conscious bureaucratic enemies. When Hasler arrived home, he was full of praise for Mary's courage and resource, but "white with fury" that she had been sent to France without a radio operator. "It was all we could do, to stop him having questions asked in the House," recalls Langley. It was never easy dealing with Mary, but Room 900 had no choice but to continue to try. It was not only that she did get results, but also that, at one point in the middle of 1943, the Marie-Claire line was the only official escape route operating in central France.

Of course, from Mary's point of view, War Office politics in London—even had she been aware of them—were the last possible reason for changing her style. As far as she was concerned, she was "untakable" and "unkillable," and she continued to have limitless faith in her own invulnerability. It was not that she thought herself too intelligent to be caught, but she recognized within herself a capacity for quick thinking in a tight spot: "I always knew exactly what to do in a corner, I could talk my way out of anything." She would have gone on living dangerously whatever London thought, and the best way—if not the only way—Room 900 could keep tabs on her was through their "listening post" in Switzerland.

Throughout the Second World War, Switzerland preserved intact an enviable neutrality in the heart of occupied Europe. For most of those—primarily Jews—desperate to escape the persecutions of the Nazis, it remained a forbidden and impenetrable sanctuary. Others were more skilled in crossing frontiers and dodging the patrols on both sides of the fence. The Swiss records show that in March 1943, Mlle. Gertrude Marie Lindell, of English origin and resident at Neuchâtel, had been granted a residence permit for one month for treatment of her broken shoulder bone. She had paid French fishermen 40,000 francs to smuggle her across the frontier on Lake Geneva. ("It was enough to last him the rest of his life—the bastard.")

The shattered shoulder in danger of becoming gangrenous was only one—the least important—of Mary's reasons for entering Switzerland. In the lining of her coat there was a coded message from Major Hasler—his report on the Bordeaux raid. It was the first news to reach Britain of the success of the raid, and the first intimation that any of the Royal Marines who took part had survived. "Loud was the rejoicing in London and Portsmouth at the news of the two commandoes," wrote Airey Neave. MI9 was "showered with congratulations."

It might have been thought that such a triumph would have ingratiated Mary forever with the British authorities in the Swiss capital, Bern, but that is to count without Mary's lashing tongue and her resistance to any imposed authority. Col. Henry Cartwright, the British military attaché in Bern, was a shrewd and capable organizer, adept at the delicate game of fighting a secret war on the territory of a neutral host. Like Langley and Neave in Room 900, he had been an escaper himself in the First World War and had written a best seller, *Within Four Walls*, based on his experiences. Such a man was ideally placed to deal with British interests in Geneva during the war. He had a good touch both with escapers (it was he who organized Airey Neave's passage through Switzerland during his escape from Colditz) and with escape line organizers. But with Mary he simply rowed.

It was the old story. Cartwright saw in Mary a head-strong maverick hellbent on compromising his delicate relationship with the Swiss. Mary looked on him, not totally without respect, "as a peppery bit of works" who on no account was going to be allowed to inhibit her freedom of movement. She taunted him with the nick-name "Cat's Whiskers"—"because that's what he thought he was." Conflict was inevitable and was not long in arriving. Cartwright was under instructions from London not to allow Mary to return to France before her injuries were fully healed. But Mary had other ideas: "I couldn't stay in Switzerland, it wasn't my business. I knew perfectly well I had to go back to France. My people were at a loose end; they probably thought I had been killed." So, with Cartwright's attention turned elsewhere, and with her arm still unmended in a sling, she jumped the border back into France. Thus her relationship with the British military attaché began, and so it continued for the rest of 1943: common cause—mutual suspicion.

There was, however, one very good reason why she had to go some way towards keeping Cat's Whiskers happy: money. Cartwright was Mary's paymaster.

The cost of resistance was high not only in lives, but in hard cash. Money was a weapon used by both sides. The Gestapo paid informers and traitors; the Resistance paid officials for documents and favours, or sometimes just for looking the other way. In a country burdened for years by hardship and strict rationing, it cost money to transport fugitives hundreds of miles, and more to buy guides to escort them secretly across the border to Spain. It was impossible to spend any time in any branch of the Resistance without realizing that idealism was not enough: There was little idealists could do that money could not do faster and more safely. There were many who made a livelihood out of this realization. What is certain is that there was a lot of money around. What is not certain is what happened to all of it. Today it is an unusual gathering of former *résistants* which does not allude in hushed voices to where the money went. And if the rumours were true, there would be few hotels on the Côte d'Azur which were not built on funds intended to fight the Gestapo.

"We did need an awful lot of money—a tremendous lot. You had to buy people, you had to pay people, and the money question was always a problem. I used to get it from Cartwright, who got it I suppose from the secret service. He used to slap this money on the table and he'd say, 'By God, I've never had as much money as this in all my life. What the hell do you do with it?'

"And I said, 'None of your business, darling.' And that was that.

Originally, MI9 channelled money to its agents through the American consul in Lyons. But since the German occupation of the whole of France in November 1942, all funds were sent through Cartwright in Bern. It was this fact that kept Mary returning to Switzerland and in loose contact with MI9. She was there in July when she received a postcard from a friend in Monte Carlo. What it said was that her son Maurice had been taken ill and was in a sanitorium. What it meant was that he had been arrested.

In fact, Maurice was being held in Montluc Prison in Lyons. He had been betrayed by an informer, and it was clear that the Gestapo already knew a great deal too much about the Marie-Claire line. "The Gestapo definitely knew all about us. They knew about my mother; they knew about the name Marie-Claire; they knew about the fact that she had been in England; therefore they were fairly well informed: There was absolutely no doubt in my mind that somebody had turned us in— somebody had been paid off.

"I've never been of the opinion that the Gestapo was

efficient—but they did so much paying to young punks that they got what information they wanted through the French. The Germans knew very well how to use people in occupied territory. They'd give you coffee; they'd give you chocolate; they'd give you money; they'd give you things that you couldn't get. And then many people who went in for selling you did it for their own personal pleasure!"

At the time, Maurice was a young, handsome, rather dashing young man, fond, he will admit, of chasing the girls. He had inherited much of his mother's confidence, which in his case revealed itself in a certain cockiness. Some of Mary's helpers in the line thought he was a little too cocky, and a little too careless. He was not easily disconcerted. He had been interrogated by the Gestapo once before, in Paris in 1941, and thought that he knew how to deal with them. He was rudely disillusioned.

"Once you'd been arrested by the Gestapo, you had to be very careful the way you talked to them because if you were any way sort of nasty or said rude remarks you could be pretty sure that you were going to get beaten up—or at least hit. Because one of the things they used to like was to give you a hit with the back of their hand across your face and that's fairly demoralizing . . . you have to avoid it if possible.

"My policy when I'd been arrested was to tone down everything, to be as cooperative as possible, to be very sorry and never to admit anything. Anything they'd say, I'd say, 'Oh, no, I was just boasting.' "

But the Gestapo in Lyons already knew too much.

"I remember I was sitting in a chair, and at a certain moment in the interrogation they took the chair and turned it round so that instead of sitting with my back to the chair, I had the chair in front of me. Then they locked my hands together with handcuffs around the chair.

"I soon realized why. They started beating me with something that looked like a piece of wire, electric wire about an inch and a half thick with a heavy, hard rubber covering. They hit me over the head and they hit me all over to such an extent that I passed out. I can tell you they beat the shit out of me."

Mary moved quickly after she got the news of Maurice's arrest. In what by then had become her usual way out of Switzerland, she dropped down over a garden wall which ran along the frontier and made straight for Lyons. Once there, she negotiated Maurice's release with the judicious use of bribery. The Germans, she remembers, were very easily corrupted. You just had to get the price right. "If you offered them too much or too little, you'd had it. And in Lyons, just as you knew how much the girls cost, you also knew how much the Germans cost."

Maurice was released on August 13, 1943. He had been in jail for three months. Mary, who had naturally dealt through a third party to secure his release, saw him for the first time in a friend's apartment. It is one of those rare occasions when her own account of her wartime experiences still betrays a sense of profound shock.

"I asked for him and they said they would fetch him. And when Maurice came through the door he looked just like God's wrath. He was so thin, the poor little devil, and as he came forward to kiss me, his glasses dropped off, and to my horror he went down on his knees and was feeling about for the things.

"Then I said, 'What's the matter?' And he told me that they'd beaten him with chains across the eyes. We thought he was going blind. He'd had a very, very cheap time.

"He'd never thought he could possibly be picked up. But it was really his own fault. You see, when you do a job like this you do not run after the girls. And he had a girl friend who happened to be a Jewess and of course that was the worst thing he could do. So he got beaten up. Not for that, of course—they were trying to find out where I was.

"They didn't get anything out of him. I'll say that for him."

Maurice was free, but the message of his arrest was clear: The Marie-Claire line was living on borrowed time. In Paris, Mary had already been sentenced to death in her absence; in the south, the existence of the line was an open secret. The Gestapo were closing in. The danger was all too apparent, but Mary's reaction was the same as it had been when she first heard of Nazi suspicions in 1940. She carried on. Throughout the autumn Donald Darling continued to receive reports that escapers passed on through the Marie-Claire line were arriving in Gibraltar, and the little information he could gather about Mary's activities confirmed London's impression of her as an eccentric and quirky operator at the height of her powers.

In fact, Mary had succeeded, despite injury and other setbacks, to build up an effective line which stretched from the Swiss border to the small border towns of the Pyrénées. She had forged an effective presence in Lyons —important because of the number of escaping airmen who passed through—and had cemented valuable relationships with a number of brave and loyal guides who escorted escapers over the mountains into Spain. She had access to money and false documents and was trusted by other resistance groups, like Blanchebarbe's in Foix, who were willing to give her assistance. She had achieved all this in spite of the fact that she was aristocratic, foreign and a woman operating in a milieu in which all of those things could easily have told against her, and she had succeeded because she was able to weave around herself an aura of confidence, determination and guts that constituted an almost irresistible charisma which fascinated all those who worked with her and for her—from Swiss intelligence officers to French peasants —and won their respect.

There were few rules in the Marie-Claire line. Her helpers brought with them enthusiasm rather than experience, and many were very young, yet nevertheless Mary relied on their initiative and discretion to an enormous degree. To the airmen she ferried through France, there was only one thing expressly and absolutely forbidden: "My only commandment was: No Women! No promiscuous climbing into anybody's bed. I said, 'If you do, you get shot, and that's the end of the story.' Otherwise, being young men—you know how stupid men are —they might have said something stupid, and they wouldn't know who they were talking to. And who gets it in the neck? Yours truly. And yours truly didn't want to get it in the neck.

"That honestly was my only rule."

Like everything else about Mary, it was a little old-fashioned. Hers was a bravura performance in the great drama of the Resistance. In the Red Cross uniform which had become her trademark, she played the part of an adventuress to a small overawed house of airmen and fellow resisters. In Mary's hands, as in Kipling's, war became not tragedy or farce but music hall. That it had the desired effect was because she had an instinctive feel for what her audience wanted when her audience was in danger.

"When you suddenly get unfortunate lost men—because, you know, even if a man is one of these wonderful pilots so brave he can't see straight—when he's shot down and he's on the run, he becomes a little boy, a little scared boy. Honestly, they are, they're all scared.

"I can still see in Ruffec two Canadians—I called them Big Canada and Little Canada. Well, Little Canada was so terrified he burst into tears and when we went down to meals I had to have Little Canada sitting at my table and say:

" 'Little Canada, eat, or I don't!'

" 'Mary, I can't.'

" 'Don't be a fool,' I said. 'You look like a fool.' And of course he'd eat. Then when we took him down, he simply sat on the train and held my hand. Not love, it was just that he thought it was safe. A little boy.

"When I handed them over to the guides, I said, 'Look, if you have any trouble with this little bastard, shoot him and forget it. We'll see about the body.' It was the first time I'd given a gun to my guides. Do you know, that little Canadian—who was so scared when he was on the run on his own—from that moment led the whole lot of them.

"I don't know if you realize the situation in a foreign country, occupied by the enemy, and not knowing anything, suddenly being handed over to something and then saying, 'Oh, God, it's a woman—this is dreadful, isn't it.'

"And yet suddenly they feel safe. It's a peculiar situation. I loved the whole lot of them. They were too sweet, too ridiculous, most of them. And I never even knew their names."

Mary was arrested on November 24, 1943. The end came quietly on the station platform at Pau during a routine security check on identity papers. Predictably, it was the result of accident and oversight. Mary had been awaiting the arrival of one of her couriers—a teen-age girl—and a party of six English and American airmen. She did not know that because of a simple mistake on their forged documents the entire group had been arrested two days before and the Gestapo alerted to be on the lookout for more members of the line. She herself had loitered on the station platform too long after the men had failed to arrive.

"I was a silly arse. I watched the train instead of walking out into my car and back to the hotel. That was stupid. It was like a cow. Cows watch trains—and that was how I got arrested."

When challenged by two Gestapo officers, she aroused suspicion by producing, accidentally, two sets of identification papers. The Gestapo also arrested a forty-four-year-old Basque peasant, Charles Lopez, one of Mary's guides, whom they had seen talking to her at the station, but Mary persuaded them that he had only been trying to sell her some potatoes on the black market. He was released soon afterwards and managed to spread the news of Mary's arrest to the rest of the line. Maurice fled to Switzerland. It was the last he heard of his mother for the rest of the war.

Mary was taken first for questioning to Gestapo headquarters in Biarritz—the inappropriately named Hôtel de la Paix et Angleterre. There she vigorously protested her innocence, and stuck to her alias as the Comtesse de Moncy, but it was clear that the Gestapo had little doubt as to who she really was.

In Geneva a young MI9 agent code-named "Victor," a "slender young Englishman of Foreign Office appearance," got himself into hot water with his superiors at the War Office by trying to raise a ransom for Mary's release, but it was no use. Marie-Claire was too big a fish. Besides, the Gestapo were already doing well enough out of her arrest. Before putting her under guard on the train for Paris, they appropriated her powder case, her gold cigarette case, a Dunhill lighter, 80,000 francs in her wallet, and a further quarter of a million francs they found rolled up in a napkin. The future did not look promising. The only choice was escape.

"I didn't want to go to Paris because I was already condemned to death in Paris, so I thought the best thing to do was to get off the train. So I told my guard that I got sick on trains and that when I was going to be sick, I'd hit him on the knee so as not to do it in his lap.

"So I hit him on the knee when we got to the place where I wanted to get off the train, and I went into the corridor to go to the lavatory. Unfortunately, I walked a bit too quickly because I wanted to get a move on, you see. He was following me—and he began shooting immediately. I saw the glass door shot, and I thought, Oh, the bastard, he's shooting. And I suppose as I turned to go through, he got me in the cheek. I didn't even feel it. I opened the door onto the rail and when you do that you can't jump at once 'cause you have to be careful of a telegraph pole, 'cause if a telegraph pole hits you, it's nasty. And when I was ready, the SD was already there with his gun out. As I jumped, he fired and hit me twice, which helped of course for getting along a bit. It was a hell of a jump."

But it was not enough to get Mary away. Her guards found her, more dead than alive, underneath a bush at the side of the embankment. She was taken to a Luftwaffe hospital in Tours. She had not escaped—but she had at least delayed her arrival in Paris.

In fact, Mary never did reach Paris. Instead, in February 1944, still not fully recovered, she was sent, manacled, to prison at Dijon. There the interrogations began once more. Yet, curiously, she was not badly treated. Today she remembers that between herself and her interrogator there grew up a kind of admiration, the respect of one professional for another. He did not hit her, she believes, because he knew it would have served no purpose. "I know who I hit," he had told her once in a moment of exasperation. She was tough—as unsentimental about torture as everything else.

"The Germans aren't stupid. They knew perfectly well that had they brought Maurice or my daughter and beaten them up before me, I should have said 'Beat away.' They wouldn't have got anywhere. And supposing I had said anything, the result would have been exactly the same in the long run. It wouldn't have saved me. We weren't very mad about the Germans, you know, and we didn't trust them."

Nobody can be sure today what happened in those interrogation cells a third of a century ago. The only eyewitnesses—interrogators, torturers and their victims, when they survive—are hardly likely to agree on their version of events. Even if the documentary records could be found, little could be said for their objectivity or completeness. In all of Mary's account of her extraordinary wartime career, nothing seems so odd to the ears of those who underwent similar experiences than her recollection of how she herself behaved when faced with interrogation and imprisonment by the Nazis. For many the idea that a stiff upper lip mixed with a large measure of English sangfroid was enough to put German guards in their place is simply too much; the high gallantry and doggedness of Mary's fight for rights that were for the most part imaginary, and where they existed at all were almost totally ignored, are just too difficult to believe. It has too much in it of the veteran's tale: a comforting yarn. Yet, astonishingly, the only British witness of the months Mary spent in Dijon Prison is still alive and confirms the picture of a doughty, snappy English-woman who somehow carved out an area of respect from her ruthless Nazi jailers.

Yvonne Baseden was twenty when she was thrown into Mary's cell in the Dijon jail. A pretty, wiry and athletic girl, she was scared and intimidated. Yvonne was a member of the French section of the S.O.E. Half English and half French, she had been trained in England for secret work in France and had been captured by the Germans a fortnight after D Day after assisting in a huge and highly successful drop of arms to the maquis at Dôle. She was roughly treated and threatened with execution, one uniformed interrogator shooting between her feet to impress her with his seriousness. By the time she met up with Mary she had grown most afraid of the guards whom she had heard whispering plans to each other about what they were going to do with her.

At first Yvonne suspected that Mary was a German plant intended to draw information from her. It was perhaps one of the very few moments when Mary's Englishness has ever been called into question, and it did not last for long. Still wearing the smart Red Cross uniform with its British medal ribbons which had provoked wonder and alarm from the Swiss Alps to the Pyrénées, Mary in her prison cell was a proud and unbowed figure. To the young girl from the S.O.E. she presented a vision that was quite incredible. "I couldn't really understand why she was there at all," recalls Yvonne. It was as if into the nightmare had walked something from a dream. "She was quite an extraordinary personality, very vivacious and very kind, who immediately took me under her wing and tried to reassure me. Of course she was an older woman and very self-possessed. She was not afraid of anyone, whatever their nationality, and the fact that she happened to be a prisoner didn't concern her at all.

"It was an extraordinary way of looking at it from my point of view. But it was marvellous to be in a cell with someone else who spoke the same language. . . ."

The need for companionship during her prison sentences was never high on Mary's list of priorities. She often gives the impression that such things are mere weaknesses of human nature. Nevertheless, she responded to the newcomer with a warmth and concern that was itself born out of respect.

"The difference between Yvonne Baseden and myself was that I wasn't brave because I wasn't frightened. Now she was scared—but she did it nevertheless. Therefore she was brave, because she definitely, most definitely was scared.

"She'd never been in prison and she hoped she'd never get in one. Whereas I, of course, had already been in one or two prisons. I knew what was waiting for me; it wasn't an unknown. Whilst for her it was an unknown. She was honestly scared, but nevertheless did it—so I think she was very brave."

Outside the prison walls the war was reaching its climax. On August 25, the Allies liberated Paris. The following day there were more advances in France, Bulgaria pulled out of the war, and Hitler ordered the evacuation of Greece. Each day brought news of fresh victories. The Americans liberated Soissons; the British took Arras; Dieppe and Rouen fell to the Canadians; Verdun, that mighty eastern fortress so resonant of the French sacrifices of the First World War, fell to the Americans. In England, despite the doodlebugs (V-1 rockets), there was an overwhelming sense of euphoria. In his diary Harold Nicolson wrote of the sheer excitement generated by the news from the Front: "It is almost impossible to follow this sequence of triumphs, and to remember what happened yesterday or today, and what will happen tomorrow. . . . All of us have a glass of gin and toast the future of France."

For the prisoners of the Reich this reversal of fortune brought great dangers as well as hope. It was not the Nazi way to allow their prisoners to be liberated when they withdrew from occupied territory. Often the approach of Allied forces was the signal for mass executions; more often still, prisoners were force-marched or shunted in cattle trucks to new and overcrowded camps in those shrinking areas over which the Nazis still had hegemony.

Late in August, Mary Lindell and Yvonne Baseden left the prison at Dijon and were transported by rail to the concentration camp of Ravensbrück, north of Berlin. They arrived on September 3. On the same day the British captured Brussels. It had been five years exactly since the war began.

Shortly afterwards, the Comte de Milleville, now living as a free man in a liberated Paris, heard a false report of his wife's fate. He ordered posters to be printed and distributed throughout the quartier announcing "with sorrow and with honour" that following her second arrest the Comtesse M. G. de Milleville had been shot by the Germans in the prison at Dijon on May 24. A footnote to the poster added the following quotation from her last conversation with members of the family. It has a characteristic ring about it. "If the Germans arrest me a second time, they will shoot me. I don't want you to go into mourning. I only want my family and my countrymen to avenge me by hunting down the Boches and smashing them completely."

Mary, of course, was not dead. She had disappeared into the *Nacht und Nebel*, the night and fog which Hitler had promised for his political enemies. More specifically, she had disappeared into the Hell for Women, as Ravensbrück was known by its thousands of female inmates. The main camp was designed only for women. It had been built shortly after the outbreak of war in 1939 in swampy land near Lake Fürstenberg in Mecklenburg, as a small cog of a concentration camp system designed to break its victims physically and spiritually by overwork, undernourishment and a thousand planned and random cruelties and humiliations. "The whole system," wrote one former prisoner, "had but one purpose and that was to destroy our humanity and our human conscience." With this even Mary, who never attached great weight to personal comfort, could agree, though not surprisingly she has her own way of expressing it. "The conditions in Ravensbrück," she says, "were pretty dim for the general public."

And getting dimmer. The system, which began as depraved and barbaric, was itself on the point of disintegration. The main camp, designed for six thousand, was overwhelmed by almost six times that number. As the war in Germany became more desperate, the meager camp rations were cut unsparingly, and conditions deteriorated rapidly. The last winter was the most dreadful of all. The "general public" perished in thousands.

But Mary had never in her life considered herself as general public. In her extraordinary way she managed—even here—to impose a pattern of respect in her dealing with the Nazis, who contained within their ranks some of the most infamous and disreputable figures in a profession that prided itself on rational bestiality.

"You must remember, I got there in a British uniform with a couple of rows of British decorations and an identity card with a title on it—which, you know, the Germans love. They were lost at the very beginning. The political officer was completely lost, and of course when I realized this, I threw my weight around a lot as you can imagine.

"They used to call me the arrogant Englishwoman: *die arrogante Engländerin*.

"I'd say, 'You're a lot of bastards.' I *was* arrogant and I consider we had the right to be arrogant, don't you, after all is said and done. We were winning the war and if there were ever any discussions with them, I used to say right at the beginning, 'You've lost it—you know perfectly well you've lost the war.' And they knew that they had too.

"Didn't stop them. They were beastly. The weaker the people, the more beastly they were."

Mary was fortunate. She was put to work as a nurse in the *Revier*, the camp hospital which had conveniences undreamed of in the concentration camp world: hot and cold running water, a lavatory with a door on it and, perhaps most important of all, exemption from the endless roll calls which took place whatever the weather, often lasting for hours at a time, and which more than anything else undermined the fragile health of the starving women prisoners. Mary's situation might not have looked that attractive. Her tasks included testing of new inmates for syphilis—"the worm's-eye view," as Mary called it. Yet for Yvonne Baseden and the other British prisoners, lodged in cramped, infested and disease-ridden barracks, it was one of the most enviable positions in the camp. It was also a position of responsibility which brought with it some influence. It was a small and limited influence but nevertheless one which, used with sense and discretion, could sometimes mean the difference between life and death. Mary's job in the hospital gave her the opportunity to do people favours. Other prisoners similarly installed in semi-official positions in the camp administration could likewise provide help. Working close to the Nazi authorities, they were in a better position to know what was going on. Like those of all the other prisoners, their lives were forfeit at the whim of the Nazi bosses, so naturally there was a limit to what they could do. There was no way anyone could possibly have stopped the erection of a gas chamber after Himmler's visit to the camp late in 1944. Nor was there any chance of saving the three of Yvonne's S.O.E. comrades who were shot on orders from Berlin in January 1945. But in other, less prominent cases something could often be done. On one occasion, for example, Mary was able to persuade an Alsatian girl who worked in the commandant's office to strike the name of a British woman off the list of those ordered to go on a death column. Mary's position and her outspokenness also brought her into contact with the camp authorities. It gave her access. This coupled with her own authoritative air made her the natural, if unofficial, leader of the small —about a dozen or so—group of Englishwomen in the camp.

She was fifty years old. Accustomed to putting a brave

face on things, she was loath to admit that the exertions of the past few years had taken it out of her. In 1942 she had been seriously injured in a car crash. A year later she was shot and badly smashed up as she jumped from a train. During her escape to England after her first period of imprisonment, she had almost died of pneumonia. Now, despite her privileged position in Ravensbrück, she was once again weakened by successive bouts of pneumonia. She was very ill when the rumours began to circulate in the camp that Count Folke Bernadotte, of the Swedish Red Cross, had come to an agreement with Himmler for the release of some of the prisoners. Mary was determined the British could be among them.

"Now I was captain of the British, but I had pneumonia and was dying, so I could do nothing. One or two of the Englishwomen used to come and say, 'What the hell are you doing?' and I said, 'Well, I'm trying not to die, you see, as far as possible.' And when at last I could get up, I can still see myself staggering across the Lagerstrasse, which was very big, and going to see the *Schutzlagerführer* and saying, 'Look—how about the British?' Well, he said he didn't know there were any there. But he knew it was a lie and then he arranged at once that they should leave.

"The following morning, when we should have left, we'd been warned not to go because we were going to be put on a death column.

"That afternoon I went back and saw the *Schutzlagerführer* again, who was frightfully ashamed of himself. He told me that it was beyond his control—which as a matter of fact I suppose it was. But he said, 'Get your people together and I personally shall see they get away.'

"And as a matter of fact he did."

This account fails to mention that the *Schutzlagerführer*, a man named Schwartzhuber, was a veteran of Dachau, Sachsenhausen and Auschwitz. That since his arrival in

Ravensbrück on January 12, 1945, he had supervised the liquidation of thousands of prisoners. Only someone who had been at the mercy of such a man can understand the dread he inspired in the ordinary prisoner, the risks involved in even approaching him, and the rashness of actually attempting to deal with him on equal terms.

Nor was it quite the end of the story. Schwartzhuber kept his word with relation to all the British women except one—Mary herself. She marched with the others to the camp gate and counted them as they stepped to freedom. Then as she headed towards the white buses sent by the Red Cross, she was stopped by a guard and told that she alone would have to remain behind. She turned back into the camp, hearing Yvonne Baseden, free but weeping behind her. "I thought you'd gone," someone said when they saw her.

"They loved me too much to let me go," came back Mary's hollow reply.

She returned to the camp hospital. There she met Dr. Percy Treite, the senior doctor in the camp, who was beside himself with fury when he heard what had happened to his nurse. Treite, half British himself, had developed respect and affection for Mary both during the period she had worked for him and the time he had nursed her through her pneumonia. Now, at some risk to himself, he escorted her once more to the camp gates and insisted on his authority that she should be allowed to join the convoy of buses which was waiting to depart.

Mary waited only long enough to bid him and the camp good-bye. Ravensbrück she never saw again. Dr. Treite only once more—two years later—at the War Crimes tribunal in Hamburg.

Today, Mary is an old English lady living alone in Paris: still proud, still—in her way—formidable. Fresnes Prison, Dijon, Ravensbrück are long ago, but Mary has never left the war behind. Like a retired general, she lives for her memories. At her apartment in the rue Erlanger, an invitation to afternoon tea can easily stretch beyond midnight as the old tales are recalled again. Once more in her eyes you can see the fire that inspired the Marie-Claire line and won grudging admiration from brutal Nazi guards. It is the Lindell style: pride and mischief. When at some point in her story she states, "I wee-weed with the Gestapo!" she is fully aware of the historical outrage she is perpetrating upon her listener. She enjoys his confusion. Mary Lindell, the Comtesse de Milleville, *die arrogante Engländerin*, is having fun. Sometimes, late in the evening, she will take from her bureau a folder of *faire-parts*, letters and cards bearing news of the deaths of her friends and comrades. It makes a sad pile. They were heroes once, but are dying now of nothing more heroic than simple old age. "You see, they're all dying off," she says without emotion. "I'm almost the only one that's living on. I'm unkillable."

On her return to France at the end of the war, Mary found both honour and sadness. The French government awarded her a second Croix de Guerre. But she also came home to discover that Oky, her second son, had been deported to Germany in 1944. He was never seen again. In 1947 she testified in Hamburg at the trial of the Ravensbrück war criminals. In the case of Dr. Percy Treite she appeared for the defense. "We English believe in fair play," she explained to the court. But she gave evidence against others in the camp hierarchy. In the event, Treite, like the others, was sentenced to death.

For many years Mary has battled with the French and British bureaucracies to win recognition for the former members of the Marie-Claire line and others in the Resistance. She remains to this day a prominent and outspoken member of the Royal Air Forces Association, Paris Branch. At the Arc de Triomphe, on Battle of Britain Day, amidst the veterans' blazers and the uniforms of the military, her tiny, neat figure stands to attention as the bugle plays out the last post and the RAF colours are dipped. The incessant Parisian traffic swirls past the scene where each year life becomes a little more like history. At the cocktail party that by tradition always follows the ceremony, Mary has a special place. "Ah, yes, our Mary," the greying officers say in English and French, "she never changes. . . ."

Back home, a bulldog portrait of Winston Churchill broods over Mary's living room where escapers hid after Dunkirk. A Union Jack hangs in the hallway. The bookshelves are full of war memoirs.

How much does she miss the war? What would she have done, this woman, without it?

"I wouldn't mind if there was another war," she says finally, "not if it was a nice one. Well, yes and no. No, perhaps I don't think so really. What's the good of hankering after something you know you can't have?"

Sigrid Lund

Christmas in Oslo, 1943. There was no end in sight, but at least the pattern of the war had become clear. Along with the Christmas mail, the clandestine newspapers spread the news of continuous setbacks and defeats for the Germans: the battleship *Scharnhorst* had been sunk; the Russians were advancing in the Kiev sector; Eisenhower had become Supreme Commander of the invasion forces massing in England.

In Oslo itself there had been a huge munitions explosion in the dockyards. Many had died or were injured. Windows were broken all over the town. Nobody seemed to know whether it was sabotage or accident, it just semed to confirm that the Nazis' luck was running out. In the hoarfrost on the fences, children had fingered in the slogan *Tyskland taper Krigen*, Gemany is losing the war. By the end of 1943 this was more than just wishful thinking.

But if a German defeat now appeared inevitable, the future remained full of uncertainty. For the armies on both sides the greatest sacrifices were still to be made, and if this were true in the main theatres of the war, it was no less so in the secret war played out between the

Gestapo and resisters of all kinds. Recognition of their impending defeat did nothing to dampen the enthusiasm of the Nazi security services. As the war drew towards its close, they became more vicious, more ruthless and more cruel.

In Norway as elsewhere a future Allied victory seemed assured, but it was what was happening in the present that continually heightened the tension and anxiety of all those working against the Nazis.

By December 1943 Sigrid Lund was fifty-one years old and had been active in the Norwegian underground for two and a half years. Already her son and others of her family were in concentration camps. Many of her friends had been arrested. Among the Christmas cards that arrived at her home in a northern suburb of Oslo was one which was sent from Romsdals Fjord in the west of Norway. It was a photograph of two children whom Sigrid had brought to Norway from Czechoslovakia with a party of Jewish refugees in 1939. They had been arrested and sent to Germany during the previous February. Since then nothing had been heard of them.

Looking at the photograph now, a photograph of two Jewish children from central Europe, a boy, Tibor, and a girl, Vera, we already have the sense that we are looking at doomed people. But for Sigrid and her family, unease at the fate of the children was still tempered with hope. They feared the worst, but in Oslo—even after two and a half years of occupation—what turned out to be the worst was still unthinkable.

In fact, thanks to the meticulous records kept by Adolf Eichmann's Reich Resettlement Bureau in Berlin, we now know with a grim certainty what happened to Vera and Tibor Tagelicht. After their arrest they had been taken to Bredtvedt Prison in the east of Oslo. Then on February 24, 1943, they were placed on board the transport ship *Gottenland*, bound for Stettin in Germany. On

board were over 150 other Jews—the oldest was eighty
and the youngest just six months. A cable to the Gestapo
chief in Stettin instructed him to expect seventy-four
men and eighty-four women and children, and to send
them to Berlin, where they were to join a transport train
to Auschwitz.

On arrival, the camp records show, some entered the
camp and were given numbers. The fate of the others—
which included all the women and children—is revealed
in the murderous, laconic prose of an unknown camp
official: *Die Übrigen wurden vergast*. The others were
gassed.

Looking at her Christmas card, Sigrid Lund knew
nothing of this. Vera and Tibor had disappeared, to
whatever fate she could only guess. What she did know
was that had it not been for the efforts of herself and her
friends in the Resistance, many more Jews—men,
women and children—would have shared the end the
Gestapo had planned for them.

Sigrid Lund (née Hellieson) was born in Oslo. Her
father was an artistically inclined and up-and-coming
young barrister who found himself in 1892, when Sigrid
was born, with a family that was growing faster than his
income. Yet there was never any impression of real hardship. The family was firmly based in the middle classes
with an enviable circle of friends both from the world of
politics (both sets of grandparents included members of
the national governments of Norway and Sweden) and
the theatre (where Sigrid's father had become secretary
to Norway's National Theatre).

As the youngest of four children, Sigrid now feels that
she was rather spoiled. But the picture she paints of her
upbringing is of an enlightened, caring family circle far
removed from the scenes of Scandinavian drama of the
period or the claustrophobic domestic canvases in Norway's national gallery. Her Swedish mother was a reli-

gious but undogmatic woman whose way of dealing with recalcitrant children was by gentle argument rather than punishment. She encouraged the children to think for themselves. They did—and quickly joined in the controversies of the day.

One of the these was the vexed question of the relations between Norway and Sweden. Norway was constitutionally linked to Sweden through a joint monarchy. But in a time of growing national awareness, Sigrid—despite her mixed parentage—had no hesitation in joining the Norwegian cause.

The children in her neighborhood split into two factions. One, which supported the union with Sweden, rallied to the defense of the so-called salad flag, which was the Norwegian standard with Swedish arms superimposed in one corner. The other side battled for the "clean" Norwegian flag. The war of the flags among the young folk of Christiania was long and harsh. It reflected the growing deterioration of relations between Norwegians and Swedes at a more adult level, which reached its crisis point in 1905. In that year a plebiscite among Norwegians recorded a 2000 to 1 majority in favour of a break with Sweden. The union collapsed. Sigrid was just thirteen. She had chosen correctly between her Swedish and her Norwegian relatives, and, not for the last time, she had had history on her side.

Hand in hand with her childhood nationalism was a growing ethical awareness. The family discussed religious and political issues with an openness that was unusual for the time. The children were expected to be independent and form their own opinions. By the time she was sixteen, Sigrid, influenced both by her mother's liberal attitudes and Tolstoy's humanist writings, had adopted a sense of values which placed a heavy emphasis on respect for the individual and the sanctity of life. Already she held these views with such conviction that she refused to be confirmed into the Norwegian state church. "The whole concept of some people being saved and others being condemned was completely against my belief in a God of love. Neither could I accept that it was right for one person to take over the guilt of another."

A few years later, when she was twenty-one, it was as an intellectually confident and aware young woman that Sigrid encountered, almost by accident, one of the key figures in the rise of Nazi racist ideology.

She was training to be a concert singer and in 1913 she travelled with her teacher to Bayreuth in Germany, the home of the Wagner cult. But it was more than Richard Wagner's music that his widow, Cosima, sought to perpetuate at the Bayreuth festivals. It was the whole pan-Germanic paraphernalia of his artistic theory: a gigantic construct of paganism, myth and Christianity laced with sporadic virulent attacks against the Jews. As a cultural center, it has been said, Bayreuth became a center of racism. As one acolyte put it: "For the first time since the scattering of the Aryan peoples they can once again gather at a pre-determined locality ... in order to witness their primeval mysteries."*

For young singers attending Bayreuth, a visit to the home of Cosima Wagner was almost obligatory, and it was here that Sigrid Lund met Houson Stewart Chamberlain, an English philosopher who had married Wagner's daughter Eva.

It was a curious encounter: the young, blond Norwegian girl, pretty, but serious-minded, already inspired by humanism and generosity of spirit; and the fanatical convert to Aryanism, the theoretician of the supremacy of the German people, and one of the fathers of twentieth-century antisemitism. One year before the outbeak of the

---

*Leopold Schröder, quoted by George L. Mosse in *Toward the Final Solution* (Dent, 1978).

First World War, the pacifist from Norway and the protagonist of a race war against the Jews sat down and had tea at Bayreuth. Nearly seventy years later, Sigrid Lund's recollection of the meeting is undimmed:

"I had read his book [*Die Grundlagen des XIX Jahrhunderts*] before I came to Germany. And when I met him I had lots of discussions with him and was terrified to hear what he actually meant about the superiority of the German race, and also, of course, his point of view concerning the Jews, which terrified me even more. That was my first meeting with Nazi thoughts, from which I took a very sharp distance from the beginning."

Thus it was that on the eve of the First World War, when she was only twenty-one, Sigrid Lund had acquired exactly those qualities of humanism, patriotism and a deep distaste of antisemitism which she would use to fight the Second World War.

By the time Sigrid was forced to put her principles to the test, a generation had passed. She had married Diderich Lund, a civil engineer, in 1923. The following year their first son, Bernt, was born, and six years later a second, handicapped son, Erik. But the cares of bringing up a young family did not prevent her from observing what was happening abroad. She was active in the Women's International League of Peace and Freedom, a supporter of the Labour Party, and she was drawn naturally into one of the organizations helping the ever-increasing numbers of political refugees from Nazi Germany, among them Willy Brandt and Thomas Theodor Heine, an illustrator of the Munich weekly *Simplicissimus*. By the outbreak of the war around two thousand political exiles had fled to Norway. It was no secret what was going on. Sigrid and her friends tried to campaign for the freedom of political prisoners in Germany. They sent money and parcels to their wives and families together with letters of support.

Most Norwegians had a far less committed attitude towards the political behaviour of their neighbours. "What Norway desired from international politics was respect for its wish to be left alone," wrote the Norwegian authors of *Norway and the Second World War*,* and throughout the increasingly hostile climate of the 1930s, most of Norway's nearly three million population put their faith in the country's traditional policy of neutrality. Their complacency meant that Norway found herself less prepared militarily for the Second World War, in which she was forced to take part, than for the First, in which she did not take part.

But while Norway slept, Sigrid continued her work for the refugees. In 1937 she joined Nansenhjelp (Nansen Help), an organization set up by Odd Nansen, the son of Norway's most celebrated international statesman. In 1939, after the war had begun in the rest of Europe, Nansen sent Sigrid and another Norwegian woman to Czechoslovakia, to bring back to Norway a group of nearly forty Jewish children. On a station platform in Prague she got her first glimpse of the true meaning of the "racial war against the Jews" which had terrified her in Bayreuth so many years before.

"It was a very moving moment when the children said good-bye to their parents, who they did not know whether they would see ever again . . . and to see these parents carrying their small suitcases with their clothes, small toys and all the things to give some joy and help and support to the children, and how they stood there alone back in the station—it was a very, very sad moment. And we didn't know at all at that time what would happen, either to the children or to the parents."

---

*Johs Andenaes, Olav Riste and Magne Skodvin, *Norway and the Second World War* (Oslo: Johan Grundt Tanum Forlag, 1974).

But just how sad a moment, neither the Norwegian ladies nor the young Jewish children could have known. There was every hope that they would be reunited with their families; indeed, they had been chosen to go to Norway because their parents already had affidavits granting them freedom to leave for the United States. The children left Prague more in a spirit of adventure than of sorrow. They were told it would be a short trip. One boy, aged seven at the time, remembers thinking that going to Norway meant travelling to a very cold country, close to the North Pole, where he would see icebergs in the street.

But not all the thoughts they carried with them were so hopeful or lighthearted. The journey would take them through Germany, and they had often heard their parents talking of the antisemitism of the Germans. They were frightened by the uniforms and motorcycles of the German troops who had occupied Czechoslovakia a few months earlier. Bertold Grunfeld, one of the children and now a pyschiatrist in Oslo, remembers clearly a warning they were given just before the journey began. "We had to be very careful," he recalls, "because we were Jewish children, not to provoke people in the streets. So they said be very careful, don't show off so that people would not get harmed by you. . . ."

They reached Berlin, where they had to change trains, at the same time as the citizens of the capital of the Third Reich were celebrating victory over Poland. The city was bedecked with flags. Soldiers from the front poured through the stations back from a successful campaign: a high point in the history of Hitler's Germany. Bertold Grunfeld remembers capturing something of the excitement and exhilaration of the moment. But for Sigrid Lund, leading the crocodile of Jewish children through wartime Berlin, there was something else in the triumphant atmosphere: the poisonous hatred of pavement antisemitism, which did not even spare the young, baffled children of a foreign country. The drivers on the trams refused to take Jews on board, and the party had to walk.

"We noticed," Sigrid remembers, "that some people, and there were lots of people in the streets, spat at these small children. And one of the boys came up to me and said, 'What is the matter that people are spitting so much here in Berlin?'

"And I knew perfectly well the reason, but I said to him, 'Oh, they've probably got a cold or something like that, don't bother about it.' And off he went. We were terrified that ordinary people could behave like that when they saw small children. I never would have thought it was possible."

The journey continued without incident. There was just one more small indication of how far, in 1939, after only six years of the Third Reich, the fear of Hitler's Jewish policies had spread. When after a stormy night at sea the children arrived at Trelleborg, in Sweden, they were met by a party of Swedish women from the Women's International League of Peace and Freedom. But Sigrid noticed at once that the children were frightened and unhappy. "They wouldn't talk to these fair, nice-looking, blue-eyed ladies. They had a kind of feeling that fair people, blue-eyed people were not to be relied upon. They were dangerous. Something that they didn't trust, quite simply. And we had to tell them that in Sweden and Norway most people were fair-haired and there was absolutely nothing to be frightened of."

The children went on to Oslo, from where most were distributed to foster homes throughout the southern part of Norway. It was the winter of 1939–40. What for western Europe was known as the phony war was for Norway a phony peace. Even as the children were settling into their new homes, a former Norwegian minister of defense, Vidkun Quisling, leader of the country's tiny Fascist Party, was in Berlin, arguing for a German invasion of his homeland. The Germans were impressed. Admiral Erich Raeder saw the need for U-boat bases in the Norwegian fjords; others were concerned to protect the routes through which Swedish iron ore reached the Reich. Above all, the Nazis were determined that neutral Norway would not fall to the Western Allies. From the beginning of 1940, when Hitler ordered plans to be drawn up for an invasion of Norway, the Norwegians were living on borrowed time.

But the Norwegians themselves remained optimistic about their future. So too did the refugees who until the last moments of peace continued to seek asylum. So too did the Czech parents of the children Sigrid Lund had brought from Prague. And so did Sigrid herself and her friends, who themselves had every reason to understand what was going on. They had worked with the refugees and knew about the concentration camps; they had spoken to political exiles from Germany; and they had no delusions about Hitler's territorial ambitions. But in each case the sadism of the camps and the logic of modern war escaped them. The children had been brought out of Czechoslovakia because "something might have happened to them," because "some of their parents had already been taken prisoner." In other words, Nansenhjelp had intervened to prevent an *envisageable* plight. No one, not even those closest and most sympathetic to the problem, realized that in bringing to Norway thirty-seven children they would be writing the merest footnote to a disaster of such great scale.

"Oh, no, we couldn't imagine that that would be possible. We thought perhaps that they would put them into concentration camps. But we did never, never think of what really happened: That would not be possible. That was not in our imagination. I think nobody believed that except for some of the parents. Some of the Jews themselves. They were afraid of it. But we were not; we didn't think of it. It can't happen here and it can't happen in Europe. Such things. We didn't believe it!"

The truth dawned slowly. But there must have been more than a vague suspicion a few months later when seven-year-old Bertold Grunfeld met an old lady who was visiting the orphanage in Oslo where he was living. He told her how much he had enjoyed living in Norway and how he liked the people he found there. But, he added, he was really looking forward to going back home to Czechoslovakia. Forty years later he has no difficulty in remembering her reply. "She looked at me very seriously and she said, 'I tell you, you will never go back to Czechoslovakia and probably you will never see your parents either.'"

The German invasion of Norway and Denmark, which began on the night of April 8–9, 1940, was the product of dream and reality. The dream was that of the Norwegian traitor Quisling, who, with Alfred Rosenberg, the overblown Nazi ideologist with whom he had conspired in Berlin in December 1939, believed in the innate superiority of the Nordic races. He wanted to create a "Greater Nordic Peace Union," based in all the states bordering on the North Sea. Politically it was nonsense; among his Norwegian countrymen it was also unpopular. Quisling's *Nsjonal Samling* (National Unity) Party (NS) received less than 2 percent of the votes in the last election before the war. But for Quisling, his ideas echoed satisfactorily the rising racism of his Nazi neighbours. To their Teutonic legend he replied with Norse saga. When he went visiting the Führer, he took a Viking warship. It was the entrance fee to a club celebrating blond barbarism and "the belief," as Rosenberg put it, "incarnate with the most lucid knowledge, that Nordic blood represents that mystery which has replaced and overcome the old sacraments."

The reality was rather different. Hitler was nothing if

not pragmatic and the motives for the invasion as listed on the directive authorized by him on March 1, 1940, predictably list only practical considerations: to preempt any British initiative; to protect the Swedish iron ore route; and to improve the strategic position of the German navy. In the end the German invasion and occupation of Norway was based on the strategic outlook of the German General Staff. The ideology and dreams of a tiny neo-Nazi minority of the tiny Norwegian population played no part. Nevertheless there was still time for Quisling to render one more service to Berlin. On April 3, one week before the invasion took place, at the Hotel d'Angleterre in Copenhagen, he met Colonel Pickenbrock of the German intelligence service, to reveal to him what he knew of Norwegian defenses. There is no reason to believe that even here Quisling told the Germans much that they didn't already know.

On the night of the invasion Sigrid Lund was out of Oslo, giving a lecture on pacifism. The war still seemed a long way away. It was a Monday. Throughout the day the newspapers and radio had reported a series of ominous developments: The British had mined Norwegian waters; one hundred German ships had been sighted moving through the straits between Denmark and Sweden. And yet such was the sense of charmed innocence with which the Norwegians viewed their pacific and neutral foreign policy that still they were incapable of believing that war was upon them. As Sigrid returned home late in the evening she heard an air-raid siren, but in common with many others did not believe it. She went to bed. The next morning she was woken by the sound of gunfire.

It is perhaps easier to imagine the act of invasion than the experience of being invaded. From the German point of view, Operation Weserübung, as the invasion was code-named, was a strikingly successful surprise attack. There were startling innovations: large-scale airborne landings; simultaneous landings all along the Norwegian coast that left the British Admiralty not so much ruling the waves as literally guessing where the Germans would strike next. There were setbacks, one or two of them embarrassing. The cruiser *Blücher*, carrying the first wave of Gestapo, whose mission was to arrest the king, was blown out of the water by the antiquated batteries of the fortress of Oscarsborg in Oslofjord. But it did not take long to overwhelm the Norwegian army in the south of the country, and it was only a matter of a further few weeks before the Allied forces sent to help Norway were withdrawn and the north of Norway too fell into German hands. It would not be the last time in 1940 that the German army would demonstrate its capacity to strike suddenly, quickly and with devastating effect.

If you are an invader, your priorities are clear. They have been worked out beforehand. This is not the case if you have been invaded. On Tuesday, April 9, 1940, in the Lund household, no one knew what to do. As the German planes flew overhead on their way to bomb Fornebu Airport a few miles down the road, there seemed three possibilities: to stay put, to run away, or to go downtown and see what was happening. In the next few hours Sigrid would try all three.

The most difficult thing to decide is, When have things stopped being normal? Diderich Lund, Sigrid's husband, was away in Sweden and she was alone at home with her two sons. The most natural thing was to send Bernt, the elder boy, to school as usual. But he was sent home again. School was closed. Something was happening. For several hours they waited at home for news. Friends came round, but no one knew what was going on. Finally the radio announced that the Germans had landed at the airport and were on their way into Oslo. Bernt, who was sixteen, asked to be allowed to go into town to see for himself what was happening. Again there was a problem: What, after all, is permissible during an invasion? "Off he went," recalls Sigrid, "to my great sorrow and dissatisfaction." But she was anxious and restless and after half an hour walked after him into the center of Oslo.

"I don't think it is possible to explain to somebody who has not experienced it what it is like to see troops, foreign troops coming with their swastikas in our streets —in our good Norwegian streets. Troops, masses of them, coming marching in this goose step, with their feet high up in the air. And it was terrible to see them. You couldn't believe it was true to begin with. It seemed to me that something strange, unbelievable had happened to us. But after a while, we had to realize, This is the truth, this is the reality now, this is the life we have to go on living with these people here in this country. And for how long, nobody knew. And what were they going to do to us, to our people, to our children, to everything here in the country? We didn't know."

What Sigrid did know, as she returned home to the suburbs, was that the refugees she had helped to bring to Norway over the past few years were now once again in danger of falling into the hands of the Nazis. That night, in the furnace of her cellar, she and the secretary of Nansenhjelp incinerated all records and papers concerning the refugees. All told, it had been a quiet invasion. The people of Oslo had taken it very sensibly for a people who had not been at war for 125 years. But now rumours began to spread that the city was about to be bombed. There was panic as people seized on any form of transport to get out of Oslo. Early the next morning, Sigrid, her two children and her young niece drove off for the countryside. Behind them, in the garden of her pretty wood-built house in the Tuengen Alle, the charred ashes of the Nansenhjelp records were still burning untidy black holes in the snow.

All victorious armies are alike, but a defeated nation is defeated after its own fashion. A country's response to defeat depends on many things: size, history, tradition, expectation, most of all upon the cohesion of the society itself. Norway was not France; Norwegians could not feel the humiliations of a proud nation militarily worsted in the latest round of a millennial contest. Nor was Norway like Poland. The Nazis did not come swaggering with racial superiority. On the contrary, they came as racial brothers. For the Poles there was only subjugation and annihilation. For the Norwegians there was a choice. They could, if they were so inclined, accept the outstretched hand of partnership. In addition, Poles were accustomed to foreign occupation. They had a tradition of conspiracy and resistance. Norwegians, as we have seen, were totally unprepared.

For the Lund family there was another important consideration which affected their freedom to decide how they should behave in the new circumstances. They were all pacifists. The single, most significant principle on which the family was founded was respect for life. As Sigrid puts it: "You should not do anything to harm another human being, whatever their philosophy, but you should try to help them in whatever way you can." Even during the bitter afternoon when she watched the Wehrmacht enter Oslo, Sigrid never contemplated armed resistance. "It never occurred to me that I should be a soldier myself and kill them to get them away. They were ordinary people, each one of them, boys, sons of ordinary mothers in their homeland. So it never occurred to me that I should be one who wanted to kill them. But of course I didn't know at that time what I could do to save our people from them and from their influence." In December 1948, looking back at the beginning of the war, Sigrid's husband, Diderich, wrote:

> Under the German occupation we found that most of us might live comparatively comfortably and undisturbed, if only we could force our eyes not to see, and our ears not to hear. But the urge to help when you see someone in distress is very strong, and just as strong will be the demand to fight for the values that make life worth living.

And he added:

> We discovered early in the occupation that a great deal depended on how we had prepared ourselves before the outbreak of war. The calm and detached exchange of views becomes almost impossible after war breaks out, and in most countries only a small minority think of any alternative to military warfare when it comes to fighting for the values they wish to defend.

In fact, the deep commitment of the Lund family to a fully articulated and well-established set of values, its awareness of the fact that "the life of the individual can be most fully and deeply developed in a democratic society," meant that they understood at once the necessity of opposing the Nazis, and from the beginning looked for opportunities to resist. After their defeat in April, it took the confused and demoralized Norwegian people a little longer to come to the same realization.

The Norwegians had little to be hopeful about. Their tiny army had had its gallant moments, but it soon became clear that the circumstances in which mobilization had taken place had been chaotic to the point of comedy. They blamed and resented their government for the lack of preparedness. Nor did the belated intervention of the Allies produce anything to restore confidence. Rumours quickly circulated that British soldiers retreated at the sight of the Germans, that they were ill disciplined, poorly equipped, and stole whatever caught their eye. A British woman in Norway at the time noted, "It will take a lot to remove the picture the Norwegians have of the British forces." Early in June, the Anglo-French forces were withdrawn from Norway. On June 7, King Haakon was taken into exile by the Royal Navy on board H.M.S. *Devonshire*. The remaining Norwegian armies in the north had no choice but to capitulate. "All our hopes collapsed," wrote one commentator, "and the people felt that they had been abandoned and deserted by their leaders and Allies." A few days later, when the news came through of the German breakthrough in France, it seemed that the Norwegians had not merely lost the battle but the war as well. The Germans were there to stay, for who now could displace them?

And so, leaderless and without a glimmer of hope for the future, the Norwegians had to decide whether to take the olive branch held out to them by the new Nazi administration. It was the key choice: whether to settle for living "comparatively comfortably and undisturbed" or to fight for those "values that make life worth living." But that choice, as formulated by the Lund family, asks for only one answer. Other saw it differently. The Federation of Norwegian Industries argued, as such business associations will, in favour of cooperation with the Germans. On June 14 they issued a statement which read, ". . . any Norwegian citizen—or any Norwegian company—is legally entitled to make contracts with the occupying power for any work or service whatever within the confines of the realm"—a collaborationists' charter. Labour organizations too sought ways of working with the Germans. The Communists (no doubt moved by considerations of the Ribbentrop-Molotov Pact, which, of course, was still in force) urged that everything should be done "to maintain the standard of living and make sure of supplies" by "an increased exchange of goods with Germany."

"The Government and the King who are sitting in London have left Norway in the lurch," wrote the leading Communist newspaper in June. "Norway needs a new governmental authority, a Cabinet prepared to make peace with Germany and to lead the people out of the present war among the Great Powers. The workers must throw their weight onto the scales on the side of peace between Norway and Germany. . . ."* The Communists were only one voice of a powerful pro-German faction within the Norwegian trade-union movement which supported an accommodation with the Nazis.

This mood of pessimism and acquiescence threatened to play straight into the Germans' hands. What Hitler wanted was a compliant Norway which could without difficulty be incorporated into the New Order for Nazi Europe. A prerequisite was that the Norwegians remove the king from his throne and their exiled government in London from office and in their place set up a new government which would make peace with Germany. On June 17, "the darkest day of all," as one Norwegian historian has called it, Hitler very nearly got his way. It was the day that France surrendered. In Oslo, the presidential board of the Storting called upon King Haakon to abdicate. His answer came broadcast from the BBC in London: No. For most Norwegians today, his clear and steadfast refusal to go, coupled with a rising sense of shame that the demand for abdication had ever been made, marks the beginning of resistance and the end of that ambivalence and purposelessness which had followed their defeat. In England the fiasco of the British

---

*Quoted by Tore Gjelsvik in *Norwegian Resistance 1940–1945* (London: C. Hurst & Co., 1979), page 7.

96

intervention in Norway had led to a change of prime minister. Now Churchill was in charge, and just as his radio broadcasts galvanized the will of the British people to fight on, so did King Haakon's transmissions reassure Norwegians that all was not lost. The rhetoric was different, but the effect was the same:

> Norwegian women and men!
> We are fighting against an enemy who does not understand us—who does not comprehend the firm-rooted love of the fatherland which lives within every Norwegian and with which we who are now in exile are more than ever filled. It is quite unthinkable for us that we should not be able to continue to build and live in a Norway where we decide ourselves over our fate and we cannot believe that the thirst for liberty and the desire for freedom will ever die in the hearts of Norwegians. The Norwegian people has never, even in times of decline, been a race of serfs and nor is it today. I send, together with the crown prince, the warmest greetings to all Norwegian women and men —in house and cottage. Let us remember the words of the national anthem: "Thank thy God whose powers willed and wrought the land's salvation in her darkest hour!"

Norway's royal family is not remote from the people. There was no long monarchical tradition. Haakon was in fact Danish; he had been invited to take the throne in 1905, when Norway had broken with Sweden. But this only magnified the effect that his resolution and steadfastness made among his subjects. Like most ordinary Norwegians who listened to the broadcasts, Sigrid Lund has no doubt that they were a turning point:

"When he had to go over to England and he gave his talk to us, he told us that he would never stop being the king of Norway as long as he felt it was the wish of the people. He became a kind of symbol for us all. He was the one who would keep it going—whatever happened.

"In one way we felt that it was absolutely what we expected from him. But on the other hand, it gave an enormous impulse to us all to continue and not to surrender in any way. I think it meant that one took up the courage and then said that when the king can say such things, then we will do whatever we can for his sake, and for the sake of the country, and for our own sake."

The Norwegian Resistance had found its hero and its figurehead. It was, at the same time, about to discover its villain.

At 7:32 P.M. on April 9—the day of the invasion—Vidkun Quisling in a radio broadcast from Oslo (which, in the words of a plaque in Norway's National Resistance Museum, made his name synonymous with traitor) declared that he and his party were taking over the government of Norway. As a coup d'état it had all the earmarks of Quisling's career for the next five years. It was bungling, overambitious and almost totally lacking in popular support.

The German ambassador, Curt Brauer, charged with coming to terms with the Norwegians and securing their cooperation quickly, understood that despite all his pretensions Quisling spoke only for himself and could offer the Germans nothing by way of getting the country back to normal. Within a week the German authorities had replaced Quisling's "national government." At the end of April, Hitler placed Norwegian destiny in the hands of Reichskommissar Joseph Terboven, the former *Gauleiter* of Essen. Terboven, a ruthless and shrewd Party boss who had learned his politics the hard way in the tough school of extremist street fights in the days of the Weimar Republic, quickly understood that in any attempt to win over the Norwegians, Vidkun Quisling was a liability.

But Quisling had friends in high places in Berlin. Hitler was anxious that he should be given recognition, as were his fellow conspirators, Rosenberg and Raeder. He spent August in Germany and impressed the Führer sufficiently to be confident that there would be some role for him in the new Norway. On September 25, Terboven abolished all political parties except Quisling's NS. From now on, Norwegians were told, there was only "one way to freedom and independence, namely through NS."*

The Resistance now had a clear and manageable target: to prevent the Nazification of their society by Quisling and his henchmen. To have attacked the German Army, at a time when no outside help was forthcoming, would have provoked massive retaliation out of all proportion to any gains that could be made. But to stop Quisling from subverting Norwegian life was a task for the whole community. It was a task, moreover, which lent itself to passive resistance; that is to say, a task fit for pacifists.

So for Sigrid there was no single moment of decision. All her life she had opposed everything that constituted the Nazi view of the world. Now the Nazi system which had come to Norway allowed the expression of only one point of view, so opposition automatically became resistance. The other members of her family found their own paths to resistance. At first it was an almost imperceptible slide into conspiracy. The simple fact was that after a few months of German occupation, the desire to speak or read or even hear the truth forced more and more ordinary Norwegians into conspiratorial and clandestine ways of behaviour.

The family home on the Tuengen Alle became in no time what Nazi police would have called a "nest of sub-

*Gjelsvik, *op. cit.*

version." But almost before any resistance activity could
get under way, the family was joined by an outsider
whom they had volunteered to take in. Early on Monday
morning, September 30, a young Englishwoman with a
green suitcase made her way up the Tuengen Alle towards the Lunds' home. Her name was Myrtle Wright.
She was a Quaker who had been stranded in Norway at
the time of the German invasion with little more than
ten kroner in her purse and a chance of getting home
which dwindled with every German victory of that dark
summer. As she entered the wooden gate and approached through the garden, everything seemed silent.
It was still early, perhaps there was no one up. But as she
rang the bell, the whole family emerged in dressing
gowns to meet her. "Come in," she was told, "you're just
in time to hear the BBC news from London."

With Myrtle Wright in the house, the Lund family had
acquired not only a friend, but a chronicler. For most of
the war their English guest kept a diary, which obliquely
and with simple coded notes followed the fortunes of a
family putting everything at risk.

It began with underground newspapers, designed not
so much as a means of communication between activists
but—in the absence of a free press—as a vital channel for
keeping the public at large aware of what was happening. Before long Bernti Lund was editing one of these
sheets from the local high school. He was just sixteen,
but there was no question of his parents intervening to
keep him out of trouble. "He was grown up enough with
his sixteen years to know what he did, and he did it
together with his friends. So it was impossible for a
mother to say No, don't do it—he wouldn't have
obeyed."

Diderich, whose civil engineering company had contracts throughout Norway, began to use his opportunities for travel, to coordinate resistance groups in the
remote north of Norway. He was, in fact, closely linked

with the central committees of the underground and in an ideal position to carry their instructions from one part of the country to another. "I became aware that Diderich had 'chores,'" wrote Myrtle Wright in her diary, "which were not strictly connected with civil engineering. But I knew nothing of the exact nature of the underground leadership until after the war. . . ."

Sigrid was involved in another vital area—the distribution of funds to the families that had been separated by the war. In the beginning, many of these were the families of merchant seamen who had defected, with the king, and who were deemed by the Germans to be fighting with the enemy. But later, more and more, the money would be passed to those whose breadwinners had been arrested by the Gestapo. The money, usually in high-denomination notes, was smuggled in from Sweden, having originated in London. There were times when Sigrid, returning home from a rendezvous, would limp past the bizarre Vigeland sculptures in Frogner Park in Oslo with 25,000 kroner hidden in her shoes. It was from the beginning forbidden work—later it carried the death penalty. But Sigrid continued. "I knew perfectly well that it was risky, but it wasn't so easy for them to work out that the lady who walked with a little difficulty, perhaps with a limp, had a great deal of money in her shoes."

Slowly, almost unconsciously, family life changed as each member of the household, except for Sigrid's eight-year-old retarded child, Erik, learned to lead a double life. "The whole family was involved in so many things," remembers Sigrid, "but it was an unspoken law that we should not tell each other anything about what we were into in this kind of secret work. None of us knew really what the other one was doing." The result was a life of tension that would last for nearly four years. Occasionally, Sigrid and Myrtle would get away to the countryside, "living as ordinary people could live" for a week or so, but as the war went on, events made it increasingly difficult to forget the threat to herself and her family.

"In one way we were always frightened, we always knew that something could happen, either to yourself or to one of the family or the rest of your friends. But that didn't hinder us from doing it. We had to do it, it was a natural thing which couldn't be avoided. When we woke up in the morning, we always thought, Oh, now a good night has passed and we are still safe. That was the feeling we had every morning. So, frightened? I think it's right to say we were frightened, even if we didn't show it to each other, and even if we didn't actually feel it as fear—but something we had to live with all the time."

It was a frightening but not a lonely struggle. After the wavering of that first uncertain summer of Occupation, the Norwegian people began to find their voice. Important figures in public life began to speak out against the New Order, regardless of the personal risk. In Stavanger, three days after Terboven's speech nominating the NS as the sole political party, the editor of the local Labour newspaper published a dangerous and devastating reply:

> We have only one choice, to serve the best interests of our people; we cannot throw mud in our heritage nor seek anything for ourselves—*No Norwegian for Sale.* Hundreds of Norwegians have already offered their lives; thousands of European youths are dying and the civilian population is drawn in also. This is no time to consider our personal good, it is our people's future which is at stake.*

---

*Quoted Myrtle Wright, *Norwegian Diary 1940–1945* (London: Friends Peace and International Relations Committee, 1974), page 37.

The paper was immediately closed down. But the challenge to the Nazis had been made and their own chosen champion was hardly in a position to rise to the occasion.

Quisling was on probation. Hitler had promised him a leading role in the new Norway, but Reichskommissar Terboven, in whom all effective power in Norway resided, was not prepared to sacrifice any of his prerogative to a native ideologue and his untested and ludicrously small band of followers. Quisling was an intelligent but inflexible man. His uncritical sense of his own destiny blinded him to the obvious fact that even a dictator, the future leader of the Nordic races, needed friends and a power base among his own countrymen. He had adopted the "leader principle" as early as 1933, styling himself *Forer* (Führer) and creating his own paramilitary bodyguard, the *Hird*, named after the retinues of medieval Norwegian kings, but consciously modelled on the SS. But there the similarity ends. Unlike Hitler, Quisling never learned to compromise, never understood that powerful interests need careful handling. Germany's Führer was a wolf: He knew the value of violence and conciliation, of stealth as well as strength. Norway's tinpot *Forer* only put on jackboots the better to put his foot in it.

The result was that in 1939 the *Nasjonal Samling* numbered only seven thousand members, no subscriptions had been collected for two years, and in most of Norway there was little or nothing happening which could justify the title of "party activity." The Nazis in Germany had steamrollered into power under their own violent momentum. In Norway a crankish group of Right Wing extremists were handed office like something to play with, wrapped up and parcelled by a foreign, occupying power.

Yet it was this almost defunct organization which now began the job of transforming Norwegian society. It was as if the Hell's Angels had taken over the White House. The political consequences were—from a German point of view—catastrophic. Quisling was not a man who would content himself with half measures. He interfered in every area of Norwegian life, with the result that more and more Norwegians reacted against him, his party and his Nazi masters. The pattern was set at the beginning when the *Nasjonal Samling* attempted to reorganize Norwegian sport. The athletes simply replied by boycotting all matches and events arranged by the NS for the next five years. When the NS "Commissioner Minister of Justice" attempted to interfere with the independence of the Supreme Court, the judges resigned. The empty seats in the Supreme Court and the empty spaces in the sports grounds symbolized the opposition of other groups and institutions—teachers, doctors, farmers, shipowners and churchmen. The attack on Norwegian institutions backfired completely—and it galvanized Norwegian resistance. By the spring of 1941 forty-three organizations had handed a statement to Reichskommissar Terboven protesting the lawless behaviour of the NS. The Party, this audacious and extraordinary letter asserted, was forcing Norwegians to compromise with their consciences and with what they considered right and proper. There was disquiet everywhere, it said, irritation and bitterness.

In the Lund household Myrtle Wright was noting in her diary the rising popular feeling of opposition. On the ski slopes there were fist fights between the *Hird* and young people wearing "red flashes" to indicate support for the king. In schools NS pupils were sent to Coventry. In Bernti's school a new boy from a Nazi family was made so miserable that he disappeared after a few days "and the Riis School had the honour of being the one perfectly 'clean' school in the town." The German authorities watched Quisling's discomfiture with annoyance and ill-concealed contempt. In the streets of Oslo it was seen that German officers would stand aside, smiling, as they watched the NS *Hird* trying to control a hostile crowd. But newly installed in their headquarters on Victoria Terrasse, the Gestapo regarded these developments more seriously. As old hands at political conspiracy, they knew that these open demonstrations of discontent required coordination, that somewhere, becoming more and more effective, there was the clandestine machinery of an underground organization. By 1941 they were ready to direct their activities not just against those eminent and conspicuous Norwegians who chose to stand up and be counted, but also against their secret confederates who remained in the shadows. For those familiar with the hallmarks of Nazi terror there are some points to be noticed. In January, Himmler paid a visit to Oslo. He was followed later in the year by Heydrich. The systematic torture of prisoners began in the spring.

It was about this time that friends of Sigrid began to be arrested. One of them, a photographer, a fellow member of the Women's International League of Peace and Freedom, had refused to take the photograph of a German officer and had made the additional mistake of declaring that she had no intention of working for "sneaking murderers." Another was put in jail for distributing "secret papers." Bernti narrowly missed arrest while distributing illegal newspapers, and Diderich actually spent five days in prison as a result of his vigorous resignation from the Engineers' Association, which had been forcibly taken over by the NS. In the space of a very short time Sigrid and her family found themselves daily committing capital offenses. Despite the fact that the German soldiers in the streets behaved impeccably, often, it was noticed, standing back in the tram queues to allow Norwegians to go first, they knew perfectly well what to be arrested would mean. At the same time, as Sigrid says, "I had to be the mother of the house, the mother of the family, seeing that everything was going as well as it could. We had our ration cards, but our meals were always difficult, because we really hadn't enough to eat." Sigrid was learning—as fellow resistance workers throughout Europe were learning too—how to combine the role of housewife and mother with that of subversive. Yet in Norway's small and oddly cosseted society, the contrast between this gentle pacifist lady and the men who operated down the road in the Victoria Terrasse, who would not have hesitated to destroy her and her family, appears exaggerated. It was a contrast echoed in thousands and thousands of ordinary Norwegian homes. As Diderich Lund put it, "The solidarity was so general and widespread that one had the feeling one might enter any door and ask for protection. I should like to be able to impress upon you," he goes on, "that strange feeling of quiet happiness that filled most of us even under hard and difficult conditions." It was the smallness of Norwegian society (in 1939 the entire population was less than that of Berlin) that gave its resistance movement, in Oslo at least, a certain quality of neighbourliness. It was heroism with a sense of proportion. The endless difficulties of war are illuminated by a curious event unthinkable elsewhere in Europe. "For instance, in this house," says Sigrid, "after a while every second Thursday a young woman came here with a suitcase. And in the suitcase she had British papers, *The Times* and other papers, which we read with the most firm interest that you ever could think of."

There was the same sense of closeness in times of tragedy. Early one September morning in 1941, two trade unionist leaders, Viggo Hansteen and Rolf Wickstrøm, were picked up by the Gestapo and taken to Victoria Terrasse. By evening they had been shot. By an underground route similar to that by which the newspapers arrived at the Tuengen Alle, Sigrid was asked to take a message to one of the widows from the king and government-in-exile in London. Within two days she arrived at Kirsten Hansteen's home with a large bunch of flowers.

Early in 1942, Sigrid became involved in the very beginning of one of the most successful demonstrations of Norwegian passive resistance. In February two teachers, Helga and Asta Stene, came to see Sigrid at the Tuengen Alle. They had heard through contacts in the Education Department that Quisling was planning a Nazi youth organization as part of a concerted attempt by the NS to introduce Nazi doctrines into the schools. The plan to block it was worked out with devastating effect by Sigrid, Myrtle Wright and the two teachers. A letter of protest was drafted, to be signed and sent from all parents of schoolchildren and to arrive at the Department of Education on the same day. The first copies of the letter were printed on the printing presses in Bernti's school; they were distributed through underground channels all over Norway. In her diary Myrtle Wright reports the result: The authorities were overwhelmed by the letters, all signed and addressed from tens of thousands of parents. "It was beyond our wildest dreams," she says. The ministry withdrew its plans. The parents' action, as it became known, had been completely successful. But once again it had shown that open public demonstrations against the Nazis depended heavily on underground organization. And the Lunds were about to pay the price for their involvement. In the summer of 1942, just after a party to celebrate his last day at school, Sigrid's elder son, Bernti, was arrested. This is how Sigrid describes now the moment that has become a European nightmare, the moment when the Gestapo bang on the door in the middle of the night:

"For us personally the worst moment during the

whole Occupation was the night when the Gestapo came to arrest our son. He was not quite eighteen years old, so he was a young man. And, of course, afterwards I regretted very much that I didn't say that 'You can't take him, you had rather take me, because he's much too young to know what he's done.' But of course he was grown-up enough to know what he had done, so it didn't occur to me to say anything like that. But they came here during the night at about two o'clock. We saw the light of the car coming up the Alle here. You know it was blackout and no cars—except Gestapo cars—were driving with lights. Then we heard the bell, not ringing in the usual way, with the nice quiet way, but a very hard press on the bell.

"I cannot just remember who opened the door, but the door was opened in any case and in they came and asked for him. And when they heard he was sleeping upstairs, they just ran upstairs to his room. I was lying in a room beside that. He was in bed, of course, sleeping, and was thrown out of the bed. I went to see what they did in my night frock.

"They said to him, 'You are arrested.'

"And he said, 'What for?'

" 'That you will know later and I'm sure you know it yourself,' they said to him, and he just shook his head a little bit and didn't say much.

"Then they said, 'Dress at once. You will have to take your clothes and be prepared to get away from here in ten minutes.'

"And I as a mother, of course, said, 'But he must have something to eat before he goes.'

"They were a little astonished and said, 'Yes, you will be allowed to give him something to eat.'

"I went downstairs, where Myrtle was sleeping, and I said to her, 'Go into the cellar and fetch a little honey.' We had some honey in a little box that was a very precious thing to have and I thought that this was the time when we should use it. And I spread some on a piece of bread with some butter we had. But he could almost not eat it. Not very much of it.

"After a little while they took him by the arm and he said, 'You don't have to take me. I'll go with you.' So the man dropped his arm at once.

"We went out with him to the gate and out to the police car, and off away they drove with him. And the three of us, Myrtle, my husband and I, went back again as poor as one ever could be.

"I think we sat and spoke . . . and didn't speak . . . and just felt as bad, all of us. We couldn't sleep anymore that night."

Myrtle Wright recorded the scene at breakfast the next morning.

> At breakfast we said nothing, but Erik [Bernti's younger, handicapped brother] was unquiet and did not start eating. "Where's Bernti?" he asked. "He has gone to town," said Sigrid. "But where *is* he?" persisted Erik. "He has gone to a big building," he was told. There was a pause. Erik sprang to his feet. "But I must go and rescue him," he said, making for the door.

It is not far from the Lunds' home to Akebergveien Prison, where Bernti was first taken, and not far from there to the Grini concentration camp, just outside Oslo. In the winter the camp, which the Germans had adapted from a pre-war Norwegian penitentiary, lies in a snow-covered valley amidst the fir-tree forests which rise up on the hills behind the city. But it was June when Bernti arrived, driven past the unused wooden scaffolds of the ski jumps towards the swastika flapping over the new red-brick barracks. "Were they depressed?" Sigrid asked a policeman when she went to collect his clothes.

"Depressed?" he replied. "They were in the highest spirits."

By the grim standards of concentration camps, Grini was not especially severe. It lacked quite that degree of Draconian sadism found in its sister establishments on the Continent. Indeed, despite the discomfort, the lice, the lack of food, and the uncertainty about the future, there were aspects of Grini life which would have astonished the less fortunate inmates of other camps. It was not long—less than a month after his arrest—that Bernti was able to write home, asking for a sleeping bag for the autumn. Myrtle Wright, we learn, a few days later was "sewing names into Bernti's clothes all day." She understood that his underclothes would be washed and mended by the women prisoners. Most extraordinary of all, by the autumn Sigrid was even allowed visits. She would ride from home on her bicycle through the pine woods to the gates of the camp, sometimes carrying a tin of sardines to bribe a guard into giving some extra concession.

"Do you know Bernti?" she asked a guard on one occasion. "The one with the red hair?"

"Oh, yes," came the German reply, "he's always cheerful."

Yet Sigrid knew only too well the dangerous and sinister reality such moments concealed. In June, before she was allowed visits, she went to Gestapo headquarters for news of Bernti. She was told nothing except the almost surrealist reply that it was permissible for him to receive a Latin grammar. A few days later she returned. This time it was to accompany a friend whose son had been sent to Sachsenhausen concentration camp in Germany. Sigrid translated the bureaucratic German of the Gestapo official to her nervous companion: Her son had died from double pneumonia; there was no question of his ashes being sent home. Sigrid remembers that the man was civil and cold. Her friend had feared the worst. Norwegians had already become familiar with this formula of reporting the deaths of their friends and relations in German camps.

In Grini itself the Germans acted with savagery when they chose. In March 1943 they shot seventeen men from the camp, one of them a close friend of Bernti's. In a letter smuggled out of the camp Bernti told his parents what had happened. On the day before the executions the camp commandant had jeered at the condemned men: "Tomorrow you will be shot and your corpses burned and spread to the winds." For the Lund family there was a note of bitterness in this letter that was particularly painful: "I was quite broken for a few days," wrote Bernti, "but now I try to see it the way Harald wanted us to see it. No sacrifice is too great for our cause. Life and Death are of no account if only truth is victorious. In this way one puts life's worth in the background, and that total pacifist attitude you have given me has had to give way to something harder and more bitter."

Everywhere things were becoming harder and more bitter. There were more and more arrests. The death penalty was extended to include even the possession of illicit newspapers. The underground press itself ran articles on how to resist torture. On all sides, Sigrid's friends, relations and acquaintances were to be found among those languishing in prisons and camps. Her home had been a meeting place for many of the finest and best in Norwegian life—Odd Nansen, Professor Didrik Seip, Francis Bull, the historian, Olaf Kullmann—all of whom had spoken out and been arrested. But there were other visitors too. Ferdinand Schjeldrup was one who, unbeknown to Sigrid, linked the household with the very center of the secret resistance movement. Schjeldrup was a member of the so-called KK, the Coordinating Committee, set up, as its name suggests, to unify the struggle against the Nazis. Through its *paroles*, secret instructions and messages were passed throughout Norway. It was this network of communication more than anything else which had enabled Norwegians to react with such cohesion in the face of Nazi threats, provocations and initiatives. With Bernti in a concentration camp, Sigrid had her own problems, but with her sense of commitment and her lifelong association with the people and institutions that had become the driving force of the opposition to the Nazis, she found herself continuously driven further and further into resistance. By now her pacifism was being truly tested. A middle-aged woman in her early fifties, she had to think in her daily life of considerations that would have been unimaginable two years before: "If one of my own circle were taken prisoner, then it was a great danger for us who worked with that person and we sometimes had to go into hiding for days, or weeks, to be certain that that person hadn't been forced—by torture—to give names, among which could be mine for instance. But we never said anything against people who spoke while they were being tortured. It was quite natural that one couldn't bear everything, and the torture was sometimes very, very heavy. So we never blamed anybody who 'burst' as we called it. We never blamed them at all. The most terrible things happened, they couldn't have been expected to resist."

It was with considerations like these that Sigrid entered another—even riskier—area of resistance. It had started as early as the autumn of 1940. Sigrid was asked to help a friend and her daughter to get over the border to Sweden. It was arranged, as at first seemed quite natural, without any fuss or special precautions. Sigrid knew a family living near the border who, it was said, frequently crossed illicitly into Sweden to do their shopping. Her friends would simply join a shopping expedition. "It was very risky," Sigrid says now, "and much more risky than we actually understood at that point." In the years which followed, with the ever-increasing Gestapo activity in the country, the "transports" to Sweden would become an enterprise run on an almost industrial scale.

Sigrid adopted the unlikely code name Suzanna. Her job, as the transport lines became more developed, was principally to arrange false papers and travel documents. But frequently it amounted to much more, finding hiding places, organizing pickups. What began as an operation to smuggle individual fugitives out of the country had already, by 1942, become an exercise in mass emigration of the victims of Quisling's regime. Whole families travelled together. Truckloads of escapees moved nightly through the forest roads towards the border. Myrtle Wright's diary becomes increasingly cryptic: There are "parties"—some of which "have to be postponed." The number of "uncles" visiting the Tuengen Alle increases. There are guests who "have to be got rid of early." By chance one of these was Claus Helberg, one of the four commandos who had been parachuted in from England to blow up the heavy-water plant at Vemork, thereby preventing the Nazis from acquiring the vital material for their own atom bomb project.

Helberg had made an adventurous and difficult escape from the scene of the raid and had arrived in Oslo injured. "He stayed with two elderly ladies who were good friends of ours," Sigrid recalls, "and they asked me whether I had any possibility of getting him over the border to Sweden. I said, 'Yes, I would think so.' I didn't know anything about him but knew it should be done as fast as possible."

Two days later he was in Sweden. "I never did see him," Sigrid remembers. (Myrtle Wright did. She gave Helberg a letter to deliver to her mother in Cambridge when he got back to England. Both the letter—and Helberg—arrived safely.)

There was one aspect of the story that was unusual. It was rare for those involved in the passive resistance (Civorg, as it was known) to have any contact at all in the armed resistance (Milorg), which was being trained and directed from London. Helberg had tripped almost accidentally into Suzanna's path after his own Milorg escape line had "burst." But for Sigrid there was never any question that the pacifist should not help the commando. "A soldier is just as much a human being as anybody else, so it was helping a human being to get to freedom and I had no doubt that this is what should have been done."

By the end of the war, 46,000 Norwegians had escaped to Sweden. The existence of the frontier—the possibility of escape denied to so many in the resistance movements of occupied Europe—must have altered the course of Norway's resistance history. But Sigrid is convinced that Norwegians acted as they did not because they had an easy escape route if the going got tough.

"If Sweden hadn't been there, the Norwegians would have behaved absolutely in the same way. I'm sure that there would have been many more people going over the North Sea to other countries, disappearing in one way or another. It wasn't at all that easy to run. It was very difficult to get away, and very, very risky. And you knew that if you were taken, you were, in the best case, sent to Germany as a prisoner. And probably—very often— you were killed. So it wasn't so easy. And secondly, you wanted to stay in Norway. No one thought, Oh, well, I can do this and then I can just run over to Sweden. We all wanted to stay in Norway. We weren't at all happy to leave and go over to some kind of freedom which we didn't look on as freedom at all. I don't think it helped the struggle at all that we had Sweden to rescue us. But, of course, it turned out to have been a good thing that it was there."

Before the end of the war Sigrid herself had very good reason for being grateful that Sweden was there.

Ironically, she had been one of the very few Norwegians who had been to Sweden legally since the war began. The circumstances of this journey also had their own cruel irony. It was 1940, a few months after the invasion. Sigrid began to receive letters from the parents of the Jewish children she had brought out of Czechoslovakia the previous year. The parents wanted their children back. They had been sent to Norway because at the time Norway had been free and at peace. Now, the parents argued in their letters, Norway was in the same situation as Czechoslovakia. In these times they wanted their families to be all together, they wrote.

Sigrid and Nansenhjelp were full of misgivings. "We were very sad, and didn't know what to do. We tried with all reasonable means to make them understand that they were safer here than in Czechoslovakia. But we couldn't—because of the censorship—write straight out that we had the possibility of taking them to a free Sweden, or that, secondly, Norway was such a large country, and they were so spread out, that we didn't actually believe anything could happen to the children here. But somehow the parents insisted—'We will have our children back again.' And what could you do? You couldn't just kidnap the children. So in the end we had to give in for some of the children. . . ."

In all, nearly half of the children Sigrid had brought to safety in 1939 were at the end of 1940 sent back to the Jewish ghettos in central Europe. Sigrid got permission from the Gestapo to accompany them as far as the port of Trelleborg in Sweden. "I must say," she recalls, "the children were rather happy. They were going home." Nineteen of the original group remained in Norway. All those who returned were gassed.

In one part of her argument with the Czech parents Sigrid was right: There was the possibility of escape to Sweden. Where she was wrong was in her belief that "it couldn't happen here." What she did not count on, that

November morning when she set out to return the children, was that such were the requirements of Adolf Eichmann's efficient machine for the destruction of European Jewry that just two years later, at a time when half a million German fighting men were desperately losing their grip and their lives at Stalingrad, the Nazis would reach out to claw into the ovens of Auschwitz a few dozen Jewish children harmlessly sheltering in a remote corner of their European empire. How could she have known? How could anyone have known?

In 1940 there were about 1,800 Jews in the whole of Norway. Around 250 of these were refugees from Germany and central Europe. Since the lifting of the prohibition on Jewish immigration passed by the Norwegian Parliament in 1851, Jews had become accepted and well integrated in the community. There was no evidence that the recrudescent antisemitism of the Continent had any appeal whatsoever for the majority of Norwegians. But as we have seen, the majority was not represented by Quisling, who by the mid-thirties was already whipping up his small fanatical band of followers with a highly developed vocabulary of antisemitic invective. Just why this intelligent nationalist had found it necessary to take on board his curious ideological baggage train this imported and dangerous prejudice, scholars have been unable to reveal. It has been said that he had been disillusioned by what he had seen in Soviet Russia, where he had worked in the twenties, and that he blamed the failure of communism on the Jews. Much of his rhetoric in later times suggests that he had read—and seemingly believed—the forged and improbable *Protocols of the Elders of Zion,* the bible of the teeming antisemitic literature of the time. In his admiration for Nazi Germany, he had fallen increasingly under the influence of Rosenberg, whose ideas even Hitler had characterized as "derivative, pastiche, illogical rubbish! Bad Chamberlain with a few additions."* (The same Chamberlain, it will be remembered, with whom Sigrid had taken tea in Bayreuth some thirty years before.)

From the time Quisling's NS was given sole political power in the country in September 1940, conditions for the Jews deteriorated. Their businesses were attacked, shops daubed with painted slogans: "JEWS WILL NOT BE TOLERATED IN NORWAY." It is, of course, extremely difficult to believe that had the Germans been left to their own devices, they would not have employed their own means of dealing with the Jewish question. But as elsewhere in occupied Europe, they preferred to act with the connivance of native puppets. Quisling was happy to oblige. In February 1942 the German authorities promoted him to the office and title of Minister-President, a usage unknown in Norway before this time. Although Reichskommissar Terboven kept all effective power in his own hands, Quisling himself clearly thought that this was the moment he had been waiting for, the moment Hitler had promised him, and from this time forth regarded himself as head of state. From his installation in Akershus Castle, a ceremony characterized by its pomposity and the utterance of National Socialist pieties ("Germany's victory is Norway's victory," Quisling had proclaimed to the assembled audience of German and Norwegian Nazis), he began to show that his belief in Nazi ideology was more than mere rhetoric.

The campaign against the Jews was immediately stepped up. From February all identification cards for Jews were marked with a large *J*. Throughout the spring and summer, individuals and small groups of Jews were arrested. At the beginning of September Rabbi Samuel was arrested in Oslo. As the antisemitic campaign be-

---

*Quoted by Joachim C. Fest in *The Face of the Third Reich* (Weidenfeld & Nicholson, 1970), page 255.

came more and more sinister, there was growing nervousness about what was going to happen. "Naturally, we hear from various sides of anxiety among the Jews," Myrtle Wright noted in her diary. "It is such a helpless feeling—what can one do?"

On October 23 a policeman was shot while checking travel documents on a train. The evening papers put the blame on the Jews. In the Lund household there was concern that it could have been a provocation. It was the very worst time for such an incident to happen. The atmosphere was gloomy and filled with premonition. The worst happened two days later. It was a Sunday. Sigrid had been out visiting one of her Czech children who had had a birthday, but by evening the family was together at home. The telephone rang. The voice at the other end of the line did not introduce itself but told Sigrid simply, "There's going to be a big party tonight and we need the big parcels. I'm going to fetch them." The line went dead. At first she didn't understand what the message could mean. She talked it over with the family. Then it became clear: the Jews.

In fact, acting on a law passed the previous day, the Nazi police were systematically arresting all Jewish men. Sigrid spent the night alerting as many Jews as possible to go into hiding. Several she sent back to the Tuengen Alle, where Myrtle Wright stayed awake to receive them. Throughout Norway others in the Resistance were spreading the same message. Precautions were tossed aside as the hiding places of the underground transportation network were quickly filled with Jews fleeing the wave of arrests.

It was a moment of the greatest significance. For the first time the Germans found a population actually prepared to frustrate their Jewish policy, and a resistance movement equipped for the problems of mass escape. Hundreds of Jews were arrested that night, but hundreds more escaped. For the next few weeks, in Sigrid's home as in similar homes throughout the country, family life was dominated by the requirements of the "parcels" and the "parties" being dispatched towards the border. But there was another question nagging in the back of Sigrid's mind: Would they start sending children away as they had in France? She didn't have long to wait for the answer.

"Just a month later, the twenty-fifth of November, a man rang at the door outside. I didn't know him at all. And he said, 'Tonight there will be a party again, and we will fetch the small parcels.' And off he ran. I didn't know the man, but I understood at once what it meant this time."

In the center of Oslo, about a mile from Sigrid's house, but only a stone's throw from Gestapo headquarters, there was a Jewish orphanage, housing refugee children from Vienna and, in addition, one other boy, Bertold Grunfeld, one of those whom Sigrid had brought to Norway from Czechoslovakia. Sigrid arrived at the orphanage to be met by a young doctor who had received the same message and come to the same conclusion. It was late in the evening. All the children were asleep.

"The whole time had been terrible, the whole autumn had been terrible," remembers Grunfeld, "because all the grown-up males had been arrested or had escaped to Sweden, so we were just waiting for something to happen. When we were woken up, we were told, 'This night is more serious for you than even the night when the Germans occupied Norway.' So we understood, as children, that something very serious was going to take place."

Throughout Oslo the air-raid sirens wailed in an attempt to keep people off the streets during the roundup. Some of the children cried, unable to understand why they had been woken, and why they could not take their toys. Dr. Nic Waal, who had a car and travel pass, drove through the deserted streets, passing the children on to families who could hide them. "It was," says Bertold Grunfeld, "a very dramatic situation. The Germans had started alarms to keep people inside, but we went on nevertheless, because we understood that the Germans were driving around arresting people. At one point we were almost stopped by German guards, but the lady who drove the car—she was a very brave woman—she just pushed on and we got through."

The diary note for the next day is laconic: "Busy day —so many guests." It was the first of many busy days as Sigrid worked round the clock to arrange transports for women and children over the border. For Bertold Grunfeld the period of waiting was "strangely calm." As he was one of her Czech children, Sigrid had come to know him well. Sometimes she worried about him, wondering whether he was happy in Norway. He seemed such a lonely child, always playing by himself in a corner. In any case, now was not the time for tender thoughts. The Gestapo had raided the orphanage just after midnight and were furiously combing Oslo to discover the whereabouts of the missing children. Sigrid could not afford to delay their departure.

"It was a beautiful day. It was cold," Bertold Grunfeld today recalls. "Many degrees below zero. We knew we were going to a new country. New things would happen to us. But of course what made it less dramatic to us was that the ladies who accompanied us were so extraordinarily clever in not frightening us. This is almost forty years ago and it may be that this somewhat romantic picture is what I want to remember because it really was too difficult to remember it in any other way."

Sigrid soon received word that the children had arrived safely in Sweden. But what she never had the chance to see was the excited first reaction of the lonely little boy she had brought from Prague and who now had so dramatically left through Norway's back door: "In Sweden you could get as much chocolate as you wished. In Norway you had no chocolate—nothing. In Sweden you could get everything. That was a fantastic experience of course. You saw no soldiers. You knew you were in a peaceful, neutral country. First and foremost you had no Germans around you."

Not all the Jews had been so lucky. At three o'clock in the afternoon following the evacuation of the orphanage, the German ship *Donau* left Oslo with 530 Jews on board —men, women and children, the victims of the first large-scale arrests and smaller *Aktionen* which had been taking place in the north of the country earlier in the year. Their fate was inscribed in the Auschwitz camp register a week later:

> *1. 12. R.S.H.A. TRANSPORT, Juden aus Bergen (Norwegen). Nach der Selektion, lieferte man 186 Manner als Haftlinge ins Lager ein, sie bekamen die Nr. 79064–79249. Die Übrigen wurden vergast.*
> [After the selection, 186 men were taken as prisoners into the camp and were given the numbers 79064–79249. The remainder were gassed.]

There is a curious entry in Myrtle Wright's diary which suggests that somehow some intimation of the fate of the *Donau* Jews did permeate back to Norway, but so vague that no one could have guessed the full extent of the tragedy. On January 7, 1943, she wrote: "The fate of the Jewish children on the *Donau* is different. News has come from some of them. The adults who can work, men and women, are in a work camp. The others and the children are separated from them."

The story did not end with the sailing of the *Donau*. Many Jews still waited in hiding to be spirited over the border, and for Sigrid there was still the last act of the drama that had begun in Prague three years before. Nineteen of the children were still in Norway, spread out with foster parents throughout the southern part of the country. Throughout the Christmas and New Year period of 1942–43, Sigrid found ways of bringing the children back to Oslo and then on to Sweden. With all but three of the children she was successful.

"That was a very sad story," Sigrid says now. "One of them had been in a family which was a Nazi family, and we did not know about that when that little boy was placed in that family. And, of course, they were very fond of this little boy and I think it was a great sorrow also to them when they really, in the end, when they understood what had happened to that child. But they turned him in to the Gestapo in the town where they were living, Stavanger, and the boy was brought to Oslo and, of course, was killed in the end."

The other two children, Vera and Tibor Tagelicht, whose foster parents would send Sigrid their photograph on a Christmas card, met the same fate. Their escape had been plagued with bad luck. "Why too is there no news of Vera and Tibor?" wrote Myrtle Wright on January 28, two months after the roundup of Jewish children. "Tibor was being difficult before we left: he wanted to know too much . . . and it is a lot to ask of a fourteen-year-old boy that he shall be kept indoors for two or three weeks, and be quiet and good-tempered. He was resentful that he had been taken away from his foster home where he was happy, though he was aware that his Jewish blood put him in danger. His nerves and impatience expressed themselves in quarrelling between the two children, and no wonder. They are a dangerous couple; they know too much and have been handled by too many people. I wish we could hear that they were over."

A fortnight later, Sigrid heard through contacts in the

police that two children named Vera and Tibor had been arrested. In the same week Quisling declared four days of mourning for the fate of the German Sixth Army at Stalingrad.

Vera and Tibor now joined the Jews who had been arrested, or had arrived in Oslo, too late to have sailed with the *Donau*. They were held in Bredtvedt Prison to the east of Oslo, where Professor Ragnar Skancke, Quisling's minister for church affairs, had described them as "unpleasant to look at and revengeful also." (It had been Skancke's department which had replied to Norwegian bishops' protest at the arrest of Jews by quoting Luther's antisemitic pronouncements.)

The Jews of Bredtvedt had few visitors, but one of them was Sigrid. She had gone to Oslo's chief of police for permission to bring clothes to the Jewish prisoners. "He was very, very reluctant to let me speak. But it happened that his little three-year-old son was in the office that day and he said, 'Excuse me, but my wife is ill so I had to bring the boy with me.' And that saved me, because I made very good friends with this little fellow. And he came and looked inside my purse and looked at photographs, and in the end the policeman, who didn't speak very much, looked at the little boy being so friendly with me and was so pleased that he said that I could have permission to deliver everything we had collected."

When this same policeman was later killed by the Resistance "for the way he had treated so many good Norwegians," Sigrid remembered her interview. "I knew from meeting his little son of his weak spots, of his human spots . . . and I was almost sorry that he was killed, because I knew there were good sides in him, which I'm sure could have been drawn out, given a different situation."

Sigrid delivered her clothes to the Jews in Bredtvedt,

but could do nothing to save them from their fate. Late in February, another German prison ship, the *Gottenland*, sailed from Oslo bound for Germany and Auschwitz. The 158 prisoners on board included Vera and Tibor and several other refugees from Europe whom Sigrid had known since her days working with Nansenhjelp before the war began.

Of the 760 Jews deported from Norway, only twenty-five survived to return at the end of the war. Of all the Jews in Norway, 43 percent had been annihilated. But there was triumph also. Over one thousand Norwegian Jews did survive, most of them smuggled over the Swedish border by the Resistance.

The mass escape of the Jews was not without cost. Many of Sigrid's friends were arrested, including both the nurse who had accompanied her to Czechoslovakia in 1939 and the doctor who had helped in the escape of the children from the orphanage. In the spring, Einar Lund, Diderich's brother, died of pneumonia in Grini concentration camp. "It was good for Einar that it went as it did," Bernti told his parents during a visit, referring to the torture of Einar and others of his group who had been arrested. It was a remark typical of the time.

The war had turned against Germany. But the Germans in Norway, as they became more and more disappointed with the ability of Quisling's NS to control their countrymen, resorted more and more to their own methods. The Gestapo stepped up their campaigns of house searches, arrests, torture and execution. On the one hand people whispered about Allied victories, on the other about the latest consignment of "instruments" delivered to the cellars of the Victoria Terrasse, about the Norwegian police who went there to interrogate their own prisoners, about their friends and relatives who had been mishandled and abused.

In the meantime, the Resistance continued to urge a

war-weary people to be on their guard against Quisling
—especially his maneuvers to form a legion of Norwegian youths and men for service with the Germans on
the Eastern Front.

"The question," as one underground writer saw it, "is
whether you can see the large in the small, the significant
in the insignificant, the matter of principle in something
casual. If not, you too or else your son may one day be
a Nazi soldier on the Eastern Front."

The problem was that the war had gone on for so long.
"Our nervous strength has been drained for a long time
now," one writer wrote. It was said that Swedes were
divided into optimists and pessimists. The optimists
thought the war would be over by the beginning of September, the pessimists that it would be October at least
before it finished. The end was always just around the
corner. In the middle of 1943 it would have been unkind
to have suggested to anyone in occupied Europe that the
war would continue for nearly two more years.

But for Sigrid the end was near. On the night of January 27, 1944, she heard once again the sound of a Gestapo
car coming up the Tuengen Alle. Another hard ring on
the bell. More men rushing up the stairs. "Where is
Engineer Lund?" they demanded. Sigrid explained that
her husband was working out of town. They searched
the house with pistols in their hands and seized the picture of the king that had hung undisturbed on the wall
in the hall since the beginning of the war.

"It has been there a long time," said Sigrid by way of
explanation.

"We have been here a long time," the Gestapo men
said, rounding on her angrily. They demanded pictures
of the family. The inquisition continued. "Where is your
son?" The fact that Bernti was in Grini interested them.
"A criminal family," they concluded. They left, empty-
handed, after half an hour. Sigrid and Myrtle Wright

came to another conclusion: that it was now only a matter of time before they too would be arrested. They began at once to prepare their own escape.

For Sigrid, who had handled so many other "parcels" and helped arrange so many "parties," her own departure was not difficult to organize. First Diderich had to be warned. Messages were sent to him not to come home through various underground channels. (Even though he was travelling at the time, he received the warning three times.) Sigrid had already prepared lists of friends who would look after her paintings in such an eventuality. Little Erik was left with friends in the countryside. A month later, Sigrid—with Myrtle—was driving through the winter night towards the frontier, squeezed into the back of a covered truck packed tight with fellow fugitives.

There is a sense in which this little convoy heading towards Sweden on the night of February 27, 1944, summed up much of the character of the Norwegian Resistance. Under the tarpaulin covers of the two lorries, thirty-six people—men, women and children, each with his own story—were leaving behind everything they had and had known to make a risky journey towards an unknown future. Each in his own way had defied the Nazis. A few perhaps, very, very few, with guns and sabotage. Most of them by writing for the underground press, or listening to the BBC, or hiding refugees, or simply by refusing to comply—or to allow their families to lapse into compliance—with some bullying order from Quisling's NS. As ordinary Norwegians, they did not know each other in everyday life, but for the few hours of their escape they recognized themselves as members of the same family.

The trucks drew up at the banks of a large ice-covered lake. There was a guide and another man with a horse and sledge. One of the party of escapees, a man with an injured back, was laid carefully on the sledge. The children, drugged with sedatives, were laid alongside him. Then, led by the guide, the three dozen refugees began walking in line, one after the other, over the snow-covered frozen lake, towards the pine forest on the other bank and beyond that the frontier. It was a moonlit night, absolutely silent: terrifying and beautiful. A family outing on a heroic scale. Exactly a year to the day since Sigrid had heard of the arrests of Vera and Tibor.

"That night there were no patrols at all," remembers Sigrid, "and we walked four or five hours until we saw over to the Swedish side. The guide said to us, 'There, that's Sweden, that means freedom for you all.' And we all felt very, very heavy that we should leave Norway, where we had done what we could to be a help to our country and our countrymen, to leave our friends and our families. I left a son behind me—two sons—one in prison and I didn't know what was going to happen with him. We were all very sad, all of us. We didn't feel freedom as something that we were looking forward to, but something that we had to take because we were forced to leave the country.

"And we came at last to the broad, open cutting in the forest which marked the border with a cairn in the middle, stone laid upon stone. And there we stood, all of us, and without actually thinking about it, we all began to sing our national anthem, 'Ja, vi elsker.' And so we continued, all of us, until we couldn't do it anymore because actually I think all of us were weeping."

It was not quite the end of Sigrid's war. That came a year later and can be placed with some precision. A month after her flight to Sweden she received news that her son Bernti had been "sent south" to Sachsenhausen concentration camp in Germany. Familiarity had made Grini almost unthreatening—during her last visits, Sigrid had found Bernti in good spirits—but no one had any illusions about life in the German camps. Sigrid, of course, could do nothing. With two Norwegian friends she opened a small center for refugees, and then towards the end of the war, as Scandinavian prisoners released under the deal worked out between Count Folke Bernadotte and Himmler began to return to Sweden, she was asked to help run a reception center. It was here, at the port of Halsingborg in southern Sweden, that Sigrid's war finally came to an end, when among the scarred and emaciated victims of Hitler's prisons and concentration camps she discovered Bernti standing before her.

Sigrid Lund told us this story in Oslo during the winter of 1979. She was eighty-seven, and it was, even for Norway, exceptionally cold. It did not stop her returning with us to Grini concentration camp, or skiing across the frozen lake where she had made her escape all those years before. Sitting in the house in the Tuengen Alle, she spoke of the war without bitterness in her gentle Norwegian accent, her old eyes alight with pride as she remembered the exploits of her friends and family, their successes and the miseries they suffered. For herself, she did not claim any special place in the Norwegian Resistance: "You just remember that I am only one whom you chose by accident of hundreds and thousands who had the same experience." For those Norwegians who had taken the other course, the NS and the collaborators, she felt only a sense of sorrow. She did not agree with the execution of Quisling and his leading henchmen and believed that most of his followers quickly saw "how wrongly they had behaved":

"We pitied them much more than we hated them. . . . I think most of the people who became Quislings were young people, many of whom had not been able to find their place among their friends and their families, and they saw the possibility to do something that was extraordinary."

Shortly after the war ended, Sigrid became a Quaker, and since then has worked for Quaker causes and with international relief organizations in many parts of the world. To this day she is moved by that same fundamental humanist philosophy that she acquired as a girl when Oslo was still called Christiania, and Henrik Ibsen was still writing his final play. For Sigrid, Nazism could never offer any choice. There was nothing in its brutal ideology that could appeal to her values: Power and race ecstasy were no exchange for the simple respect for life. "I'm afraid that I have to say that I never had any doubt that what I did was the right thing."

Yet however intense her patriotism or profound her disgust at what the Nazis were doing, she never lost sight of the fact that the German soldiers "were ordinary people . . . sons of ordinary mothers in the homeland." She extended to them, as to the collaborators, Quislings, informers, profiteers, and torturers, the same rights that she felt belonged to all men. Throughout the bloodiest war in history she never wavered in her belief that the pacifist way was the right way and that there were never any circumstances in which it was right to take a life.

And even today, to those who suggest that the only way to end such a war was by military means, she has a defiant reply:

"That may be true. It may be true that the only way of winning the war was the military way, in any case in such a short time. But if the war was about principles—Nazi principles—I think we could still have won many Germans to our way of looking upon the meaning of life and then we could have won in another way.

"We see now what the world is like. It is not at all more peaceful because the war was won by military means, but maybe if we had won it by other means it could have been quite a different world."

Maria Rutkiewicz

Moscow. Christmas 1941. Russia's first winter of the war. The great socialist experiment totters on the edge of oblivion.

Since mid-November the daytime temperatures have never been much above zero. For weeks the endless greatcoated regiments have filed through the streets on their way westward to the bloodiest battlefront in history. A million civilians have fled the city in the opposite direction. Now at last there is a breathing space. The German panzers have been turned back at the very gates of Moscow itself.

In such a winter, in such a place, at such a time, only the gigantic is conspicuous. Yet in Red Square, among the wintry silhouetted figures in the snow, one group stands apart. Under the threatened towers of the Kremlin, they wander aimlessly, like tourists, as if, in this most critical moment of the war, they have nothing to kill but time.

They are ten men and a girl, students of the Pushkino School, to the north of the city. They are not Russian but Polish, and already they have seen in their own country a terror far worse than the citizens of Moscow will ever know. Pushkino is no ordinary school, and these are no ordinary students. They are being trained by Comintern —as saboteurs and spies. Their mission is about to begin and they have come to Red Square to say farewell. Their task is simply the transformation of Poland.

What follows is the story of the only woman in the group. Her name is Maria Rutkiewicz. She is pretty, twenty-four years old, and she has been a Communist all her life. Within three days, with ice in her red hair and tears of cold streaming down her cheeks, she will parachute with her friends from the hold of a Soviet Dakota and jump out into the darkness above her homeland.

Forty years later, Maria is the only one left alive to tell the tale of what happened after that.

Maria Rutkiewicz (née Kamieniecka) was born in Warsaw on August 22, 1917. It was a time full of promise for both Poland and communism. Within weeks Lenin had swept into power in Russia. Not long afterwards, Poland, which for 130 years had been partitioned among her powerful neighbours, regained her independence. At almost the same moment in history, a century of nationalist and socialist aspiration had been fulfilled. It did not take long to discover that the one was incompatible with the other.

Both of the new states were expansionist and restless: Poland in pursuit of her historical inheritance in the east; Soviet Russia in the quest for world revolution. A clash was inevitable. In April 1920, not eighteen months after the end of the First World War, a Polish army advanced purposefully on Kiev. The Red Army counterattacked with even greater determination. For a moment, not just Poland but the whole of Western civilization held its breath as Bolshevik hordes threatened Warsaw from the banks of the Vistula. But finally it was Lenin who had to sue for peace, and in 1921 he signed the Treaty of Riga, ceding vast territories to the Poles and thereby almost doubling the size of the Polish state. So began an unpromising and uneasy relationship between the two countries which has lasted to this day.

Maria grew up in a middle-class family in a Warsaw rejuvenated by independence, once again established as the cultural capital of a free Poland. Her parents were people of sensibility rather than education, and she remembers her father as a man more interested in poetry than politics.

It was her older brothers and sister who were drawn towards the Left, and it was their commitment and the sacrifices they made for it which were to have the deepest influence upon her life. From her earliest years, Maria's young imagination was fired by the two great movements of her time: the twin sirens of nationalism and communism, Poland and revolution. It was a double calling of extraordinary complexity and danger.

Between the wars, communism was the ugly duckling of Polish politics. In the recrudescent Poland, earnestly grappling with the problems of statehood, the party represented all that was disaffected and divisive. Its main strength came from the ethnic minorities in the eastern territories, recently overrun in the war against Russia, who owed only a dubious allegiance to the Polish state. Its membership was disproportionately intellectual, and, worse—from the point of view of popular support— conspicuously Jewish. Antisemitism was rife and nothing could have put the party at a greater electoral disadvantage.

"From long observation," wrote Professor W. J. Rose, the author of a Penguin Special on Poland published in 1939, "I am convinced that the antagonism which is everywhere latent and at times flares up, is neither religious, nor racial, nor class, nor economic *as such*, but lies simply in the fact of difference . . . The Jews are *different.* . . ."* What he meant was that they were unassimilated,

---

*W. J. Rose, *Poland* (Penguin Books, 1939).

distinct. They had an exotic and cosmopolitan background. Before the Great War they had been citizens of Austro-Hungary, Russia and Prussia. Poland, with its powerful Roman Catholic Church and popular antisemitism, had no claim on their loyalty. Instead, many Jews were drawn naturally to the internationalism of communism. "Most Poles," one historian has remarked, "took a more prosaic view. To them communism was not international, but Russian."* The presence of so many Jews in the Party's ranks merely confirmed Poles in their deepest suspicions: Communism and Russian imperialism were synonymous; Communists themselves were little more than agents of the Soviet Union; Polish communism therefore was a contradiction in terms.

Polish parliaments did not come by their reputation lightly. In the first flourish of independence, Polish parliamentary democracy was characterized by incompetence, violence, corruption and inflation. The country was brought to the brink of disaster as no fewer than ninety-two political parties scrambled for power. In May 1926, there was a coup d'état. It was led by Marshal Joseph Pilsudski, a romantic and cavalier figure who had become a national hero in both the struggle for independence and the Polish-Russian war. He came to power with little respect for politicians, but with the air of a man who would make the trains run on time. He was not quite a dictator, more an authoritarian. The western European press saw him, approvingly, as "Europe's new Mussolini," and he soon began to demonstrate similar ways of dealing with his Communist opponents.

In the late twenties, Pilsudski's police arrested Maria's elder brother and sister. They were sent to prison for their activities in the Communist Youth. For Maria, who

---

*Nicholas Bethell in *Gomulka: His Poland and His Communism* (New York: Longman, Inc., 1969).

had thought for a time they would be executed, their imprisonment was both frightening and an example of the sacrifices that must be paid for idealism. Far from being deterred, she began while still at school to help with Party work. It was an early introduction to conspiracy. "We had to be very careful with our activities," she says in her halting English, "they were arresting even young people like me at school. So it wasn't easy. . . ."

Nothing was ever easy for Polish Communists, and Pilsudski's arrests of young people in the Party did have its point. It was, after all, still an important part of KPP (Polish Communist Party) policy that the Party should defend the Soviet Union against attack. In the 1930s, when the pressure of collectivization had brought the Russian countryside to the point of civil war and Stalin feared foreign intervention from the West, the party decided that young Polish members should be trained to perform acts of sabotage in the event of a new Polish-Soviet conflict. Maria, of course, was still very young. What she saw as a struggle for social justice was viewed in more conservative eyes as little short of treason.

Warsaw, the world in which Maria grew up in the twenties and thirties, has been swept away forever. For the traveller from England, writing in the moment before catastrophe, it was a romantic and fascinating place:

> On arriving in Warsaw from London one cannot fail to be struck by a certain peculiarity of aspect and character. The furs and fur hats worn by both men and women in winter, the strange presence of Jews in their medieval garb, and of peasants in their top boots and sheepskins emphasises this impression. A London crowd, in view of the sameness of dress, seems rather monotonous by comparison with a Warsaw crowd.*

---

*A. T. Lutoslawski, writing in *1938 in Europe*, edited by Eugene Fodor (London: W. Aldor, 1938).

Life was cheap. "Amusements," wrote our guide, "are cheaper in Poland than almost any other commodity"— a view endorsed by the Polish Tourist Office, which boasted, "Poland is one of the cheapest countries in Europe."

What it meant was that Poland was one of the most backward countries in Europe. Her weak economy had been ravaged by the depression of the 1930s. The people for whom Maria and her friends fought were not those who could afford the "cheap" amusements of the Café Club, the Paradis, or the Pink Room at the Hotel Bristol. They were the unemployed, the poor, those who could hardly afford to clothe or feed themselves.

"I think it was mainly idealism," she remembers, "feelings of humanity, a very strong sense of social justice. We wanted to save people from poverty, from humiliation."

As time went by she became more and more committed to the Party. She was arrested, briefly, for organizing illegal meetings at school. Later, in 1938, she married Wicek Rutkiewicz, another Party activist. She was twenty-one. It was hardly an auspicious moment to start out on life. Within twelve months Maria's three worlds —her party, her country and her marriage—were overtaken by disaster.

The first surprise came from an unexpected direction. For many years Stalin had distrusted the Polish Communists. From time to time they had deviated dangerously towards his rival Trotsky, and he suspected their long and close association with the Old Bolsheviks, whom he was busy purging. In 1937 he liquidated a large part of the Polish leadership. A year later he diagnosed more radical defects among his Polish comrades. In the vicious idiom of the purges, they had become "contaminated with hostile elements." He ordered that the Communist Party in Poland be completely disbanded. Several hundred more of its members simply disappeared.

However, in 1939, Stalin was ready to spring an even greater surprise—and this time not just on Communists. Throughout the 1930s nothing had been more certain in the diplomatic world than the fact that fascism and communism were the two most hostile and irreconcilable forces of the day. In the summer of 1939 all that suddenly changed. On August 22, at the invitation of Stalin, Hitler's foreign minister, Joachim von Ribbentrop, flew to Moscow with the text of a nonagression pact between the two countries in his briefcase. As a diplomatic tour de force it has seldom, if ever, been surpassed. Its implications were immediately recognized as devastating and sinister: An end to peace was almost inevitable. Hitler, who had already swallowed Austria and Czechoslovakia, had spent the summer barking his fury at the Poles over Danzig, and over their supposed maltreatment of the German minority in Poland. Now with this cynical deal with his archenemy under his belt, he was free to take action. For Poles, the outlook could only have been worse had they been able to examine the text of the secret clauses of the pact. They read: "The question of whether the interests of both parties make desirable the maintenance of an independent Polish state can only be determined in the course of further developments."

Only a week later, there were further developments. On September 1, 1939, Hitler invaded Poland.

In 1918, Poles had regained their freedom after 130 years of foreign domination. Now it took them just twenty-nine days to lose it. The campaign was a disaster: "Their mobilisation was slow, their leadership poor, their communications flimsy, their reserves thin, their aircraft obsolete, and their tactics—cavalry charging tanks with the aim of dashing into Germany—hopeless."*

---

*Peter Calvocoressi and Guy Wint, *Total War* (New York: Pantheon, 1972).

Hopeless optimism turned within weeks into dreadful defeat. In Warsaw alone, 60,000 people were killed and injured in the bombing, over a tenth of all buildings flattened. In the last days of September, the largest city in Poland, its cultural and intellectual center, lay smouldering at the mercy of the Nazi Army.

"We had very mixed expectations," recalls Maria. "First of all, it was our deep conviction that we must win, but after some weeks everything happened in an absolutely awful way.

"We couldn't imagine what it would mean to lose the war in such a way as it turned out. Nobody was prepared to believe that anything could happen so tragically. Of course, everyone knew that it would mean the losing of independence of our country—and that was something very difficult for people.

"But that it would happen that over six million people would be killed, that we would have these camps, Nazi camps, that we would have everything which happened afterwards—it was absolutely unimaginable. So we didn't have any real feeling of what it would be like to lose the war."

Hitler had a clearer idea, and so did his new ally, Stalin. Once again Poland was partitioned. The extreme west was annexed to the Reich. In the east, the Russians —under the secret terms of the Ribbentrop-Molotov Pact—occupied the territory up to the River Bug. In the middle there was a territory designated as the Gouvernement Général. It was here that the conquerors reacted with their full fury against those they regarded as the "racially inferior" Poles.

"Poland is to be treated like a colony," Hitler had proclaimed at the start of the invasion. It was soon clear what he meant. Within two days of the surrender of Warsaw, the Gestapo moved in, and the order went out to begin the elimination of the educated classes in Poland.

In case there was any confusion about what this involved, a memorandum issued by the NSDAP (Nazi
Party) Race Policy Office in Berlin spelled out exactly
what was meant:

> The term "Polish intelligentsia" covers primarily Pol-
> ish priests, teachers (including university lecturers),
> doctors, dentists, veterinary surgeons, officers, execu-
> tives, businessmen, landowners, writers, journalists,
> plus all persons who have received a higher or second-
> ary education.

In the circumstances Maria had little choice. The war
had already struck two hard blows at her family. Her
brother had been killed in the fighting in Lvov, and her
husband, Wicek, had been one of the thousands of Polish
soldiers marched off to prisoner-of-war camps. Now, as
did many of her Communist friends, Maria fled east to
Russian-occupied Poland. There she began to play her
part in an area of Polish history still clouded by mystery
and bitterness.

From this point there are two violently opposed ways
of looking at Maria's story. The first is that it is the tale
of a patriot and heroine who paid a heavy price for her
part in the struggle to liberate Poland and to create there
the kind of society she believed in. The second view is
that of the thousands of Poles in exile, and the thousands
more within Poland, who have never accepted the Communist state that was erected in Poland after the war,
and whose hatred for the Communists who built and run
it remains, a generation later, virulent and unabated. To
them Maria is a traitor, the agent of a foreign power and
an alien ideology which has enslaved their country. Her
story is no more than the chronicle of one of those who
manipulated the heroic and tragic struggle against Hitler and the Nazis in order to deliver Poland into the
hands of Stalin and the Soviet Union. For Maria, the goal
was a Communist Poland. For many if not most Poles

this meant, as we have seen, a Russian Poland. The chasm is unbridgeable. It reflects the real tragedy of Poland, which began in September 1939, and which has persisted to this day.

By the end of September, Maria found herself caught in what would become an historical and ideological minefield. From her point of view, as a Communist, the Ribbentrop-Molotov Pact was merely a device by which Stalin could buy time to prepare for the inevitable conflict with the Nazis. The Russian annexation of eastern Poland had to be seen in the light of the fact that most of the population in these provinces was not Polish and that the Soviet Union acted to protect its own people.

For non-Communist Poles this has a bitter ring about it. The Ribbentrop-Molotov Pact was nothing more than a charter for the rape of their country. They saw only that the two great powers which had dismembered Poland once before had jumped at the first opportunity to divide the spoils again. Why, they ask, if Russia was acting in the interests of the Polish people, did Stalin now begin to deport thousands of Poles from the Russian-occupied sector to camps inside Russia? Why (though this has never been proved) was it necessary for the Soviet secret police, the NKVD, to travel to Cracow to discuss cooperation with their colleagues in the Gestapo? Why was it necessary for the two victorious armies to draw up another treaty which specified: "Both parties will tolerate in their territories no Polish agitation which affects the territories of the other party"?

"No wonder," writes Bethell, "this period [from September 1939 to June 1941, when Germany invaded the Soviet Union] is not one that is covered in any great detail by modern Polish historians."

For about two years, from 1939 to 1941, Maria, exiled, cut off from her family, found herself in an extraordinary position. As a Polish Communist she was living under the rule of the leader of world communism, a remote and terrible figure, who had disbanded her party, occupied her country, and was allied to her enemies. In the end it was not Communists but the Nazis themselves who made Stalin see things from Maria's point of view.

With the German invasion of Russia, Stalin agreed at last that he might have some use for Polish Communists. In Moscow a small cell of Party members, led by veteran Communist Marcelli Novotko, began to plan a return to Poland. Maria, who had met Novotko and others in the group while in exile in Bialystok, now bombarded him with telegrams, asking to be allowed to join whatever enterprise was being planned. In October 1941 she joined him in Moscow. He told her she was to be trained as a radio operator. So began a relationship that would end in tragedy in less than a year.

"He was then, I think, forty-five or forty-six," says Maria, describing Novotko, "but he seemed to us an old man, and all of us would call him Old Man. He was not a man of high education, but he had a great strong character, with strong feelings towards Poland. He had spent many years in prison before the war in Poland, but it didn't matter for him, he was so deeply committed to the nation. He was very good-looking, very charming, liked singing and poetry. So, you know, he was a very nice man—and a very deep Communist. . . ."

For Maria, Novotko was more a legend than a leader. He "had hardly ever lived the life of a normal human being but had nearly always been hunted, living under assumed names, an outlaw." To her he was a father figure and a friend. It was a relationship that was cemented by the roles they were to play in the Resistance. Their forged papers would show that they were father and daughter. If Maria called him Old Man, he called her daughter; it was a relationship which combined tenderness and Party discipline. The cell was known as the

Initiative Group. It consisted of ten men and Maria, the youngest member. All of them had been in the Polish Party before the war, and many, including the leading members, Novotko himself, Pavel Finder and Boleslaw Molojec, had been imprisoned by Pilsudski and were liberated only when the country was invaded by the Germans. The old leadership of the Party had been liquidated in the purges. To these men now fell the task of re-creating the Polish Party, and of unifying and increasing its scattered support, a task which had proved difficult enough when Poland was at peace, but which now had to be accomplished in the face of ruthless German terror. They called themselves human torpedoes—the first agents from Soviet Russia to be dropped into Poland for resistance work.

It was evening, December 28, 1941. The weather report at a military airport near Moscow was favourable. Maria began to put on extra pullovers and jackets for the flight. It had been over two years since she had left Poland, two years in which she knew that much had changed. Maria had made only one parachute jump before. That had been in daylight from the icy wing of a small single-prop trainer. She felt a sense of exhilaration and fear. There had been no special treatment of her because she was the only girl. She remembers that she felt rather like a young boy, "one of the lads." But now she felt apprehensive. "We were happy," she says, "because we had waited so long for this moment to go back, but at the same time we knew that perhaps it was our last day of life."

As she was checking her equipment and her dress, a colonel in the Soviet air force who had been watching intently approached her and gently removed the big Colt revolver from her belt. "This is far too big for you," he said, and in return he gave her a small, ladylike pistol. "It's a fly-killer," her comrades joked. As she walked with the others towards the black outline of the plane, she felt the hand of Novotko on her shoulder.

"At the last moment—it is a moment I will always remember—when we saw the plane and we were sure at last that we were going back, I remember my feelings when the Old Man caressed me and told me, 'Oh, you are very brave, you are a hero, my dear girl'—'my daughter,' as he put it.

"Then suddenly I told him, 'No, it is not true, I am not a hero, I am afraid of all this.'

"And he answered me: 'You know, it's no surprise what you are telling me. We all of us are a bit afraid because you only live once. Courage isn't not being afraid of death. It is to be sure that what you are doing is worth being done, and then being able to overcome yourself and your fear so that your decision is really firm.'"

The Douglas Dakota took off. It was cramped and cold. Maria lay on a fuel tank, vaguely conscious that they were flying over the battle line, and then, when the searchlights had vanished once more, the noise and the freezing cold continued interminably into the night. Suddenly the plane lost height. They took their places—Maria behind Pavel Finder, Novotko behind her—and then, at a prearranged signal, Maria, who today says that she is too nervous to ride a bicycle or drive a car, threw herself into the darkness.

"How can I describe what it was like to fly back into Poland? We were very happy that we were in our country. But I'll tell you something very intimate—something I'm a bit embarrassed to repeat in other circumstances. But I think it will be enough to understand. When we landed and we found each other—because it was some minutes before we could find each other—we all came together, to Novotko—he was a huge man—and we stood with him for a moment and our first word was for all of us, for all of us, the same one word. It was *Poland, Poland, Poland.* It was something I will never forget. It was my first flight to my Polish soil."

The Initiative Group had landed near the village of Wiazowna, about twenty miles from Warsaw. They split up and approached the capital separately. It was the evening of the following day before Maria arrived at Warsaw Station on a suburban train. She had not seen the city since the first dreadful month of the war. Her memories were still of a time when Warsaw was free. She was completely unprepared for what she found. "I met something that was so changed. The German voices in the street, and the German soldiers. And the people, my Polish people, were so poor, so miserable, it broke my heart.

"It was a feeling not only of fear but it was the feeling of humiliation, of something that I hadn't seen, that had changed. It was a feeling of bitterness."

It is impossible to re-create the atmosphere and mood of that doomed city. By the time Maria arrived, Warsaw's unfortunate inhabitants had already fallen victim to a sustained and unprecedented reign of terror. Already the numbers killed in the murderous blitzkrieg at the beginning of the war had been exceeded many times by those who had been killed, executed or dragged off to camps by the murderous SS gangs. Warsaw was regarded by Hans Frank, the ruler of the Gouvernement Général, as a nest of subversion to be singled out for special treatment. Frank was in some ways a weak man, a lawyer, out of place in the Nazi hierarchy, but he had little hesitation in making huge Caligulan gestures if they were to be paid for in Polish life and blood, and he entered fully into the letter and spirit of his Führer's instruction: "to assume the administration of the conquered territories with the special order to exploit this region as a war zone and booty country, to reduce it, as it were, to a heap of rubble in its economic, social, cultural and political structure." His diaries reveal an almost pantomime megalomania: on May 30, 1940, he writes (apropos the "extraordinary Pacification Action"):

> There is no need to send these elements to Reich Concentration Camps, since we would only be involving ourselves in additional difficulties and unnecessary correspondence with their families; we shall settle this matter on the spot and we shall do so in the simplest way possible. Suspected persons are to be liquidated immediately . . . we cannot saddle the Reich Concentration Camps with our problems.*

He was talking not about the liquidation of criminals but of "all Poles with any kind of influence among their compatriots."

At a later date, replying to the correspondent of a German newspaper who had asked about the differences between Nazi rule in Czechoslovakia and Poland, Frank said:

> I can tell you a graphic difference. In Prague, for example, big red posters were put up on which could be read that seven Czechs had been shot today. I said to myself: If I put up a poster for every seven Poles shot, the forests of Poland would not be sufficient to manufacture the paper for such posters.†

Today these insane utterings seem hyperbole or even parody. But translated literally onto the streets of Warsaw, they produced a kaleidoscope of suffering: a wild and random terror. What in Frank's diaries might almost

---

*Quoted by Władysław Bartoszewski in *Warsaw Death Ring 1939–44* (Interpress, 1968).

†Quoted Joachim C. Fest in *The Face of the Third Reich* (Weidenfeld & Nicholson, 1970).

be dismissed as literary conceit in reality was expressed in ghoulishness. This is an eyewitness account of the scenes following a mass execution of hostages in 1942:

It was a windy day, with occasional gusts of rain. The bodies of the hung men swayed in the wind like ghastly pendulums. Little groups of people approached the terrible place, the site of the appalling crime committed a few hours earlier. "Oh God, oh God, don't let Janek be there," an old man whispered to the youngster in his twenties leading him by the arm. "Don't let Janek be there. . . . Do you think, Tomek, it could have happened to him, he was arrested the day before yesterday so they wouldn't have touched him yet, would they?" The old man kept his eyes fixed on the ground, not daring to look up at the gallows. He only raised his eyes when he heard his young companion say: "Janek isn't there." His eyes gazed distractedly at the dishonoured bodies. But then his look hardened, his fingers stiffened into a fist, his jaw clenched so tight that it looked as if his teeth would be crushed. The rapid vengeful breathing of the old man was matched by the same vengeful breathing of the younger. . . .

A little further off, a woman was approaching leading a small boy, perhaps twelve years old. Both their faces were pale, their features drawn, their features showed alternate waves of excruciating fear, pain, and anger. Eventually they stood under the gallows. The woman's fingers bit into the hands of the boy: "Look up there, son. Force yourself to look. All your life remember what you see—and never forgive. Never forgive."*

---

*Aleksander Kaminski, *Biuletyn Informelyjing* (Information Bulletin), quoted by Władysław Bartoszewski in *Warsaw Death Ring* (Interpress, 1968) page 145.

It had been two years since Maria had been in Warsaw. Her own encounter with the terror was just beginning. When she arrived just before curfew at the home of her husband's family, it was as though she had come from another world. She was received with wonder and amazement. Friends were called, old comrades reassembled. All of them understood that her arrival could mean only one thing: that the Communist Party was to be re-formed. An old family friend lifted her glass to Maria and to the New Year: "May this year be the last of our enslavement and our defeats. May all those who have been lost or imprisoned be returned to us this year." "Her voice broke," Maria wrote much later; "it was too early to believe in its possibility, yet too heartbreaking to accept its impossibility." It was not long before Maria was reading another, equally optimistic declaration. It was the Party proclamation:

> THE POLISH WORKERS PARTY summons all its countrymen to unrelenting battle with the German Fascist invaders . . . to selfless preparation for a national rising . . . to a struggle for a new and independent Poland, where the nation is free to decide its own future, for a Poland in which there is no fascist or oligarchic exploitation, in which there will be no concentration camps or degrading ghettos, in which there will be no oppression, no hunger, no poverty, and no unemployment.
>
> To arms! To arms for a free and independent Poland!
>
> We shall overcome!

If Maria and her comrades had parachuted from the icy skies expecting a welcome, they were to be disappointed. Rarely can avenging angels have received so lukewarm a reception. The Communists arrived with their newly found sense of purpose to discover that their fellow countrymen, far from abandoning the long-held suspicion towards them, now regarded them with increased bitterness and hostility. There was in fact some satisfaction among Poles that their two traditional enemies were now at each other's throat, and for many this satisfaction outweighed any thought that Poland and the USSR were now in the same boat, threatened by the same Nazi menace.

For Maria and the Initiative Group it was clear that the tactics of the Polish Resistance should be to attack German supply lines to the Eastern Front. But for many Poles who had been resisting against hopeless odds during the cruel period of the Ribbentrop-Molotov Pact, this was not nearly so obvious. Why risk the lives of Polish hostages to help the Russians? Had they not amply illustrated only two years before that their historical appetite for Polish soil remained unabated? It was not as if the Initiative Group arrived as reinforcements. The existing Polish Resistance, soon to be called the Home Army, which owed its allegiance and derived its authority from the Polish government in exile in London, numbered 300,000 men under its direct control. By comparison, in the early months of 1942, Communist strength was puny. All that the Initiative Group's coming heralded was that Moscow had at last begun to take an interest in Polish resistance. To men and women who had been fighting the Germans for at least two years it was an interest that appeared more sinister than gratifying.

In these circumstances it is not surprising that relations between the two groups never became cordial, and that on occasion their rivalry almost took on the form of open conflict, with each side accusing the other of betrayals and deception. As the war continued, the propaganda battle between the two groups intensified. The Home Army continually portrayed the Communist underground as agents of Moscow; the Communists insisted that the London government was comprised of fascists.

It was a setting for double tragedy: Pole was set against Pole on a stage which the Nazis were preparing for genocide.

Maria had been well prepared to enter this world of violence and double cross, of torture and sudden death. Her years as a schoolgirl and young woman in the Communist Youth had developed in her the reflexes of conspiracy and caution. She had strong feelings of solidarity with her comrades and a sense of mission as yet untrammelled by doubt. But as a radio operator of a small and none-too-popular resistance movement she faced from the outset certain elementary difficulties.

In the first place, she had no radio.

The transmitter dispatched with the group from Moscow had been lost during the parachute jump, and it was not until May of 1942—five months after the drop—that she succeeded in piecing together an apparatus powerful enough to send the first messages back to the Soviet Union.

It took a little longer to acquire some of the other useful furniture of subversion. But it came, slowly. One of the early recruits to the Party was a qualified metallurgist, Mietek Lasocki. "He had," remembers Maria, "a passion for ornamental work in metal, which proved a very useful skill in underground work. And it was thanks to this passion of his that I had a superbly concealed false bottom to my powder case, a table lamp with secret cubby holes and a splendid hiding place for my revolver."

By mid-1942 the operation was well under way, and German soldiers whose heads were turned by a beautiful girl on the trams and pavements of Warsaw might have discovered, had they delved more closely, that under the pretty bouquet of fresh flowers in her basket were the working components of a radio transmitter.

It took them just over a year to make that discovery.

It was an extraordinary year. On the global stage the

summer of 1942 was the last in which the Nazis could look forward to victory. By the following year the war had turned irreversibly against them. But in Warsaw the turning of the tide was distant, almost mocking. Victories on fronts a thousand miles away did little to alleviate the present danger. The outcome of the Battle of Alamein in the deserts of North Africa on October 23, 1942, did nothing to prevent the executions a week later in reprisal for a Communist attack on the Café Club in Warsaw. The German surrender at Stalingrad on February 2, 1943, did not prevent Himmler from issuing orders only a fortnight later for the destruction of the Warsaw ghetto. However, these German reverses did encourage the Polish underground to take up a more aggressive and adventurous stance. Increasingly, terror was met with counterterror. But in terms of Polish lives lost, the Germans ensured that each and every act of resistance was also an act of sacrifice.

It was against this background of arrests, street roundups and executions that Maria relearned the geography of her native city. At a time when simply to be Polish was crime enough, when every shopping trip could end in arrest, deportation to Germany or worse, Maria dragged her heavy radio equipment from safe house to safe house to avoid the attentions of the Gestapo detector vans. Throughout Europe young men and women were doing the same job, disguising their aerials in the same ways, experiencing the same narrow escapes in order to send a few minutes of ciphered Morse to secret offices in Allied capitals, where its significance would be determined by unknown men who no doubt hoped, but did not expect, them to survive.

If Maria had any hopes for her own survival, she could draw no encouragement from what was going on around her.

It was a time, she recalls, thinking of the atmosphere

of those days, when heroism and greatness mixed naturally with the ordinary and everyday. But it was also a time when the scale of the tragedy frequently transcended anything that heroism or greatness could do to counteract it.

"In the spring of 1943, there was the rising in the Warsaw ghetto. It was a very difficult experience for us because we knew that it was a struggle that must be lost.

"I have been only once in the ghetto, but it is very difficult to describe what I saw there. It was a crowded district of the city with thousands of Jewish people. There were people dying on the street. I have seen corpses lying on the street, small children crazy from hunger. We saw these children. Sometimes the Gestapo or soldiers beat them to death on the street.

"Nobody could help them, because to help Jewish people meant to be condemned to death, because the Germans not only killed the Jews, but also the Polish people who defended the Jews.

"When the uprising broke out we knew that this was the end of some part of our nation. Because for us it was a Polish population—of Jewish origin, but Polish.

"It was a tragic experience because, you know, the most difficult moment is when you can't help."

On May 16, 1943, SS Maj. Gen. Juergen Stroop reported to his superiors that the Jewish quarter of Warsaw no longer existed. In all, he remarked in his official report, only eight buildings were left intact, one of them the prison building at Dzielna Street, known as Paviak.

The rising of the ghetto had been an interruption, an interlude in the normal course of police activities. Now the SS detachments and police units which had spent almost the whole of the previous month in putting down the Jews could return to the equally serious business of ensuring that the cells and execution yards of Paviak were kept filled with "bandits" from the various sections of the Polish resistance movement.

But before they caught up with Maria, she too experienced an interlude of an altogether different kind.

In the autumn of 1942, Maria's husband, Wicek, was one of a group of Polish prisoners of war released by the Nazis. He returned at once to Warsaw and to Maria. They had not seen each other for three years. For the few months that now remained to them they worked side by side in the Communist underground. They lived in a small flat in Wilcza Street. It had been found for them by an old friend, a comrade as all their friends were, and it was filled with pictures, antiques and bric-a-brac. It was here that in between Maria's radio transmissions and Wicek's intelligence reports, which kept him busy late into the night, they found each other once again. They knew the net was closing in but the danger added to the bond between them.

"In this short time, we were very much conscious that every day we could be separated or even killed. We had a very strong feeling that every day was special for us and we remembered that, even if we were very busy because I was working and he had his own work, his own job and responsible Party duties. We always knew that it could be for a short time."

Despite the pressure—or maybe because of it—they decided to start a family. Wicek especially, Maria remembers, had a real desire for children. So they went ahead. But the net *was* closing in.

One by one the original members of the Initiative Group were rounded up or killed. As early as November 1942, Marcelli Novotko had been shot in mysterious circumstances in Trzech Krzyzy Square. Pinkus Kartin, another member of the group, had been arrested by the Gestapo and executed. Anastazy Kowalczyk had committed suicide after being arrested and tortured in Crakow. Feliks Paplinski had been hanged in Warsaw. These were the casualties only from among the Initiative Group itself; in what was known as "the terrible spring" of 1943 many more of Maria's close friends and comrades were hunted down by the Gestapo. Then, one morning in July, Wicek left the flat in Wilcza Street to go to work. Maria never saw him again.

By the late summer, it is reasonable to suppose, the Gestapo knew all about the Initiative Group's mission from Moscow. They would be looking for the radio operator. Maria changed locations for her transmissions with increasing frequency, moving the apparatus from house to house, the risk increasing all the time. "Moving the apparatus—it's an easy thing to say now, but how much human suffering is hidden behind it all?"

At the beginning of September another comrade, Janek Krasicki, was shot dead when the Gestapo broke into his flat. He had been high-spirited, brave, everybody's favourite. A fortnight later, Maria herself was taken. "Yes, in some ways we expected it. All of us were involved in the resistance movement. We were prepared to be arrested and killed. But expectation is not the same as reality. I had been prepared, but when it happened, I had a shock, a real shock."

The date was September 14, 1943. Maria and her friend Renia had set up the transmitter in a house in Miedzeszyn, a suburb of Warsaw. Following instructions, Renia left before the transmissions began. Maria, alone in a first-floor room which overlooked a small garden yard, began to send the Morse signals to Moscow. Once, not many months before, she had looked out of the window of her station and seen a German search party combing the neighbourhood. That time they had passed by. This time she did not hear as a detector van took a fix on her position; she did not hear the soldiers surrounding the house underneath her window. On the pillow of a bed close by lay a large revolver, but this time they came so suddenly that she had no time even to reach for it. "I remember that the door opened and many Gestapo men ran in. I don't know how many, maybe not as many as it seemed at the time. I managed to smash all my apparatus from the table. That was my first duty—not to give them my apparatus."

The men were shouting. They grabbed her, but she wrenched her arms free and flung herself over the verandah into the garden below. It was a useless gesture. The Gestapo were there too. They dragged her back into the bedroom. It was now filled with people. They were searching wildly for anything that would tell them more about the "Bolsheviks' " work. Maria sat on a stool in the corner of the room. She watched them empty the contents of her handbag out onto the floor; they cut open the mattress and its straw filling floated in the air. They grabbed at her hair and threw her across the room. In a strange way, convinced that these were the last moments of her life, she watched what was happening in front of her as though it were a violent pantomime.

"I tried not to show them that I was afraid. There is something in the ambition of people who fight not to show their unhappiness or anxiousness.

"They put me some questions and I didn't answer at all because I knew that I could not answer anything. And then they started to beat me and they found in my bag a paper from the doctor which said that I was pregnant. And then they tried to say, 'You are pregnant. You know you will be shot, so you must tell us everything.' I was sure that I would never help them."

During this time Maria's attention was hardly on her tormentors at all, but on another small slip of paper that had fallen from her handbag onto the floor. It was a note from her husband smuggled out of the prison at Paviak. She recalled its message over and over again: "You must preserve our greatest treasure. . . ." For Maria there seemed very little hope of that now.

More Gestapo men arrived. Their commanding officer began to ask more questions. Maria refused to answer. He hit her hard across the mouth. She was taken downstairs once again and made to stand in the yard facing a tree. "I was sure that I would be shot. They had found proof that I was very much involved with the resistance movement, so I was sure that this was my last moment, and as I stood in front of the tree, something unbelievable happened. I have never since had such a feeling, but I remember it very well. Every leaf of the tree was separate, every patch was like a picture, separate and big. I could see every detail of the little flowers in the grass. I was sure that this was my last view and that in a moment I would feel the bullet in my head, here in the back of my neck."

Beyond the verandah covered with vines, the Gestapo continued their search. Their prisoner, the young Polish mother-to-be, stared at the bark of the tree in front of her and waited to die.

"Frightened? Yes, I was frightened as well. I am not a hero. I'm a—I was a girl, a young woman, and I was afraid as well. But there was something else. You could be afraid but at the same time you must be brave and remember that you are a part of your nation, of your friends, of your party, of everything: that you are not alone. Of course, to die is difficult, but with such feelings it is not so hard."

By the tree in Miedzeszyn, Maria came to terms with the inevitable. It was more than composure. It was a kind of peace, a calm, an acceptance of her fate. "I had decided that this will be the end." She had made the wrong decision.

Without warning she was snatched from the tree and thrown into the back of a Gestapo car. Suddenly everything had changed. "I went with them to Warsaw and I understood that I would have more time, long or short, and that I must fight again from the beginning. But I knew very well that it would be a very tough and difficult time for me."

Today, 25 Szucha Avenue houses the Polish ministry of education, an off-white unobtrusive building constructed in a style of somber classicism appropriate to anonymity and bureaucracy. Doubtless these were characteristics which commended it to the Gestapo as both a headquarters and an interrogation center. As such it became the nerve center of the German terror, and the name Szucha itself inspired and became synonymous with an immense dread. Here the victims of the Gestapo were stripped of everything: the fellow feeling of their compatriots, the support of their families, friends, comrades, the reassurance of strings which can be pulled and of proprieties which will be observed. Above all they lost the powerfully held but unspoken belief that there are some things that one human being will not inflict upon another human being. In Szucha you stood naked before the uniformed agents of an alien race: men who did not speak your language, who did not share your beliefs, who did not share your humanity. Men who looked upon you like meat and would not hesitate to do to you all the things that men can do to meat.

On the Eastern Front the Russians were advancing on Novorossisk and Smolensk. In Italy the Allies had just landed at Salerno. In Warsaw the doors of Szucha shut behind Maria Rutkiewicz. There a message scrawled by a prisoner on a cell wall read:

> *It is easy to talk about Poland.*
> *It is more difficult to work for her,*
> *More difficult still to die for her,*
> *But most difficult of all is to suffer for her. . . .*

An iron grill door opened and Maria was placed in one of the cells known as the "tramways." Inside there were others sitting in wooden stalls screwed down into the ground, their backs towards the door, their eyes staring straight ahead at the wall at the end of the cell. They waited, sometimes for hours, sometimes for days. They were forbidden to turn round and forbidden to speak. In the dim light they could have been mistaken for worshippers in a chapel praying in their pews. In reality they were, almost all of them, waiting to be tortured.

For Maria there was an even greater anxiety than the prospect of what was waiting for her in the interrogation room at the end of the corridor. Ever since the note from Wicek had dropped to the floor when she was arrested she had been uncomfortably conscious that if the Gestapo realized that now they held both her and Wicek, there would almost certainly be a confrontation. To make her talk they would beat Wicek to death before her eyes.

"I had no right to turn," Maria remembers, "but I asked in a very low voice, 'Is anybody here from Paviak, from the hospital?' because I knew that my husband was for some days in the hospital.

"And a man sitting here answered me, 'Yes, I am from Paviak.'

"I asked him, 'Do you know Rutkiewicz?'

"And he answered me, 'Yes, we were together in the hospital and I will tell you some details. He has a wife, and she's pregnant, and he's very, very anxious about her.'

"So I answered him, 'It's me. I'm his wife.'

"And then he gave me a small roll and a small piece of chocolate, I don't know how he managed to have it, but he gave it to me. And he told me, 'You must be very happy. He will not be shot. Yesterday he was sent to a good camp: to Auschwitz.'"

* * *

In 1978, Maria was in Szucha again. A small part of the ministry basement has been turned into a museum to commemorate the generation of Polish martyrs who died and were tortured there. The tramways were empty. She sat alone, talking of the events of thirty-five years ago. She spoke softly, not much above a whisper. There were no longer jailers and torturers to hear her. They were all gone, dead long ago, or else returned to Germany. It was the spirit of their victims which lived on in those empty cells set out as a museum piece, and Maria spoke for them and with them and to them, seeking in a foreign language to express their truth, answerable to their cumulative experience of suffering.

"In a place like this it was impossible to appeal to humanity or human feelings. Impossible. When I was beaten, the Gestapo men, Rudolph and the others, told me that they were humane because they beat me only in the face, but not here [indicating her stomach]. So, they said, they were very humane.

"They told me that the child was condemned to death as I was condemned to death. They were sure I would not have the baby, and that we would be dead together."

After each interrogation Maria would be hustled into a prison van known as the *budy*, kennels. The vans leaving Gestapo headquarters took a predictable course. They turned left outside the gates and travelled north along the heavily patrolled and barricaded Szucha Avenue. They continued across the Aleje Jerozolimskie, which the Nazis had renamed Reichstrasse Ostland. At the central square, which had become Adolf Hitler Platz, they turned away from the River Vistula. Inside the *budy* the prisoners, tired and hungry, had no doubt about where they were being taken. On their right the Old Town, the heart of Warsaw. On their left, as they moved down Bielanska, they came to the ghetto wall and the ruins of the Warsaw synagogue, destroyed by the Waffen SS in the very last moments of the Jewish rising. A little farther on, at the corner of Ogrod Krasinik Park, the prisoners entered the devastated wilderness of the ghetto itself. The *budy* travelled on down Dzielna Street until it came to a halt outside the gates of the largest building still standing amidst the rubble in the heart of the ghetto: Paviak.

In the early days of her captivity, the daily journey between the prison at Paviak and Szucha became almost routine: "My interrogation lasted seven days. Day by day and night by night, and I was beaten very hard so that when I was sent back to the prison, the woman supervisor of the corridor, she couldn't recognize me and didn't know what number of the cell to send me."

Maria did not tell them anything. It is something she is still proud of today. She knows that her interrogation was not as severe or brutal as many. She did not have to bear the sophisticated systematic tortures which destroyed her best friend and many thousands of others in those same cells. But she still glows with satisfaction and pride when she remembers that her comrades, on hearing of her capture, decided not to change the ciphers because they trusted her not to talk. For her it was a question of responsibility. "People could resist not only such interrogations as I've had, but much worse. Hundreds of thousands of people resisted in camps and prisons because of the feeling of responsibility for the job they had done in the resistance movement."

These convictions did not lessen the agony, but perhaps they made it easier to bear: "To be beaten is something very hard. To be beaten by another man or woman, to be put in a position unlike a human being, that is something very hard. It was hard to be in a solitary cell, to be alone day and night. It was very difficult not to know what had happened to your family, your husband, to mother, to father, to friends.

"And it was very difficult to wait, wondering what will happen, knowing that it is the end of your life."

Maria's interrogation ended. Under sentence of death she was placed in a solitary cell in Serbia, the women's section of Paviak. It was late September. Maria was in the fifth month of her pregnancy.

Paviak had long before established its notoriety as a clearinghouse for political prisoners of the Third Reich. For many thousands it was a point of transit, a stepping-stone to the concentration camps. Thousands more were taken from Paviak to be shot in the killing grounds in the woods and villages just outside Warsaw, or latterly, since the destruction of the ghetto, in the ruins which surrounded the prison itself. At night the cell doors clattered as prison guards worked their way down the lists of those to be executed the following morning. Night after night, Maria waited for the guards to come for her. Alone in her cell, she could only wonder why they took so long.

It was not long before she realized that, hopeless as her situation certainly was, she was not entirely alone. One day she found a piece of bread left in her cell. Another time it was a flower. After about two months she received a letter smuggled into the prison from her friends Malgosia Fornalska and Pavel Finder, who after the death of Novotko had taken over the leadership of the Party. "They told me how much they loved me and how much they cared about me," remembers Maria, "and that they would do everything they could to save me."

There was something else, something which she had discovered when she had been examined in the prison hospital: Maria was expecting twins. The Polish prisoner doctors, who largely ran the hospital, had promised to do everything to save her—at least until the children were born. And there had been a German doctor, Dr. Bomeier. He was trusted by the Poles. Unofficially he slipped the Polish doctors drugs and medical books. He too had said that he would do what he could.

But in the balance between life and death, Maria was realistic enough to know that all this was too little to constitute hope. The Nazis were no respecters of a woman's delicate condition. When so many innocent were being slaughtered at random, why should she, a Communist, caught red-handed, be spared? Today Maria believes that it was the twins that saved her, that some curious sensibility led her captors to put off the date of execution. In a way she is right. But one of the Polish prisoner doctors, Dr. Krystyna Ossowska, who looked after her throughout her confinement and after, has a more prosaic explanation for German behaviour. She had worked in the prison hospital since 1940, and she knew how the Nazis operated: "The mothers and the children born in prison were not specially considered by the Germans. They were the same as other prisoners. As far as Mrs. Rutkiewicz was concerned, when she was arrested she was far gone with child. I do not remember the details, but it was a hanging matter. She survived because she had twins. After several interrogations they simply forgot about her."

The randomness of terror works both ways. If the innocent perish arbitrarily, the guilty must sometimes be allowed to survive. Nevertheless, in the last months of 1943, this could not have been a thought that offered Maria a great deal of consolation.

Outside the walls of Paviak, the German terror reached a new pitch of ferocity. At the beginning of October 1943, Hans Frank had issued a new decree. No one by now was in any doubt as to the seriousness of his clownish utterances. The street public-address systems spluttered out the implications of the new policy: "A

German policeman may shoot anyone encountered in the street who arouses his suspicion."* A new wave of street roundups began on an unprecedented scale. Those caught were held as hostages, to guarantee the good behaviour of the population. In the event of resistance activity either these hostages or others, taken from among the two to three thousand prisoners held in Paviak, would be executed publicly in the streets of Warsaw. The executions began in the middle of October. The names of the victims were posted on the walls or broadcast over the loudspeakers as a warning to others. No attempt was made to link them directly with the crimes for which they were being put to death. Ludwig Landau, an economist and social researcher, kept a chronicle of events in Warsaw throughout the Occupation until his own arrest in February 1944. In this period he paints a picture of a city gripped by fear: "Anyone who can stays home," he wrote on October 25, "if he has to go out he scuttles down the street fearfully; the slightest sound of a car is enough to cause panic. The shops are empty. It's not only the customers who stay away; even the assistants keep far from regular hours."

And three months later he was writing:

> Warsaw has again suffered a harrowing experience: an execution in the city centre. Executions are an everyday occurrence, but no descriptions can possibly compare to the shock made by what you actually see even if it is the ominous preparation or the traces of an execution, or even what you hear—the crash of the volleys bringing death to innocent people.†

---

*Władysław Bartoszewski, *Warsaw Death Ring 1939–44*, page 196.

†Quoted by Władysław Bartoszewski, ibid.

In Paviak, Maria's time was almost due. The prisoner doctors successfully persuaded the German authorities in the prison to transfer her from her solitary cell to the prison hospital to await the birth. They showed her X rays and she saw for the first time the "two little backbones" of her twins.

On February 16 it was reported from Paviak that five Jewish women and three children had been shot. On the same day Maria gave birth to a son and a daughter.

"Oh, how to describe it. It's difficult to describe for you as a man because women understand that when you give birth to a first child, your attitude to life changes very much. And that happened to me. It changed everything. Suddenly I was not alone. I had the responsibility for two little human beings. I thought of my husband who wanted so much to have the children and that now he had them but he didn't know it."

The mother and children were alive and well. But in Paviak no one could dare to hope that that was a situation which would be allowed to continue for long. "Every day and every night I spent sitting near them I knew well that it could be the last time. Often the Gestapo would tell the doctors that I could only be with them for another two weeks. Every day I wasn't sure that this could be the last day."

The birth of the twins caused something of a stir in Warsaw. The news spread from mouth to mouth and quickly travelled beyond the prison walls. The underground press printed an article: "Twins Are Born in Paviak." From that dark prison house in the middle of the ghetto the news represented cheer; it indicated a kind of hope. Bomeier, the kindly German doctor, told Maria that he would not be able to help, but that he would do nothing to harm the twins. From outside, brandy and cigarettes were sent to bribe the guards to favour Maria and her children. The Polish doctors inside the prison began to wonder whether even if the twins would not keep Maria alive, their existence might lead to further postponements of her execution. No opportunity was lost to tell the German guards that the twins were still weak, that they needed their mother for a little while longer. Throughout the spring of 1944, as the Russians drew nearer and nearer Warsaw, Maria and the babies grew stronger, and healthier.

But there was the problem of Wicek. In Paviak prisoners had organized an underground communications system of marvellous efficiency. A massive volume of illicit mail passed in and out of the prison, some of it intelligence sent to outside resistance groups, some just correspondence between relatives. In this way Maria received news from her husband in Auschwitz. Wicek had been arrested seven weeks before Maria and had heard no news of her or the children since he had been sent to the concentration camp. Month after month he had received no letter. He became dispirited and told his friends if Maria did not write, it meant that something was wrong. His friends in the camp, knowing too well that in Auschwitz a man could die from depression more quickly than from the brutalities inflicted by the Nazis, sent an urgent message through the grapevine to Warsaw. They wanted Maria to send evidence that she was alive and well.

The result was a small photograph, no more than a snapshot. It shows two women sitting on a bench, holding on their laps two young babies clad in white. One of the women is looking towards the camera, smiling; the other looks down at the child on her knee. The face of one of the children is blurred, but he or she appears to be asleep. The other is quite clearly crying heartily. The atmosphere is free and easy. The photo could have come from a million family albums. In fact it could claim to be one of the most remarkable documents to survive the war.

It was taken with the camera of a German criminal prisoner in Paviak and shows Maria and her two twins with Dr. Krystyna Ossowska. It was taken secretly in the prison yard and it was intended to lie:

"I'm sitting with Doctor Ossowska, a very dear doctor, and we are smiling a bit because I thought at that moment that this was a trick for my husband. He would think that we are in a forest or perhaps in a village and he will believe that I'm free. So I said, 'Smile with me' —and we are smiling. That is why this photo is so gay, so cheerful. We sent this photo out of Paviak to my brother-in-law and afterwards he managed to send it into Auschwitz. My husband got this picture and he was very happy. But then he ran to his friend Dr. Alfred Fiderkiewicz, an old doctor friend of ours who was several times imprisoned in Paviak—he was a gynecologist so he was often in the women's part of the prison—and he recognized that it was not taken anywhere else, but that it was in Paviak.

"And he told my husband, 'It's Paviak.'

"So all this arrangement was for nothing, because he was very sad. After the war Dr. Fiderkiewicz told me how he had taken the news. I know that it was very hard for him. He was a very brave man but in some way he lost his hope."

At the end of 1943 only one member of the original Initiative team remained at liberty. Most were already dead. Among the last to be arrested were Pavel Finder and Malgorzata Fornalska, Maria's closest friend. They had been picked up days after smuggling their secret letter to Maria in her solitary cell. "We will do everything we can to save you," they had written. It was this message more than anything else that had told Maria she was not alone. Now they too were being held somewhere in Paviak, shuttled back and forth to Szucha, where both were subjected to the most horrific tortures.

Throughout the spring of 1944 the military position of the Germans deteriorated steadily. In Warsaw too they faced setbacks. At the beginning of February, a Home Army commando, code-named Parasol, ambushed and killed the Warsaw SS and police chief Franz Kutschera, the man responsible for the recent wave of public executions. The Germans retaliated with the execution of three hundred Polish hostages; a fine of a hundred million zlotys was to be levied on the residents of Warsaw; and all Polish restaurants would be closed for an indefinite period. Nevertheless, the death of Kutschera ("The Butcher," as he was known) brought an end to the public executions. It was not a change of policy, but it was a modification: Henceforth, most of the killing took place behind the ghetto walls, in the ruins surrounding Paviak.

The battlefronts were no longer remote. In January the advancing Russians crossed over the 1939 Polish-Russian border. For the first time since the Wehrmacht had swept into the city in September of 1939, Warsaw braced itself for battle.

All over Warsaw the painted slogans splashed on the walls warned the Germans: PAWIAK POMSCIMY—Paviak Will Be Revenged. The Home Army, the main Polish underground movement, was preparing to rise against the Germans in a bid to seize the city on behalf of the London government in exile before the arrival of the Soviet armies. The Germans too sensed that their tenure of power was coming to an end, and began to plan accordingly. All over Warsaw there was a climate of expectation, a feeling that deliverance was imminent.

Yet Paviak was a world in itself, cut off in the middle of the ghetto. Inside the prison rumour and anticipation infected everybody, but few could entertain hope of personal salvation. The prisoners watched as the Gestapo incinerated documents and records in the prison yard and had little doubt how they themselves would be disposed of. Throughout July the lucky ones were evacuated to concentration camps. Many hundreds more were executed.

It was a critical moment. Bomeier had warned Maria that it would be difficult to go on protecting her once the children were six months old. On July 16 they had reached that age. Maria had repeatedly asked the Polish doctors to send the children to her relatives outside the prison, but they had refused. They knew that the twins were the only thing standing between Maria and execution. But Maria was desperate. She realized that in the battle for the liberation of Paviak, the twins would be quite defenseless. "There's going to be fighting," Maria told the small group of mothers in the hospital block in Serbia, "and we won't be able to save them." She wrote a last secret letter to her family:

> My dearest ones,
> The last days have brought us so much news and given us new hope. If we were not so hopelessly cut off from the world, I might believe that I will soon be with you. But our situation is extremely poor. We can be executed the moment before relief comes. So after long hours of thinking, I have come to the conclusion that I must send the babies to you now. It's not possible to save all three of us and I want them at least to be with you. I know I am putting you in a difficult situation—but only you, my dearest ones, can save them.

It was the end of July. In the distance the remaining prisoners of Paviak could hear the Russian guns pounding the German positions east of the Vistula. Most of the inmates had by now been evacuated to other prisons or camps. The executions of the remainder continued until the very end. Among them, on July 26, were Pavel

Finder, Malgorzata Fornalska, and a twenty-year-old girl, Krystyna Matysiak, the operator of a secret Communist radio station just outside Warsaw.

The prison was almost deserted. Of the male prisoners, only about one hundred were left. In the women's wing, perhaps fifty—mothers with their children, the sick and the disabled. Most of the Germans had disappeared. In their place there were men from the Polish police—collaborators. No one was in any doubt: It was the end of Paviak.

On July 31 the prison gates opened to admit a horse and cart. It was driven by a woman who had visited the prison many times before, Helena Danielewicz, who worked for the prisoners' aid organization Patronat. Orders were given to the mothers to come to the yard and place their babies on the cart. Then came the moment no one had predicted.

"Some Gestapo men approached," recalls Maria, "and they shouted, 'Mothers together! Mothers together with the children!' So we went together. It was so unexpected that I didn't have the feeling of how marvellous it was to be free—because I didn't feel it. I wasn't prepared for it. My sister was waiting for the children at the ghetto wall—because, you know, Paviak was in the ghetto—and when she saw me she was so astonished that she was absolutely convinced that I would have to go back, and that I would only give her the children.

"And I told her, 'No, I am going with you, Natalie.'

"And she cried, 'It's impossible, no, it isn't possible!' Many of us were in the same position, condemned to death after years of imprisonment ... and then suddenly to be free. It was another kind of freedom. It was not real freedom but we were ... free. So it was at that time, the time of war, the time of the Nazis. Everything could happen.

"Everything. The worst could happen. Then suddenly, there happened something that was very good, very unexpected."

A day later, the Warsaw rising began. It was the culmination of five years of resistance, the last splendid but desperate act of Warsaw's tragedy. But for Maria the war was already over. Freed from Paviak, she left Warsaw to stay with relatives near Crakow, in the south of Poland. There is another photograph of her there in 1945. A family group. The pose is a little stiff, unlike the photo taken in Paviak. Maria in the back row is holding her young son, whom she had named Wicek after his father. In the front an old aunt is holding her daughter, named Malgosia, after Maria's best friend, shot in Paviak. But this time the smiles are ingenuous, the cheerfulness genuine. It is a photograph taken for no other purpose than to be included in the family album.

A footnote on Paviak: Dr. Krystyna Ossowska was one of the very few prisoners to remain in Paviak to the end. She had the opportunity of witnessing what happened there after Maria had left: "Only those prisoners who couldn't walk and two mothers in the very last stages of pregnancy were left behind. They decided that they had to have somebody to take care of them so they kept me and one midwife. On August 13, 1944, the Germans took them all in fives and shot them in the ruins of the ghetto. I saw them passing the prison gate from the quarantine building. Before that execution two children had been born. One was six days, the second ten days old. They took the mothers and shot them separately outside Paviak. And the children . . . they simply smashed their heads to pieces."

Maria returned to Warsaw the following year. What she found was a moonscape: a vast, depopulated city in a state of almost total devastation. When, after sixty-three days, the Germans finally succeeded in crushing the Warsaw rising, Hitler had ordered the complete destruction of the Polish capital. Not one stone was to be left standing on another. His general obeyed the order with such enthusiasm that they even made a film of the operation. Maria surveyed the scene of the city where she had been born and brought up, loved and fought. "There was no trace of the past. No road, nothing but ruins, and we had to climb, like in hills, from one part to another. No houses, no streets, no squares. Nothing but ruins.

"What did I tell the children?" she asks. "I didn't have to tell them anything. They were brought up in the ruins. Everything which surrounded them told them the story of our lives."

Today Warsaw has been rebuilt. Parts of the city—the old town square, the royal palace, and elsewhere—have been lovingly reconstructed. But most is entirely new, the streets bearing no resemblance at all to those after which they were named. It is a new city. The pre-war traveller from London would recognize buildings but would not rediscover the old Warsaw. "The strange presence of the Jews in their medieval garb" no longer lends to the city that peculiarity of aspect and character which had so delighted him. As he watched the drab Warsovians queuing outside butchers' shops for meat, he would be unlikely to conclude that the London crowd "seems rather monotonous by comparison." Looming over the new Warsaw, its highest stories frequently obscured by cloud, is the huge skyscraper, the Palace of Arts and Culture. Built in the early 1950s, its bleak utopianism is a constant reminder to the people of Warsaw that their country has once more passed into Moscow's sphere of influence. They call it, sardonically, Stalin's Gift. Nothing could represent more concretely that the rulers of Poland are not the successors of Pilsudski and his regime of colonels, or even of Władysław Sikorski and the London government in Exile, but of that eleven-man Initiative Group, dropped into Poland on an icy midwinter night at the end of 1941.

Of these, the original human torpedoes, only two survived the war and Maria is the only one still alive today. They had paid a high price to create a Communist Poland. Maria lost her mother, and her two brothers, one killed in battle in September 1939, the other in Auschwitz. But in Poland, she reflects, to lose many members of one's family was nothing special: "Everyone lost somebody." Her husband, Wicek, never saw the children he had wanted so much. He was killed in Sachsenhausen concentration camp, near Berlin, at the very end of the war.

It was an enduring loss. Thirty-five years later she wrote "Distant by Death," a poem about her feelings towards him:

> I sculpt the memory of you
> in the most frail substance of thought
> I do not search for words to name you
> I do not struggle with stubborn matter
>
> enough to touch with my senses
> our once common world
> enough to be bewitched
> by a new experienced good—
> and you are with me
>
> enough for everyday pain
> to reach and hurt me
> enough for someone's lie
> to besot me with fear—
> and you are with me
>
> I look in my son's eyes
> and in them is the sparkle of your eyes
> I touch my daughter's hand
> and feel the warmth of your hand

wherever there is wrong
you are among the fighters
wherever brutality—
they aim at you

I find you in human magnanimity
in the bravery and goodness of those
*   who are ı. ,t indifferent*

you are only a little distant
by the camp death too far
by the whole death too far

I sculpt you in the most durable substance
in the live tissue
of imperishable memory

After the war Maria married Artur Starewicz, a high-ranking Communist official. She worked for the Party for a time, studied history and became a journalist. In 1971, when Starewicz was appointed Polish Ambassador to the Court of St. James, Maria accompanied him to London, where she lived throughout most of the seventies. In 1978 she returned to Poland and now lives in a comfortable apartment in suburban Warsaw.

From time to time people ask her whether the time has come to forget the war. The answer is always the same:

"Forget all that happened? It isn't possible to forget—even if we wanted to, it's impossible. How do I forget all my relatives, all my close friends who were killed? How do you forget that over six million people in this country —my country—were killed, how do you forget this experience? For my generation it is quite impossible.

"But there's another question. I don't want to remember who did it, because, of course, I remember quite well. But it's not a matter of who did it, but why it happened. And we must not only remember the cruelties—we have a duty never to allow them to be repeated. I think that my generation, the generation which suffered during the war, not only in Poland but in Germany and in every country in Europe, must not only remember that something so cruel could happen, but we must prevent a repetition of this awful experience."

The story of Maria Rutkiewicz is the story of a brave woman. But she herself remains something of an enigma, trapped inside the question marks that still hang over the true story of the rise of the Communist Party in Poland. Maria portrays herself simply as an idealist, an innocent: "We were just strugglers after understanding," she says, "we wanted to be here [in Poland] to struggle with my people, my nation." But in Poland the Communist struggle has never been simple. What does Maria tell us of the Stalinist purges of the thirties which liquidated the top layer of the Polish Party? Nothing— she learned about them only after the war. What of the Soviet deportations of Poles from eastern Poland between 1939 and the German invasion of Russia? Once again, nothing. Maria says that she is unaware of the existence of camps in Russia and suggests that the only people the Russians took prisoner were the big landowners. Ask her whether the idealism of her pre-war days has remained intact and her answer is parabolic:

"Is the idealism of my younger days the same now? In some ways, yes, in some ways, no. It is the difference between your dreams and reality. You can never manage to create reality in the same way as your ideals. I put it this way: When you are young and you are in love, you love a girl and you are sure that you must marry her and that your life will be beautiful and you will love her all your life. And perhaps your marriage will be very happy. But of course reality is not the same as dreams. You will love your wife and your children, but at the same time it will not be the same. Because life is life, and it is impossible to create the world you dream of."

Poles have always paid a heavy price for their dreams,

and the politics of the Polish Communist Party have never been for the squeamish or fainthearted. For Maria the worst moment of the war was when she heard the news of the death of Marcelli Novotko. He had led the Initiative Group from Moscow and been first secretary of the Communist Party in Poland. Maria had loved him —the Old Man—as a leader and friend. Today he is a hero in the Communist Poland he fought to build. But the circumstances of his death have never been fully explained. He was killed—in the middle of the war—not by the Nazis, but by one of his Communist comrades, in fact by a senior member of the original Initiative Group.

For what purpose he was assassinated, and upon whose orders, it has never been revealed.

Every year on November 28—the anniversary of his death—Maria accompanies Novotko's widow to his graveside in Warsaw's Powazki Cemetery. There on a cold winter morning, among the jumbled crowd of aging tombstones, the last member of the Initiative Group pays her respects to the first. Her sad glance is all that reveals the love and the experience and the secrets they share between them.

Hiltgunt Zassenhaus

September 1944. Germany was approaching breaking point. In the east and west, Germans saw the armies of their enemies massing to pour over the frontiers of the Reich. The unthinkable was about to begin. Albert Speer, minister of armaments, sent an urgent message to Hitler from the west: "In the vicinity of Aachen one sees the miserable possessions of evacuees, setting out with small children and the old, exactly as in France in 1940." But in Berlin this reversal of fortune seemed to pass with very little sympathy for war victims. "Rather a terrible end than an endless terror," they had said in the old days of Brownshirts and street fighting before the Nazi seizure of power. Now the Nazi leadership contemplated the terrible end. The *Völkischer Beobachter* pointed the way in an editorial on September 7: "The enemy is to find every footbridge destroyed, every road blocked—nothing but death, annihilation and hatred will meet him." There was no hope. The Führer himself had dictated the editorial.

Trains do not run on time when time is running out. For many months travel inside Germany had been almost intolerable. Nevertheless there were still trains, and thousands of passengers hardy and desperate enough to wait for them however long they took to arrive. One day late in September a train finally pulled out of Lübeck bound for Rostock, a journey of about one hundred kilometers, far enough across low-lying, flat countryside exposed to attack by British and American fighters. The train was in a sorry state. At Lübeck there had been the usual fights on the station platform to get on board. The windows had been shattered by the bombing, and in some places the doors were only held on by rope.

Sitting silently in the corner of a compartment was a fair-haired woman in her midtwenties. She was pale and appeared ill and tired. For much of the time she studied the medical textbook on her knee, only occasionally lifting her eyes to look out at the flat beet fields of Mecklenburg passing by. She seemed drained of energy and life. It was a look that was becoming familiar in Germany. War weariness, fatigue, rationing, too many nights in the bomb shelters—they had taken their toll. She was not the only one who was exhausted, but at least, in a country which had become used to being careful not only with strangers but with neighbours—and even friends—she looked harmless enough. Had her fellow passengers known who she really was, they would certainly have treated her with more respect.

The name on her identity card was Hiltgunt Zassenhaus, an officer of the Nazi department of justice. She was travelling under orders from the Gestapo. In her handbag, next to her travel documents, there was a gun.

The train stopped at Bützow Station. Fraulein Zassenhaus left her compartment, carrying a large, heavy suitcase. Bützow was a small, damp agricultural town lying in swampy ground in the middle of the northern German lowlands. She walked directly from the station towards the town jail. With her was a young man. They had travelled together in the same compartment, though throughout the journey they had said almost nothing to each other. Now they were deep in conversation. As they approached the prison a change came over Fraulein Zassenhaus. She became alive. Her eyes became brighter.

At the prison gate she presented her papers and instructed a hesitant guard to take her to the warden's office. There she showed the warden a list of prisoners and instructed him to produce them in the visiting room.

One by one, they were produced.

She inspected them as they came through the door: thin, emaciated men, enemies of the Reich, political prisoners from the Danish Resistance, who had been sent here after the Gestapo had finished with them. Now they were suffering from the familiar effects of solitary confinement and semistarvation. She waited until they were all assembled and then sent the prison guards away.

Suddenly the grim faces of the prisoners broke into smiles. They greeted one another in Danish.

"Knud," said Fraulein Zassenhaus, approaching one of the men, "I have news for you." She handed him a photograph. "You are a father. You have a girl, born on September the fourth."

He looked at the photograph in his hands. It was of his wife in Denmark and his baby daughter.

Thirty-five years later, Knud Christensen, sitting in the Langelinie Pavillionen restaurant in Copenhagen, retells the story of how he heard that he had become a father for the first time. Outside, the peaceful waters of Copenhagen harbour lap the statue of Hans Christian Andersen's "Mermaid." "You know," he says, "the Germans blew this place up to teach us a lesson. It had to be rebuilt after the war." His mind goes back to his days as a prisoner in Bützow, meeting Hiltgunt Zassenhaus for the first time.

"I was placed all alone in a cell which was dirty with fleas. I was very surprised when this beautiful young lady asked me in a charming, perfect 'inter-Scandinavian' language if she could help me."

The danger did not seem to bother her, he remembers. She had smuggled in medicines, letters, food. She spoke about anything, families, news of the war. "We never thought of her as a German, but as a human being, like a good friend. She was called the Angel," recalls Knud, "the German Angel."

In the spring of 1979 the German Angel, then aged sixty-two, a doctor from Baltimore in the United States, flew back to Europe to retrace the steps of her life in Hitler's Germany. It was not the first time she had come back, but it was the first time she had returned with the object of facing the past. She had agreed to make a documentary film for British television describing the course of her long and lonely resistance to the Third Reich, a story of quiet determination and dogged courage which began when she was a young schoolgirl out of step with her classmates, and which grew slowly until after five dangerous years she helped twelve hundred men to survive.

A new Germany has now been built on the ruins of the old, but for Hiltgunt, back in her hometown, Hamburg, after half a lifetime, it was the old Germany that kept on seeking her out.

Then, as now, Hamburg was Germany's largest port, a great center of international trade, cosmopolitan and outward-looking. It was said to be "the most English of German cities" but it was what happened to the hearts and minds of people here that had put Hiltgunt on the road to resistance and which eventually led her to say good-bye to Germany forever.

She was born in 1916, the youngest of four children. Her father, Julius Zassenhaus, a former Lutheran minister, was the headmaster of a girls' high school. He was a man of deep moral purpose, a writer on Christian theology and a follower of the teachings of the Alsatian missionary Albert Schweitzer, whose humanitarian ideals and especially his belief in "the reverence for life" he passed on to his family. Her mother, Margaret, was twenty years younger than her husband, a lively, intelligent woman who was an active supporter of the reforming Social Democratic Party.

Hiltgunt and her three brothers were brought up in a home where intellectual freedom went hand in hand with a clear sense of the rights and duties of the individual. In the Germany of the late twenties, these were beliefs and attitudes which were about to become unfashionable and dangerous.

The aristocracy of Hamburg's society had always been drawn from the shipping people: ship builders, export traders and stockbrokers. The city's character, the way it was built and set out, reflected their solid bourgeois values of probity and sound business sense. Traditionally, this patrician class had exercised its sway over Hamburg's society from exclusive clubs, but in the troubled and divisive economic climate of the 1920s these clubs—*Gesellschaften* or *Vereine,* as they were known— began to lose their hold. With the great slump of 1929, Hamburg's giant shipyards laid off their workers by the thousands. Blohm and Voss, the city's largest yard, retained only a skeleton workforce to carry out a program of scrapping out-of-date vessels. With growing unemployment came growing impatience with Weimar's democratic remedies. On the streets there were demonstrations from the Left and the Right for more totalitarian solutions. In the industrial areas and dockland, membership in the Communist Party grew rapidly. But others were determined that the Communists would not have it all their own way.

Throughout the twenties the Nazi Party (NSDAP)

had had little influence on Hamburg's life. Now that was changing. By 1931 it had become the city's second largest party. The momentum of the Nazis' advance was fuelled by constant scuffles and fights between Nazi Storm Troopers and their Left Wing opponents. These incidents multiplied at an alarming rate. In one month, January 1931, the Storm Troopers calculated that 64 of their own men had been injured. In March a Communist member of the city parliament was murdered, and three Storm Troopers arrested. Communists retaliated by attacking Nazi pubs. The most infamous of these incidents took place on July 17, 1932; it became known as Bloody Sunday. A Nazi march through a predominantly working-class area of the city ended with 19 people dead and over 250 injured.

Hiltgunt Zassenhaus, the doctor from America, stood reflectively outside the Lyceum, Altona, the high school in the harbor section of Hamburg where forty-six years before, as a schoolgirl of sixteen, she had come into contact with Nazism for the first time. It had been in July 1932, three days after the Bloody Sunday demonstration. Hitler had come to the Victoria sports ground in Altona to address a rally, and Hiltgunt was sent by her political-studies teacher to write a report on the meeting. It was a key test of her political maturity. Hitler had already acquired a reputation for being able to achieve a mesmeric grip on the women in his audience, for sweeping them off their feet. His effect on women, described as a form of "mass eroticism," has been explained in many ways, from the erotic nature of Hitler's gestures to a specially female response to his pent-up frustration. "One must have seen from above, from the speakers' rostrum," wrote one observer, "the rapturously rolling, moist, veiled eyes of the female listeners in order to be in no further doubt as to the character of this enthusiasm."

Hiltgunt remained dry-eyed and unimpressed. She watched the ranting and the saluting. She watched the crowd's swelling anticipation of what has been called "the collective debauch" and went home to write her essay. If Hitler had, as he said, "systematically adapted himself to the taste of women," he had failed in this case. "The loudness of his voice can silence you," she wrote. "But it cannot convince." Hitler, she added, was a psychotic.

Six months later, Hitler had become Chancellor of Germany.

All this was in her mind as Hiltgunt returned to her old school. She walked along the Max Brauer Alle towards the entrance, her raincoat flapping, her handbag dangling, and her eyes scanning the street for signs of the neighbourhood she knew. In the new Germany she looked out of place—a foreigner, an American tourist. Once inside, she climbed the wide staircase and found her old classroom. The class of 1979 was there waiting for her, young German boys and girls, seventeen years old, as she had been in the same classroom in the year Hitler came to power. Dressed casually in the international blue-jeans style, they greeted Hiltgunt with easygoing informality. They were distant from the war, from the old Germany; not the children but the grandchildren of the Germans who had occupied and terrified Europe. This was the new Germany, the disco generation, at home anywhere in the world, casual and confident. Hiltgunt looked into their fresh young faces. Could they really be the heirs of the Hitler Youth.

No, they told her, it was different now, it couldn't happen again.

Besides, they argued, it was not just a German problem. The Americans killed the Indians, and look what was happening in Cambodia.

"We young Germans would say No to a system of

dictatorship," said a young girl from the back of the class.

And another added, "Now we are living in a democracy, and I think we would say No!"

The headmistress and one or two teachers looked on, smiling indulgently at the wisdom of their pupils. They had learned their lesson well.

Hiltgunt's mind travelled back through the years. She could not forget that she too had been living in a democracy. The lesson she had learned was that head mistresses could be replaced, teachers could change their minds, and pupils could be brought in line.

It was early in 1933 in the same classroom. Hitler had been in power a few weeks when the headmaster issued a new regulation. Henceforth each morning pupils were to greet their teachers by standing to attention and declaring, "Heil Hitler!"

"Originally," remembers Hiltgunt, "I thought I would not follow that order, and on our way home I talked to my schoolfriend about it. And she said, 'Why don't you do as I do and just raise your right arm and mumble something?' I didn't think I could do this, and the next day when we came to school, I stood there with my arms glued to my side.

"The teacher looked in my direction and told me to salute. I said, 'No. I cannot do it.'

"So she sent me to the principal. The principal said, 'Well, an order is an order and we are here to obey. I give you twenty-four hours. Tomorrow you will come and you will do it.'

"I went home in a turmoil. My father looked at me and said, 'You must decide for yourself.'

"The next day I went to school.

"I remember that it was May and the trees were becoming green. I came to the class and my hands shook and I was trembling. And in comes the teacher and behind her the principal.

"All the thirty girls stood up, but instead of looking towards the teacher they all looked in my direction. What would she do? They all shouted, 'Heil Hitler!' In my desperation I made such a forceful movement with my arm that I hit it right through the window. Blood poured from my arm. They all screamed and I was rushed to the hospital.

"From that time on, no one looked in my direction. They simply ignored me."

It was an extraordinary, brave, even foolish gesture. By May 1933 the brutality of the new regime was obvious to everyone, and these were intelligent, politically aware young girls. The pressure on them was enormous. It was not that Hiltgunt could have been unconscious of the possible consequences. One of her schoolfriends—who did salute—explains why:

"I could understand why Hiltgunt had not said 'Heil Hitler'—but hers was the only case in the whole school. The rest of us, in the meantime, had learned our lesson. For one reason or another we were all scared in '33. People were vanishing. People were killed and our parents begged us not to be conspicuous.

"We had four Jewish girls in our class and they said, "We cannot say 'Heil Hitler.' And we said, 'No, you can't—and no one can expect it of you.'

"Whereupon our teacher said, 'Tell these girls to do it. We do not want to draw attention to ourselves—or to them.'

"So from then on, the Jewish girls, at our request, said 'Heil Hitler.' "

Why Hiltgunt? She herself had asked whether the gesture was worth the possible consequences. Was it not possible to show her opposition to everything Hitler stood for in some more positive, constructive way? At seventeen Hiltgunt was serious-minded but romantic. At home the family had discussed the political changes taking place in the country. They fully understood their implications and each of them knew where he or she stood. They had read aloud to each other from Albert Schweitzer, and they knew that his values, which they so much admired, were held in contempt by the new regime. But Hiltgunt's mother had also read her *A Tale of Two Cities* by Charles Dickens, and there was something theatrical in her nature that drew her to the lonely figure of Sydney Carton at the foot of the scaffold and his thoughts as he mounted the steps to the guillotine: "It is a far, far better thing that I do, than I have ever done...." Hiltgunt still remembers identifying with this man who gave his life for the woman he loved. "I thought it was so beautiful, the sacrifice of his life."

Hiltgunt never wavered in her belief that individual liberty was worth any sacrifice. But in the next few years she learned a great deal more about the value of discretion. The Third Reich itself claimed the monopoly of posturing and the great, empty gesture. It would not tolerate any free-lance activity, however lowly the source. Hiltgunt's opposition remained as steely and resolute as Hitler's armoured columns, but only once again did she attempt such an open gesture of defiance. That was much, much later—and the result was almost disastrous.

In Hamburg generally, there was little debate about individual responsibility. In contrast to Hiltgunt, the people in the street had few scruples about saluting, and when Hitler paid a state visit to the city in 1934, it was an occasion for mass celebration and a collective affirmation of the Third Reich. The fact that all the Gestapo cells in the city were full, that half the local prisons had been transformed into a concentration camp, and that an empty peat-processing factory had been taken over to accommodate the surplus of political prisoners—all this had little effect on the average Hamburger. What was more important in Hamburg was that the Nazis had promised to save the shipyards, and Hitler told the dense and admiring crowds on the waterfront exactly what they wanted to hear. "One thing is clear," he bellowed triumphantly, "in one way or another we will bring work to every German who seeks employment."

One man would never work again. Hiltgunt's father was a marked man. On the day the Nazis came to power, the family house was smeared with swastikas. Shortly afterwards he was dismissed from his job as headmaster and the family were forced to leave their home in the schoolhouse. His books and writings were burned and he himself only managed to avoid imprisonment because he was too ill to be moved when the SS arrived to arrest him. The Nazis had no intention of leaving alone a man whose political views were so well known. "There is no time for even the smallest criticizing in the New Germany," Robert Ley, the leader of the Labour Front, had said. And Himmler took up the theme: "The only private life for a person is when he is asleep."

Hiltgunt and her family now began to pay the price for a crime the Nazis found intolerable—the crime of not joining in.

The German terror began first in Germany and it was astonishing how quickly it struck roots. "You have to have lived in it to be able to imagine it," recalls Hiltgunt. "It's just as if it closes in on you from every side. It was not so much the boots, the brown shirts, the SS men on the streets. It was really more subtle than this. It was between the lines. It was that suddenly you were being moulded into a people who were marching at the same pace. It was this demand to give up your individuality, this is what hurt. The fear that you would lose yourself. I think that the majority of people just went silently along out of fear and those that joined the Party did so not because they had convictions, but because they had none."

The pressure was insidious and pervasive. Dr. Carl Stromberger, a close friend of the Zassenhaus family and someone who was very much in sympathy with their way of thinking, recalls how nervous he felt in the street. He had had polio as a boy and could not return the Hitler salute with his right hand. "Oppression and fear," he says, "it's very important not just to hear the words but to feel them to know what it was like in Germany. It made it difficult to think and to act.

"I'll give you a small example of how such a common feeling was spread. You know they introduced this funny thing, 'Heil Hitler' and this replaced the normal greeting between people. And this name, this word got into every mind, every day. Everyone had to say 'Heil Hitler,' so his name was always in the brain. This—I want to say diabolic—greeting was associated with loss of freedom and oppression. It paralyzed the capacity to act.

"This was the background on which all other things developed."

For Dr. Stromberger, and for a small circle of friends who thought and felt as he did, the Zassenhaus family was like an oasis in the desert of National Socialism. They were now living in reduced circumstances in a small modern house in the Bahrenfeld district of Hamburg. Outwardly, they did nothing to provoke the curiosity of informers or the hostility of the authorities, but inside the home their independent spirit remained unchanged. "Inside our home it was really like a fortress," recalls Hiltgunt, and once the doors were closed the family and their friends spoke out without restraint.

"It was gay in their house," recalls Stromberger. "You felt absolutely free."

But it was a diminished freedom, and for Hiltgunt it only cast into relief what had been lost. It was the change in people that depressed her most. At school her political-science teacher told her to burn her essays which had once earned top marks. She listened as *Mein Kampf* and the pompous works of the racist Rosenberg were accepted as unassailable authorities. Where once there had been free discussion, now all dissenting opinion was silenced. She could not understand why people were willing to trade their personal liberty and their freedom of expression for what Hitler had to offer. She saw her friends apprehensive and their parents afraid of their own children. She knew of people who had lost their jobs, who had been informed upon, and some who had simply disappeared. But what she feared most, with a sense of almost physical revulsion, was the uniformity which the Nazis had succeeded in imposing so quickly on the whole of German society. Individuality had been overtaken by the unit, the units were controlled by the state, and the state was controlled by men whom it was impossible to respect. "Everything has changed, everything has changed," her teacher told her, as if she were a simpleton. But for Hiltgunt the difficulty was simply to understand how people could have let it happen at all.

"From now on, after Hitler came to power, I was always against everything—and that's very hard for a young person because the basic feeling of a young person is to want to belong. You want to be in a group. But from then on, I was always the outsider, and somehow I arrived at a point where I was in continuous fear and anxiety. I didn't feel accepted by the girls in my class; the teachers looked at me disapprovingly.

"I remember one day the teacher asked me, 'Should you think objectively or subjectively as far as it concerns your country?'

"And I said innocently, 'Objectively, of course.'

"She just shook her head and told me, 'You never learn.'

"You see, this continuous pressure made me want to get out."

In 1934, to escape the feeling of oppression and isolation which she now felt everywhere in Germany, Hiltgunt hitchhiked to Denmark for her school holidays. It was in effect a holiday from Hitler. For three weeks she rediscovered the sociability and conviviality which she now associated with the lost world of the Weimar Republic. People chatted and laughed with each other in quite a normal way. They didn't wear the so-called German look, that turn of the head right and left to make sure that no one was listening. Even the cows, she thought as she crossed the border, looked happier in Denmark.

She stayed in a beach house near Copenhagen with a house party made up of writers and artists and refugees from Nazi persecution in Germany. There she became infatuated with an artist who indulged her and chatted to her throughout the days about the political situation. One day he painted her portrait, and when it was finished she stood back amazed at the result. In place of the romantic picture she had hoped for, she saw instead the frowning image of a young, serious-minded schoolgirl. "For a schoolgirl," her friend told her, "you're far too preoccupied with Hitler."

Hiltgunt was hurt and disappointed. "I know what's going on in Germany," she told him. "I love freedom just as much as you do."

Leaving aside romantic setbacks, the contrast Hiltgunt found between this free-and-easy group and the fearful populace she had left behind at home left a lasting impression. She even considered for a time whether to stay permanently with these interesting and bohemian exiles. But Germany was her home, and she decided to go back. Denmark, however, had become a symbol of freedom and hope, a place where life went on as it had before, and Hiltgunt decided that when she left school she would go on to the university to study Scandinavian languages. It was a decision which gave her life a new purpose and a new direction.

Back in Germany there was a very clear idea about the proper direction a young girl's life should take. The Nazis had a very simple view of girls and women in general: They were inferior. It was an attitude admirably summed up when women were barred from jury service on the grounds that "they cannot think logically or reason objectively since they are ruled only by emotion." It was not a situation that the Nazis had any intention of remedying. Hitler himself declared that the emancipation of women was a symptom of depravity on a par with parliamentary democracy and jazz. On the other hand, the female sex was not entirely useless: "Woman has her battlefield too," the Führer told them. "With each child she brings into the world she is fighting her fight on behalf of the nation." There was also a National Socialist view of what women should look like. *Haute couture* and lipstick were considered signs of decadence. Nor were German women encouraged to look after their figures. The ideal German frau was blond with wide, childbearing hips. It was all part of a world view which celebrated simple Teutonic values: Men were warriors and fought for the fatherland. Women were decorative and produced children.

The result was that the new German woman was half Amazon, half domestic servant, and widely held to be the most ugly in Europe. Their "finishing school," the feminine counterpart to the Hitler Youth, was the B.D.M., the *Bund Deutscher Mädchen*, or the German Girls' League, one of whose favourite slogans, "Supple as leather, hard as steel," says a great deal about its aims and aspirations. Among their other accomplishments, including a high degree of athletic prowess, Leaguers were expected to acquire a sound knowledge of bed making, route marching, the history of the Nazi Party, and the "Horst Wessel Song." In order to continue her studies, Hiltgunt was obliged to join the B.D.M. She allowed her membership to lapse after precisely one week.

Meanwhile, Hamburg itself was enjoying the fruits of the Nazi renaissance. By 1935 the economy was already beginning to pick up and Blohm and Voss, the shipyard that was a barometer of the city's economic climate, started to benefit from the beginning of full-scale rearmament. Although within Germany, Hamburg was regarded as being lukewarm in its support of the Nazis, this did not prevent the Führer from visiting the city once or twice a year throughout the thirties. In 1935, for instance, he "dropped in" unexpectedly for the last performance of *Die Neistersanher* at the Hamburg State Opera House. In 1936 he came to launch a training ship, the *Horst Wessel* for the navy, named after the Nazi Party's first martyr. A year later he was back at Blohm and Voss to launch the *Wilhelm Gustloff*, named after another leading Nazi, who, it was said, though never proved, had been killed by Jews in Switzerland.

Meanwhile, the Zassenhaus family kept themselves to themselves in their little house in the Lyserstrasse. Julius Zassenhaus was a sick man. He was suffering from Parkinson's disease, the onset of which had been traced to a bout of influenza he had contracted during the great epidemic of 1918. Dr. Stromberger noticed that while his patient retained his sincere and open mind, his condition grew steadily weaker. He noticed too how Hiltgunt's mother took over the responsibility for the family with a brightness and vivacity that somehow balanced the incapacity of her husband. The family lived frugally. There was no carpet on the floor and there were no extravagances for the table, yet while Hiltgunt's father watched on helplessly as his countrymen turned their backs on the ideals and beliefs he had held all his life, her mother preserved the animus of the family intact, and also, unbeknown to the rest of them, was also the first to put the family's convictions into action.

"My mother was a very special person, I don't think anyone who knew her will ever forget her. You may think this is the blind adoration of a daughter, but it is not. She helped to shape the lives of many people by her example and her kindness. I remember, before the war, when the Jewish people started to be arrested and little by little had to leave the country. One day, quite by accident, I learned that my mother was helping Jewish friends. I'd noticed that at times she went away for days, and that she sometimes looked very pale and exceedingly tired. My father had told us that we must help Mother as much as we could, but I did not understand why. And when the moment came, and I found out, I felt insulted and hurt. Why had she not told me?

"Later on I understood why she had to do it in secret. . . ."

The Nazis had never disguised their attitude towards the Jews, and throughout the thirties attacks on their property and infringements on their liberties had steadily mounted. Their suffering had little effect on their fellow German countrymen, who, if they were not themselves actively involved in the persecutions, preferred to turn a blind eye. It has been noted that in the entire history of the Third Reich no single body—civic, academic or even religious—ever made any protest against the regime's inhumanity. Those who—as Hiltgunt's mother did—helped Jews acted on their own behalf and at their own risk.

Hamburg itself was not an antisemitic city by German standards. But when the greatest pre-war catastrophe hit the Jews late in 1938, the characteristic response in Hamburg was the same as elsewhere: indifference. At one o'clock on the night of November 9–10, a householder looked out of his window overlooking the Adolf Hitler Platz, the central square of Hamburg, and watched as a large body of men in civilian clothes were marshalled in front of the town hall by uniformed Storm Troopers. The men were separated into groups and sent off under different leaders.

It was the beginning of what was to become known as *Kristalnacht*, the night of broken glass. Throughout Germany similar gangs of SA thugs went on the rampage, attacking both Jewish property and the Jews themselves. In Hamburg the British consul sent this report back to London: "Shop windows were demolished, and the shops themselves were then entered and wrecked. The synagogues were also entered and smashed up. . . . The main synagogue on Grindelhof, the centre of orthodox Jewish worship, was burned down."

A seventeen-year-old Jewish boy remembers: "I had only been in the shop a short time when the Gestapo arrived and asked where my father was. That morning he had gone to the doctors: He was already suffering from a weak chest. A short time later someone telephoned to say that my father had been arrested in the waiting room at the doctor's surgery. He was sent to Sachsenhausen concentration camp, where he was held prisoner for several months. A short time after his release he died.

"During the course of the morning of November the tenth, while I was out of the shop, the Gestapo returned and arrested all the Jewish male assistants working for my father."

In all, the Hamburg Gestapo arrested 2,500 Jews during that night and its aftermath. In each of the next two evenings, a train loaded with 700 prisoners left Hamburg station bound for Sachsenhausen, near Berlin. On arrival the Jews were savagely brutalized and forced to stand at attention for over twenty hours.

Protests never rose above a whisper. The Gestapo mixed with crowds which had gathered outside the wrecked shops and arrested anyone who voiced dissent. Whether the "average" Hamburger approved or disapproved, we do not know. It is most probable that he did not care. What is certain is that after *Kristalnacht,* he could not say that he did not *know* even if nothing of the events of that dreadful night was ever reported in the local press.

Those with eyes to see watched helplessly, conscious of a rising sense of outrage inside them which was forbidden expression.

"I remember my brother Willfried went to town one day and saw a Jewish woman with a yellow star on her lapel. And in the baby carriage was her baby with a star on as well, but because the baby was so small the star covered not only his lapel but it was spread over his whole chest.

"And Willfried came home and said to my mother, 'Mother, you have taught us many things, but there's one thing that you didn't tell us: that there are some people in this world who are simply just evil."

It was not what he had been brought up to think. It was a conclusion of despair.

By 1938 the family had grown up. Hiltgunt's eldest brother, Hans, had graduated with a degree in mathematics and already appeared to have a brilliant academic career ahead of him. Guenther and Willfried had both studied medicine and qualified as doctors, and Hiltgunt herself had graduated from the University of Hamburg with a degree in Scandinavian languages. For the first time she found herself in demand, and though she was still only twenty-two, she was appointed interpreter in Danish and Norwegian at the court of Hamburg. It was a grand title for a small office—in fact, Hiltgunt had no office, she worked from home. But it was her first step behind the closed doors of the Reich.

Overlooking the harbour of Hamburg and the River Elbe, his vast stone hands resting on a sword, stands the huge statue of Count Otto von Bismarck, the Iron Chancellor, the founder of the modern German state. His scale is monstrous; his posture, conquering; his attitude, uncompromising. On February 13, 1939, Adolf Hitler returned to Hamburg for the launching of the port's most formidable contribution to Germany's rearmament program: the battleship *Bismarck*, at the time the most powerful warship the world had ever seen. There was little doubt now in what direction the Führer was leading Germany. It is interesting, however, to see how he at that time regarded his achievement. In the early months of 1939, in these remarks addressed to President Roosevelt, Hitler spelled out his record.

> I once took over a state which was faced by complete ruin, thanks to its trust in the promises of the rest of the world and to the bad regime of democratic governments.
>
> Since then, Mr. Roosevelt, I have only been able to fulfil one simple task, I cannot feel myself responsible for the rest of the world, as the world took no interest in the fate of my own people. I have regarded myself as called upon by Providence to serve my own people alone.
>
> I have conquered chaos in Germany, reestablished order, enormously increased production. . . . I have succeeded in finding useful work once more for the whole of seven million unemployed. . . . Not only have I reunited the German people politically, but I have also rearmed them. I have endeavoured to destroy sheet by sheet the treaty which in its 448 articles contains the vilest oppression which people and human beings have ever been expected to put up with.

I have brought back to the Reich provinces stolen from us in 1919, I have led back to their native country millions of Germans who were torn away from us and were in misery, I have reestablished the historic unity of German living space—and, Mr. Roosevelt, I have endeavoured to attain all this without spilling blood and without bringing to my people, and consequently to others, the misery of war.*

This was the powerful case of the man who was about to plunge Europe into war. What price the freedom of the individual when compared to the annexations of the Rhineland, of Austria and of the Sudetenland? How could private moral scruple be compared to the fifteen-inch guns of the battleship *Bismarck* as they gleamed in the sun? By 1939 the vast majority of Germany's sixty-six million people had made their choice. And for those who had not, it was too late.

On September 1, 1939, Hiltgunt was at home in the Lyserstrasse. It was not what she heard, it was what she did not hear that told her something was wrong. "I woke up and it was peculiarly quiet. It was such a deep silence and it did not come from inside the house. It came somehow from the outside."

She opened the door. There was no milk and no newspaper. The street was empty. She returned indoors and switched on the radio: German troops had invaded Poland.

The family gathered round the bed of Hiltgunt's father—the three boys, all of them eligible for call-up, Hiltgunt and her mother, each thinking the same thought: What was going to happen to them now? "This will be the end of Hitler," her mother said quietly.

For most Germans it was the beginning of the sec-

---

*Quoted in Alan Bullock's *Hitler: A Study in Tyranny* (Odhams, 1952).

ond war of their lifetimes. It was very different from
1914. This time there were no cheering and jubilant
crowds. The same odd silence and empty streets which
had woken Hiltgunt in Hamburg stretched across the
country. The British Ambassador noted as he left Berlin: "My impression was that the mass of the German
people—that other Germany—was horror struck at the
whole idea of the war that was being thrust upon them.
. . . the whole general atmosphere in Berlin itself was
one of gloom and depression." At ten o'clock on the
morning of September 1, when the Führer drove
through the capital to address the Reichstag, the streets
were emptier than usual and passersby stared at his
motorcade in silence. "There was no crowd on Wil-
helmplatz shouting for Hitler," wrote Speer. "None of
the regiments marched off to war decorated with
flowers as they had done at the beginning of the First
World War." "God help us if we lose this war!" Goering declared as he heard of the British ultimatum. It
was a widespread anxiety. It did not, however, corre-
spond entirely with the anxieties of the Zassenhaus
family in the Lyserstrasse. They too, as they experimented with their bread cards and blackouts, felt the
general sense of uncertainty and apprehension. But did
they—a family from which two sons were immediately
called up for active service—want Germany to win the
war? It was a question that had its roots in troubled
loyalty and addressed itself, often with tragic consequences, only to a small minority of Germans. For
Hiltgunt and her family there was only one answer:
No—not if a German victory meant also a victory for
Hitler. This feeling is summed up by Dr. Stromberger,
who by 1939 was very much part of the Zassenhaus family circle:

"It may be a very strange question, whether at that
time we wanted Germany to win the war. But really—

when we thought about the situation—we didn't want it. I mean it's not very easy for a citizen and patriot to want to lose the war. But during this time, we knew it could not go otherwise. Our misfortunes would not disappear without losing the war."

But Hiltgunt, however much she hated Hitler and despised everything he stood for, never thought of fighting against him. Even today she objects to being described as a resistance fighter: "Frankly I never fought against anything, I fought for something . . . I tried to think of what I could do to relieve the situation." It was not long before she was offered an opportunity.

All letters between Germany and abroad were now being vetted, and Hiltgunt's qualifications made her an obvious candidate to censor Scandinavian mail. She was ordered to report to Chilehaus, a large office building near the Hauptbannhof which housed the postal censorship office. Most of the work was done by civilians under the supervision of retired army officers. The instruction manual too was a leftover from the Great War. The work was routine and tedious. Then one day a Gestapo officer entered the sorting room and thrust a packet containing about fifty letters into Hiltgunt's hands. With them came "special instructions." It was these that were to take her over the line from silent opposition to active resistance.

The letters were unlike any she had ever seen before, scraps of paper, sometimes toilet paper, almost falling apart. They had been sent to relatives in Scandinavia from Jews in the Polish ghettos. Hiltgunt's "special instructions" ordered her to strike out any requests for food and clothing. At last she felt she had her opportunity to help. She began smuggling letters out from the censor's office and delivering them to an old friend of her father's, a ship's chandler in the port of Hamburg. He forwarded them through his own contacts with seamen on to their destinations. To emphasize the plight of the senders, Hiltgunt would write on the letters her own message: "Send Food. Send clothing!" Months later, she began to find evidence that the letters were getting through. "Thank you," read the occasional note from Poland, "we got your parcel. . . ."

"Then one day I came to work and there were no letters from the Jews and I went to the captain and said, 'Where are my letters?' and he just said, 'There are no more letters.'

"And so I asked him why. And he replied, 'We are not here to ask questions, we are here to follow orders!' "

Hiltgunt recognized in his tone not only the sickening euphemisms of the Third Reich but Prussian militarism itself, which reached back to the looming statue of Bismarck at the harbour. How she hated it, overlooking the River Elbe, a threat to the morning and evening, the first and the last sight of shipping, his hand on his sword "as if this was the only answer to the problems of the world." Bismarck might have unified Germany and founded the Kaiser Reich, the German Empire, but for Hiltgunt he remained the man who elevated belief in authority to the point of principle and planted the notion of the Germans' superiority over their fellowmen. Hiltgunt did not intend to stay at the censor's office "to follow orders." She enrolled at the university as a medical student, thereby excusing herself, for the present at least, from further war service.

Hiltgunt's attempt to avoid working for the Nazis was short-lived. On April 9, 1940, Hitler launched the invasion of Denmark and Norway. It was the prelude to a summer of spectacular success. Denmark capitulated almost at once; Norway offered some resistance backed by Anglo-French expeditionary force, but the Germans were quickly in control. It was not long after the arrival of the Wehrmacht on the streets of Oslo and Copenhagen that the first political prisoners began to be transported to Germany.

In Hamburg, Hiltgunt was summoned to the office of the district attorney. Once again she heard the words "We have a special assignment for you." Several hundred prisoners from Norway were expected at Fuhlsbüttel Prison. Hiltgunt was to censor their mail. She had the feeling once again that here there could be a chance to help the victims of the Reich. It was a chance which expanded dramatically a few months later when she was given additional duties. Instead of merely dealing with the prisoners' letters, Hiltgunt was also ordered to supervise their visits. "We trust you," the district attorney told her. But Hiltgunt already knew that she had more in common with the men inside the cells than with the men who were guarding them.

"These people were the cream of their country and their only crime was that they had offered resistance to Hitler. Of course any country would have arrested people who resisted—but the point was how you treated a prisoner. If you had seen these people, as I saw them, if you had known how they were starving, how they were riddled with sickness, how they needed help in any way —you would understand why I had to help them.

"This was something I could do because I was the only woman in Germany with a degree in Scandinavian languages. So it was I—with my convictions—who was hired."

In 1979, Hiltgunt walked towards the gates of Fuhlsbüttel Prison once again. With her were two tall Norwegians, both of whom thought that the prison gates had closed behind them for the last time long ago. At the age of nineteen Bjoern Simonnaess had been arrested by the Gestapo while trying to escape to England. He had been sentenced to five years' hard labour in Germany. His companion, Christian Hatlivik, had been arrested in Bergen in 1941 for distributing underground newspapers. He had been given twelve years. Now as they waited for the gates to open, each of them felt the raw edge of apprehension.

"Are you scared? . . . Are you scared?" Hatlivik asked Hiltgunt.

"A little bit. Aren't you?"

"I have a feeling," he replied softly, "a special feeling."

The guard opened the gates and cheerfully wished them *guten Tag*. "We don't have many of our old boys come back to see us," he joked.

Hiltgunt's mind went to her first visit to Fuhlsbüttel. It was different then. Then as she rang the bell she knew that her life depended on her performance inside. "I had to be very official. For example, as much as I hated it to say 'Heil Hitler' when I came in, I mumbled something. I said, *'Drei Liter'* [three liters], which almost sounds like 'Heil Hitler.' And the reason why I was treated here with more or less reverence from the guards was that they always thought I was a member of the Gestapo. They took it for granted and thought that I might report on them.

"The whole system was based on fear. The one feared the other. That was why I could succeed in what I was doing. They feared me and I feared them, but the important thing was who feared the most."

Fuhlsbüttel has changed little since its construction at the turn of the century. Its high walls and fortress gates conceal the familiar pattern of cell blocks with their regular rows of small barred windows. In 1933 the Nazis had walled off one section of the prison and turned it into a *Konzentrationlager*, a concentration camp. It had been judged that the conditions were too lax for political prisoners. By 1936 the block held about eight hundred men: Communists, homosexuals, Jehovah's Witnesses and the so-called antisocial—drunks and Gypsies. It was upon them that the Nazis refined the brutalities of their concentration camp system. The Norwegians, as foreign resistance fighters, were counted among "the worst ene-

mies of the Reich," and suffered accordingly Fuhlsbüttel's fiercest regime. They were held in solitary confinement. Bullied, ill and undernourished, they were almost
permanently in a state of semistarvation.

On that first visit Hiltgunt was led farther and farther
into the jail, through an endless series of doors and cages
which opened before her and were locked behind her.
She feared two things most: that the prisoners would not
trust her and that she would never get out of the prison
again.

She sat waiting nervously in the visiting room. "I
heard this very deep silence and then suddenly this *tap,
tap, tap* of wooden shoes approaching. I went out of the
room and there were twenty prisoners all lined up with
their faces to the wall. And the guards just said. 'OK,
here are twenty pieces. I looked at the twenty pieces and
I saw these emaciated faces, the pale, almost yellow skin,
the rags they had on. I looked at their legs, swollen with
edema, and the wooden shoes pressing into the flesh.

"I saw at first their cold stares: Who are you? And I
thought, If only I can make them trust me."

Hiltgunt was under strict orders from the department
of justice. Only the pastor of Hamburg's Norwegian
Seamen's Mission was officially allowed to visit prisoners, and he was not allowed to give them encouragement,
bring news, say prayers or read from the Bible. It was
Hiltgunt's responsibility to ensure that these regulations
were enforced as unrelentingly as possible. It was her
intention to ensure that they were not enforced at all.

"I am in charge here!" she told the visiting-room
guard. "There will be no guards present during the
course of the interviews."

Surprised and intimidated by her air of authority, the
guard went out of the room, leaving Hiltgunt along with
the Norwegians. The pastor whispered to the prisoners,
"She is a friend. She is one of us."

"She came towards me and took my hand," remembers Bjoern Simonnaess, "and she said, 'I have cards from your father and mother and your sister,' and I . . . I couldn't understand how she knew all my family. She talked a little Norwegian but mostly Danish, and I asked her how she could know my family and she told me that she had been the censor for a long time and that she had read all my letters and remembered almost every word. It was a fantastic memory and we were good friends at once."

Bjoern was not the only one who would be surprised. By the end of the war Hiltgunt was in contact with over twelve hundred Scandinavian prisoners and had committed to memory all the details of their families and background. She became an open channel to their families back home, bringing them forbidden news and photographs and passing messages from them back to Norway.

This was her first claim on the hearts of the prisoners, but there were others. "I looked on her and she was very beautiful indeed," Christian Hatlivik recalls. 'I hadn't seen a woman for many months and so we spoke and I got the news and it was very interesting and I thought, Maybe you can rely on this woman. The next time I looked upon Hiltgunt as a member of the Norwegian resistance movement, as a comrade, fighting the same war as we had fought and fought still with all our hearts —not against the Germans, but against Hitler, against the Nazis, against the system. That was the main thing for me and I always took this point of view: Nazis, Hitler and Germans—and Hiltgunt was a very fine representative of the real Germany."

From the beginning it was clear to Hiltgunt that the men would need more than just moral support. She began to bring a suitcase with her on her visits, filled with homemade bread, vitamins and medicines (provided by Dr. Stromberger), pencils and paper, chewing tobacco, letters and photographs from Norway—anything she could find to make life easier inside the jail. When questioned by a suspicious guard she answered that it contained her "air-raid luggage" and that she had to have it with her all the time. But she remembers thinking constantly that she had to walk straight so as not to reveal to the guards how heavy it was.

Perhaps the prisoners understood, more even than she did, the risks she was taking. They knew that they themselves were safe, but Hiltgunt faced dangers on every side. Outside the prison she risked denunciation by informers. Inside, the guards had only to search her suitcase or, worse still, a starving prisoner betray her for a piece of bread. "It was a fantastic thing," Bjoern told her when they revisited the prison. "We were sitting in our cells in quiet and safety, but in my imagination I felt your dangers all the time—you risked it."

The risks were enormous. Nazi justice had always displayed a cruel instinct for punishment but by the middle of the war the instinct had become a passion. The number of capital crimes had risen from three to forty-six, and in many other cases courts passed death sentences at their own discretion. As the war wore on, the judicial reflex became even more Draconian. Death sentences were handed down for anything from petty pilfering to making an anti-Nazi joke. By 1943 the number of executions counted 5,336—nearly six times greater than at the beginning of the war. Bjorn had every reason to be afraid for Hiltgunt. There was no doubt what would be in store for her if she were discovered.

Yet despite warnings from the prisoners and the Norwegian pastor, Hiltgunt continued, if anything taking more risks as time went on. She developed an almost fatalistic attitude towards fear. It was something to be overcome. A part of her that believed that as long as she was so needed, no harm would come to her. What she felt more than fear was loneliness: "In such work you are very alone. That's the nature of it. You cannot share it with anybody because you would endanger them. I could not even tell my own family, because had I done so and been caught, they too would have been arrested and tortured."

There were times when arrest and torture seemed very close indeed.

May 1979. A main street near Hamburg University. It is late afternoon and raining hard. The light is not good. Hiltgunt is looking for an old Hamburg house that she used to know well. She knows it is in the neighbourhood but the problem is that she cannot ask anyone for help. In May 1979 you cannot ask a passerby for the way to Gestapo headquarters.

During the war Hiltgunt was interrogated by the Gestapo three times. The summons always arrived by post. It contained no details: simply an order to report to their offices. Each time she took her Bible and her gun. Each time the interrogation began the same way: "You know why you are here, don't you?"

"I remember they had the lights on you, and in one hearing I had these lights for only three hours, and I began to get hot and cold. The idea is that you finally stop thinking and just have the feeling, Somehow I have to get out of here. Fortunately, when I was in danger I turned very cool, somehow as if I were guided by a director onstage. I just knew exactly what to say. It was a question of survival. I was very nice, very harmless, as if I had no worry in the whole wide world—just sitting there, relaxed. I am a tense person, basically, but in those moments of great danger I was totally relaxed and I think that saved my life."

After the first interrogation the Gestapo instructed Hiltgunt to write them reports about the prisons and especially the prison officials. In later interrogations she was reprimanded because her reports were not incriminating enough. The guards at Fuhlsbüttel were right to be suspicious of Hiltgunt. She was working for the Gestapo.

All this went through her mind as Hiltgunt searched in the rain for the offices of her old interrogators. She stopped in front of a gate and walked up the pathway towards the front door. Hamburg is a smart city, but this house had a faded air. The plates on the doorway showed that it had been taken over by several small enterprises. There was no clue as to what it had been in the past. Hiltgunt climbed down a small flight of steps to a basement door. She pushed it open. A warm damp mist wafted out into her face. When it had evaporated she realized she had walked into a sauna. A heavy blond girl lay face down on a pallet, and another figure—possibly male—sat leaning against the light wood panelling near the door. Their skin was clammy and appeared almost green. Slowly they turned their eyes towards Hiltgunt. "Do you know," she asked before they could utter anything, "if this is the house where the Gestapo had their headquarters?" They did not reply. They gazed at her in silence but without surprise, as though she were simply another part of their reverie.

"I don't think we'll find it," said Hiltgunt, stepping out into the rain. "The whole area round here was bombed . . . it must have been rebuilt after the war."

Late in the autumn of 1941, H. W. Flannery, the American correspondent of CBS in Berlin, reported that for the first time since he had arrived in Germany a year before, he was able to find a seat on the train to Hamburg. The German people, he observed, were not travelling towards bomb targets. He had been told to expect a great deal of bomb damage, but when he arrived at the city he was more impressed by the measures taken to defend it than by the destruction brought by the RAF. The glass roof of the railway station had been painted over to look like a park. In the river, cardboard islands had been constructed, and the entire pattern of the two city-center river basins, the Binnen Alster and the Aussen Alster and the bridge between them, had been transformed by massive camouflaging. It impressed Flannery, but it was not enough to save Hamburg.

Throughout the following year the bombing raids—terror raids, as they came to be known—increased in number and intensity. The wailing of sirens and the cramped discomfort of the air-raid bunkers became a monotonous feature of the night. During the day rumour and loose talk added to the strain and tension. At the beginning of May, for instance, on the anniversary of the fire that had destroyed Hamburg in 1842, there were whispers that the RAF would light the torches of a new conflagration. The English bombers did not disappoint the rumourmongers: They attacked the city in greater numbers than ever.

In 1942 the optimism of the early years disappeared. The war turned sour. Newspapers were full of casualty lists from the battlefields—and in Hamburg, as elsewhere, the price was also being paid on the streets. People appeared shoddy and downtrodden. Their coats were threadbare, their stockings unmended and their shoes down-at-heel. The traditional Hamburg Spargelzeit, the asparagus festival, had passed by with just one small portion of asparagus per person. Everyone looked unhealthy and prematurely old. "How different the atmosphere is," wrote one old lady to her children in 1943, "from the first war year, when at the slightest provocation red Nazi flags were flown and drums were beaten on the radio, and everyone bragged outrageously. Since the capitulation of Stalingrad and the realization of total war, all is grey and still. Shop after shop has closed down. . . ."*

Hamburg became even greyer as the authorities experimented with a new anti-aircraft device: a thick artificial fog which covered the city like grey soup when the sirens warned of an attack and left the parks shrivelled up and discoloured.

The summer of 1943 was damp and cold. It was said that the war had changed everything, even the weather. Life in Hamburg went on. There were even optimists who persuaded themselves that the English would not destroy the city because they would need its harbour later. The RAF dropped leaflets which did little to inspire confidence in this idea. "You have got a few weeks' respite," they warned, "then it will be your turn. There is peace now; then there will be eternal peace."

There is a report of a conversation Hitler had at a dinner party in the Reich Chancellery in the heady days of 1940. "Goering," the Führer told his guests, "wants to use innumerable incendiary bombs of an altogether new type to create sources of fire in all parts of London. Fires everywhere. Thousands of them. Then they'll unite in one gigantic area conflagration. What use will their fire department be once that really starts!"

It was not the people of London but the people of Hamburg who would be the first to judge the effectiveness of Goering's idea.

On July 24, as Hamburgers admired a perfect sunset over the Elbe estuary, one of the greatest armadas of

---

*Mathilde Wolff-Mönckeberg remained in Hamburg throughout the war. Her children were in England. Her regular "letters" to them remained unposted until the end of the war. Mathilde Wolff-Mönckeberg, *On the Other Side: To My Children from Germany, 1940–1945*, translated and edited by Ruth Evans. London: Peter Owen, 1979.

bombers which had ever been assembled was preparing for takeoff on airfields in eastern England. It was the beginning of Operation Gomorrah. Its aim was the destruction of Hamburg. Gomorrah was not the largest raid to date—simply in terms of the number of aircraft used, the raid on Cologne in the previous year had been larger—but two new features transformed its impact. The first was a new scientific device, code-named Window, which confused German radar so successfully that most of the bombers got a clear run at the city. But more important, the bombers returned, night after night, for seven nights. The result, as Goebbels wrote in his diary, "was a catastrophe, the extent of which simply staggers the imagination."

"The very first night of the firestorm," recalls Hiltgunt, "I got out of the bunker and the first thing I saw were these huge flames—the sky full of flames. The whole sky was red and it was reflected in the windows so you didn't know what was real flame and what was just the glare of the flames in the sky.

"We stumbled out and staggered. I was petrified.

"Later the wind came up, and then it became a hurricane. The trees in our yard were swaying and the branches were cast to the ground. The letters to the prisoners were blown from my desk into the yard. You can't imagine it, you have to hear it. It was not just the wind, it was the explosions, the smell, and the noise. . . .

"The next day there was no sun, the sky was not grey but yellow and the sun just stood out like a yellow spot. There was an awful smell, of corpses, of fire, of death, of total destruction.

"People were screaming, 'My feet, my feet!' The phosphorus which had come from the sky was creeping around their shoes and just eating its way through to the feet.

"I remember an old woman crying, 'It's the end, it's the end'—that's all that she could say, and that's what we all thought."

The result fully confirmed Goering's expectation. For a week the people of Hamburg huddled in their shelters with wet clothes across their mouths and noses, watching babies frozen with fear, while aboveground a quarter of a million homes, nearly three hundred schools, fifty-eight churches and twenty-four hospitals were burned to the ground. In one week over forty thousand people lost their lives, and a million people fled the city.

"Hamburg," said Speer, "put the fear of God into me."

For the prisoners in Fuhlsbüttel the raid was a gratifying reminder that they had powerful friends. They watched the fantastic fires as Hamburg burned from one side to the other, the lost searchlights scanning the sky in vain for the British bombers. Bjoern Simonnaess recalls his feeling of "cruelty and revenge" when one of the guards who had lost all his family came weeping to him and tried to shake his hand.

Hiltgunt's reaction could not be so simple. "I loved this city. I had been here all my life. Then suddenly everything disappeared in front of my eyes and I could see how the people were suffering. But it was the only way to end the war and I must tell you that it came to this, at least in my family, that we almost had to hope that we would be bombed—suicidal as it was to think that way—but how otherwise could we hope the war would come to an end? As a German I had to hope continuously for the demise of Nazi Germany."

In the shelters people were numb. They did not sing any longer, they hardly even talked to each other. They stumbled through the days and nights, exhausted. Occasionally someone would attack people who were wearing Party badges with screams of "Let's get that murderer!"

But mostly there was weary indifference to everything except survival. When Nazis tried to encourage their neighbours in the shelters, they were met with blind stares. The people had forgotten how to listen, they had forgotten how to sleep, for a time they forgot even to be cautious:

"The amazing thing was that as the air raids got heavier the restrictions of the government eased up, because where was the government? There was not much of a government. The newspaper didn't arrive in the morning, the radio was quite often off for days at a time. You almost felt like a school class without a teacher. Certainly there was no authority. But as soon as the first trickle of water came through the pipes again, as soon as the electric light and the telephone came on again—there was the hand, the all-guiding hand of authority. People got very quiet again. They didn't even speak up a little here and there. A little hope was gone again."

Hiltgunt watched the city she loved crumble into dust, convinced that at least the end of the war had come at last. Nothing could continue after such devastation. Ten days later in Hamburg's bombed-out station she realized her mistake. Trains passed by loaded with soldiers for the front. In the countryside she saw peaceful homes and farms where crops were growing and cows grazing. It seemed that all the dying had been in Hamburg. The war went on.

So too did Hiltgunt's underground war. More and more political prisoners were being transported to the Reich's proliferating prisons and camps. Hiltgunt's work expanded. Her visits were no longer confined to the prison in Hamburg, but took her all over Germany. The food she brought the prisoners in her suitcases was now bought with the family silver on the black market. Her memory of the details about their families which had so impressed her first prisoners at Fuhlsbüttel was supplemented by a card index system in which she also kept track of them as they were transferred from prison to prison in the labyrinthine Nazi penal system. Soon there were over a thousand prisoners to take care of, more than fifty prisons to visit, and more than fifty prison governors to deceive and intimidate.

"I am not very intelligent, but I had a good instinct for people. I always have had. I had this sense of knowing when my life was in danger and I used this in dealing with the guards. I knew exactly what I was saying in the prisons. I knew when to be kind to them and when to intimidate them. I knew how to play one against the other. It was almost like being dishonest—but it was a question of survival."

Hiltgunt was twenty-seven years old. For ten years— ever since she had first refused to give the Hitler salute —she had had no real social life. With that one gesture she had distanced herself from her generation of fellow Germans. She had missed almost entirely the everyday pleasures of growing up: the boyfriends and dating, the parties and dances. With the outbreak of war and her clandestine work with the prisoners, the isolation was almost complete. She did not even think about a social life. It was a totally trivial thing. It did not enter her mind. Her life centered more and more on the prisoners themselves.

Once, still shaking after an interview with the Gestapo, she had thought about giving it up. She speculated about being an ordinary student like everyone else, about not worrying anymore, about what it would be like to be able to sleep, about not being afraid. But when she arrived once again at the station and saw the trains, she knew it was an impossible dream. Her prisoners were waiting for her; she could not let them down. Her work and her purpose was with them.

"Once they were being transferred to another prison.

I didn't know about it and I arrived and suddenly I saw them all in the prison yard in civilian clothes and with their luggage. Some of them were even smoking cigarettes. And for a minute I thought I had gone mad—I didn't believe it. What was happening? And then they told me they were being transferred. But it was a very peculiar feeling that suddenly came over me when I saw them in civilian clothes because for the first time I realized that one of these days I would be without them.

"And I must be honest. For a minute it struck me: How could I go on living without them?

"I had to get hold of myself and realize that actually this was really the whole idea."

On August 22, 1944, Hiltgunt's youngest brother, Willfried, was killed in action in Russia. In her grief Hiltgunt realized that she had been so preoccupied with her foreign prisoners that she had hardly thought of her own brother at all since he left for the front.

Lyserstrasse was a changed and sadder place. Hiltgunt's father had died at the beginning of the war. Guenther was away, stationed with the Luftwaffe in Holland, and now Willfried had gone forever. The air raids had divided Hamburg into two classes, the victims and those who still had homes. As the homeless increased in number they were billeted with those who still had roofs over their heads. Hiltgunt remembers when the first lodgers arrived at Lyserstrasse. They came with looks of ill-concealed envy and hostility, as if to ask, "By what right do you still have a home when we have lost everything?" "This house shall be our fortress," Julius Zassenhaus had declared when they had been forced to move there in 1933. But now Hiltgunt and her mother could no longer close their doors on the world outside. Now there were strangers inside their home, strangers who were embittered by bad fortune and whose political sympathies were unknown.

When suspicion arrived through the front door, the oasis of freedom shrank to a couple of rooms on the ground floor. Everything was dangerous now. Total war had brought total surveillance. Even Nazi officials reported an increase in anonymous denunciations, in which "individuals try to denigrate their fellows from low motives of hatred and envy." Whispers, signs and nods replaced conversation. Hiltgunt and her mother crouched in a corner with blankets over their heads to listen to the BBC from London.

They were right to take precautions. In the jittery last stages of the war, radio criminals, as those who listened to foreign radio broadcasts were called, were savagely punished. There was another problem too. Hiltgunt cooked the prisoners' bread at home from flour which she obtained from the black market. These were hungry times. It was hardly tactful to excite suspicious lodgers too often with the rich aroma of baking loaves.

Throughout 1944, in newspapers, in letters, in diaries, in a hundred million conversations, in prayers, in sermons, in speeches, in communiqués, in the underground press, in taxis and tanks, in cafés and concentration camps, in cabinet rooms and bunkers, millions upon millions of people had consoled themselves with the idea that the war would be over by Christmas.

Christmas Day arrived and there was still fighting on all fronts. Incredibly, the Nazis had even launched a massive new offensive in the Ardennes. Christmas Day in Hamburg was frosty and sunny. There was not much of Hamburg left anymore; there was not much of anything left anymore. For the past year the main diet had been turnip. The monthly allowances of everything else had dwindled with the Nazis' declining fortunes: three-quarters of a pound of butter a month; half a pound of meat. Only the rats which had infested the bomb sites and had now moved into the houses were getting fatter.

With little enough to celebrate, just to have a Christmas tree was celebration enough. "I remember the last Christmas when my mother and I were alone. We did the same as we always did. We had a little Christmas tree. We had no candles anymore, but we still had one or two apples on the tree and we had an angel on the top which we'd had right from my childhood.

"My father had gone. Willfried had been killed. My other brothers were not there. So my mother took the Bible and read the story of Christmas and we two together sang our Christmas songs, as we'd always done."

Nineteen forty-five. The gas in Hamburg was turned off two days a week. There was no electric light on Wednesdays. Rations were cut still further and the air raids were so "totally unpredictable" that Mathilde Wolff-Mönckeberg wrote to her children that "one cannot plan for anything."

Through all this Hiltgunt planned her journeys to Scandinavian prisoners throughout Germany. She was determined that not a single one of them should disappear into the *Nacht und Nebel*, the night and fog, of the Nazis prison system. When a group of her Scandinavians were transferred, she doggedly tracked them down and reestablished contact—with or without the cooperation of the prison authorities.

Exhausted and ill, she carried on, driven by a sense of purpose that had become an obsession. She was too tired to be afraid. She was too tired even to care about the risks she was taking. She just went on. "I was not so frightened because everything was frightening. You were frightened of the Gestapo, you were frightened of the bombs, you were frightened of everything, it became one blur of fright. . . . I was so fatigued that sometimes I didn't think clearly, it was as if I no longer cared what would happen to me. I became less cautious. . . ."

The nightmare continued. The prisoners were being

scattered around Germany almost faster than Hiltgunt could keep track of them. No sooner had one group been traced to a new prison or camp than there would come news that other prisoners had moved to an unknown destination. It was in that last frenzied winter of the war that Hiltgunt realized that she had lost thirty of her men. They were Norwegians, some of them among the very first she had visited at Fuhlsbüttel Prison in Hamburg. She knew them better than almost anyone else—at this point in the war she felt that she loved them better than anyone else. She began a desperate search to find them. It was not that she knew yet what she could do to help, but she was fully aware that she could do nothing at all if she did not know where they were.

It was dangerous to ask questions in the Third Reich. But Hiltgunt was by now too involved to think of the danger and too tired to measure the risk. From jail to jail she inquired about the Norwegians. Sometimes she would play the naïve, innocent German girl, loyally working for the department of justice. On other occasions she would employ the veiled threats of a Gestapo agent. Both roles she stretched to the limits of credibility. The evidence accumulated. It pointed to a prison to the east of Dresden, a prison which even in Nazi Germany had a grim reputation for its harsh discipline: Bautzen.

"We came there and I found immediately the hostility of the warden. Somehow he resented me and somehow he suspected me although I had never seen him before. And he said right away, 'Well, I will put a guard on you during your visits.' That meant I would have to follow the rules. I would have to speak German and I would not be able to allow the reading of the Bible.

"I don't know what came over me. I saw the prisoners coming in so very much changed from the last time I had seen them. So deathly pale and the legs, thick with edema

—just staggering in, barely holding themselves upright.

"I saw these people who I loved and I saw that they really were at the very end, that they didn't have much further to go. Suddenly I did not care for myself anymore. I spoke in Norwegian to them and I let them know that they were not abandoned. 'We know exactly where you are, we'll keep track of you, even if you don't see us for months.' (Because I knew we would not be allowed in there again.) 'We will make sure you will get out.'

"What came over me? I don't know because at that time I didn't even know if we could really get them out. But somehow I believed it so strongly—and I think I conveyed that hope to them.

"And then I asked the pastor to read from the Bible. He looked at me and paused and then he read 'The Lord is my Shepherd.' "

It was the same Hiltgunt who had refused to salute in the classroom. That time it had been the impetuous gesture of a seventeen-year-old schoolgirl. Her stand in Bautzen Prison was the decision of a mature conscience, pushed beyond the limits of endurance. She left the prison with the warden's words ringing in her ears: "I knew there was something wrong with you. I will send my report direct to Himmler."

It was February 14, 1945—St. Valentine's Day. It was also the day that the Allies decided to bomb the nearby city of Dresden out of existence.

Hiltgunt left Bautzen the following morning. Her train crawled towards Dresden through eastern Saxony. At every station along the route the rumours grew that there had been a catastrophe in Dresden. The train came to a halt some distance from the city and Hiltgunt walked the last few kilometers. She found the city that had been called the Florence of Germany in ashes. There was total confusion. The numbers killed were higher even than Hamburg. In fact, they would be higher even than Hiroshima.

Hiltgunt surveyed the devastation. Maybe, she thought, this is what will save me.

Whether the destruction of Dresden was necessary or justified remains a question of bitter controversy. However, the chaos that the English and American bombers left behind them certainly helped to save Hiltgunt's life. We do not know if the report of her misdemeanours in Bautzen Prison ever reached Himmler, or, if it did, how it impressed him. By that time he had a lot on his mind.

Germany was on the point of collapse. Speer had already sent the Führer a timetable of defeat based on the unavailability of essential minerals and raw materials. Hitler had told him to destroy everything. "If the war is to be lost, the nation will also perish. There is no need to consider the basis even of a most primitive existence any longer." In those places where Germany's armies did not retreat, they did not continue to exist. The air raids had made travel and communication impossible for days at a time.

Hiltgunt's first reaction on leaving Dresden was to go into hiding. She went to Berlin and remained for some weeks with a friend of her mother's. It was a bizarre retreat—as much a flight from reality as from danger. The house had been badly mauled by bombing. There was a gaping hole in the back wall. But her mother's friend belonged to a wealthy and well-connected old German family and had managed somehow to reserve a curious gentility. While a few kilometers away, in the *Führerbunker*, Hitler was ordering an orgy of destruction, Hiltgunt sipped ersatz coffee from delicate porcelain demitasses served on a silver tray by an old family maid still wearing the well-starched uniform of her position.

Nevertheless, Hiltgunt had lost the habit of being safe —even of being still. She was impatient and restless. She felt instinctively the insane apocalyptic spasms of the dying regime and feared that this death wish would destroy the men she loved most: her prisoners. When the expected denunciation did not come, she decided to return to Hamburg.

Incredibly, she had decided that the prison visits must go on.

Hiltgunt was no longer alone. Concern for the fate of the Nazis' political prisoners was widespread and moves were already afoot to help them. From Sweden, Count Folke Bernadotte, of the Swedish Red Cross, flew to Berlin to negotiate with Himmler for the lives of the thousands of prisoners from Denmark and Norway. Reluctantly, the leader of the SS agreed to release his grasp on this small portion of his lethal estate. As a preliminary move Red Cross buses were allowed into Germany to collect all the Scandinavian concentration camp prisoners in one place.

But there was a hitch. Many prisoners had been swallowed up into the system and could not be found. Now Hiltgunt performed her final and greatest service to the men she had been helping for years. Throughout her travels with the Danish and Norwegian pastors, she had built up records of the movements and whereabouts of over twelve hundred prisoners. Her secret files now assumed a life-and-death importance. They were handed over to the Red Cross.

Throughout April the Red Cross buses picked up Scandinavian prisoners from prisons and camps all over the Reich. First they were taken to prisons in Denmark and then on to neutral Sweden to await the end of the war.

In Hamburg, Hiltgunt too was waiting. There was little else to do.

May 1. The wind howled and the rain poured down on the forty-three million cubic meters of rubble which had once constituted the proud city of Hamburg. The British waited at the gates of the city. Their ultimatum was simple: "Surrender or we will bomb you into oblivion."

From the shells of bombed houses the radio could be heard playing the somber and magnificent Seventh Symphony by Bruckner. Without warning the broadcast was interrupted with an announcement: Hitler was dead.

"I was sitting with Mother in the living room. It was the moment I had looked forward to for twelve years. I had waited for it and thought about it and imagined what I would do when it happened.

"But I remember, when it actually came through, I was totally numbed. I didn't feel anything: no joy, no hate. Nothing.

"I remember Mother sat opposite me and she looked at the picture of my brother who had died in Russia. And we both sat there, very silent, and said nothing."

One week later the Thousand-Year Reich came to an end. A struggle of a different kind began.

Germany was starving. In Hamburg, as late as the end of 1946, one hundred thousand were suffering from edema due to malnutrition. Only a fraction of the children were of normal weight. Soon after the war ended, Hiltgunt took up work looking after the war orphans who were roaming the streets. She appealed to her ex-prisoners in Norway and Denmark for help and they sent food and clothing. In 1947, Hiltgunt was the first German after the war to be invited to Norway and Denmark. By this time her story was well known in Scandinavia and she was welcomed in both countries as a heroine. She resumed her medical studies, first in Bergen and later in Copenhagen. But her spirit remained restless. She was no longer at home in Germany, and even in Scandinavia there were too many reminders of the past. For years she had been cut off and alienated. With people who in normal times would have been her neighbours and friends, she had been compelled to act and pretend. She felt that she wanted to find herself. She needed a new start. In 1952, after she had qualified as a doctor, Hiltgunt left Europe with her mother and emigrated to America, where today she still practices medicine in Baltimore.

May 1979. Hiltgunt is back in Hamburg. The rubble has somehow reconstituted itself into a city again, finer and more beautiful than ever. Around the Alster, the noble buildings have regained their smart air of prosperous restraint. The hotels, the Vier Jahreszeiten and the Atlantic, have resumed their place among Europe's grandest places of resort. It is the middle of the Spargelzeit, and at home and in a thousand busy cafés and restaurants, Hamburgers celebrate with as much asparagus as they can consume, specially cooked for them in a hundred different recipes. In the newspapers it says that the Mercedes car company is concerned because its product—once a luxury to which everyone aspired—has become simply boring.

It is as if the war never happened.

Hiltgunt's mind drifts back to one of the questions she was asked by the schoolchildren in her own school. "Germany is good now. We're a democracy. Why do you still live in America? Why don't you come back?" But Hiltgunt decided long ago that she could not live in Germany anymore. Her trust in the people has been lost forever; she could never be the same in her relationship with other Germans. "It was just as if you had a friend who had somehow disappointed you so much that it could never be the same."

For twelve lonely years Hiltgunt fought her private battle to be free. Today, in America, she fights another battle to persuade people to use the freedom they possess. In talks and articles, she repeats a simple message:

There are two enemies of freedom: those who impose their ideologies upon others by force; and those who stand idly by and let them. Individuals have a choice to defend their liberties or watch their freedom disappear; that freedom which is lost through indifference is regained only by suffering.

The message is simple, but it was hard won. It is directed at free men and women everywhere, but it is based on private anxieties:

"I still dream of these things now. I dream of my home, the home I was born in. I can't forget the day when they tried to get my father—when the three SS men came to our house. I dream of our locks, and each time I think we have to put new locks on the door. At night I am bathed in sweat thinking of it. There must be other locks! There must be better locks!—so that they can't come in. When I came and saw my house now, after all these many years, that was the first thing that I did. I went to the basement door and to the other doors and thought, These are still the old locks, they must be replaced.

"I have another dream. I dream of the trains, these endless trains I saw, and the stations. I still see my brother in the train—the very last time he left us—when my mother said to him, 'Remember, you must still serve Life,' and he didn't give any answer. He just looked at us and then he disappeared. He went to Russia and we never saw him again.

"I also dream another dream that haunts me. I am back in Germany—these days I dream it quite a lot—and suddenly I discover I have lost my passport. I rush over to the American consulate general. I try to tell them I don't have my passport and they look at me and say, 'We have never seen you.' 'But I live in America . . . I have a home there! I have a profession there—I am a doctor!' 'We have never heard of you—you can't get a passport!' "And I get this feeling—I have to stay in Germany. Nobody knows me in America. I am lost. I must stay here.

"It's a nightmare."

Kitty Hart

Gentlemen, I must ask you to arm yourselves
against all considerations of pity.

—Hans Frank

The first time Kitty Hart arrived in Auschwitz she was
in a cattle truck. The second time she came in a white
taxi. In April 1943 she was sixteen years old and she arrived with her mother to be exterminated. In November
1978 she returned with her son to make a television film.
So it was that at eleven o'clock on a cold winter morning
a Polski Fiat taxi crossed the rail junction at the small
Polish town of Oswiecim, rounded a bend in the road
and approached once more the barbed wire and watchtowers that make up that terrible, but familiar horizon.
And so it was that Kitty Hart, the lady next door from
the suburbs of Birmingham, stepped falteringly back in
time to be reclaimed by that vast swampy compound
where long ago it had been decided she was going to die.

There are tribes in Africa who do not share our notion
of memory as a mental wardrobe of experience through
which the sensations of a lifetime can be relived like a
series of costume dramas. Instead, they believe that
memories have a separate and independent existence in
their own right, and that bad memories—like evil spirits
—must be propitiated if they are not to return and trouble us.

There are many survivors of the concentration camps who would make any sacrifice to rid themselves of the nightmare of their past experience. What was it then after nearly thirty-five years that led Kitty Hart to leave behind her comfortable home and the engrossing routine of a radiography post at a private clinic to stir the memories of the eighteen months she spent as a teen-ager in the worst place on earth? There was a stated aim, a public purpose, which was always passionately expressed: It was to remind the world of what had taken place at Auschwitz and so help to prevent it happening again. But could this entirely explain the motives of a woman who could also say: "For me, Auschwitz was a worthwhile experience. Something that I wouldn't want to go through twice in my lifetime, but something I'm extremely grateful not to have missed." And what did she mean when she said that although she was psychologically prepared for Auschwitz the first time, she was not sure whether she was psychologically ready to face it a second time?

Kitty's return to Auschwitz had a private as well as a public purpose. It was undertaken to discover something about herself. In the war Kitty triumphed in a horrific struggle for survival, but she knew that neither then nor afterwards had she ever wanted to confront the experience directly. "Right through the postwar years I've felt completely detached from this particular part of my life. I have not felt any emotion about it whatsoever," she said in an interview before she returned to Poland. "I have always felt that I had to be the sort of person that would not get involved emotionally in thinking that this actually happened . . . I didn't allow my brain to take it in . . . I couldn't go on living if I did."

To go on living was the task Kitty set for herself in Auschwitz. She was very good at it. In such a place endurance was so unusual a quality that it conferred upon a prisoner a terrible primacy. By the tattooed numbers on their forearms, prisoners could tell how long each had been in the camp. A low number brought its bearer a kudos and respect from which not even the SS were wholly immune. Survival was not the highest or the lowest but simply the final denominator. Even today Kitty claims to be able to tell within minutes of a stranger entering a room whether he or she would have been able to survive in Auschwitz. "Newcomers," she says, "were the lowest form of life in the camp. Newcomers were despised by everyone because they had to prove themselves first." This attitude is scarcely surprising. In a death factory—which is what Auschwitz was—survival is the only possible form of sabotage. Kitty was— and is—a survivor. Emotional detachment was the keystone to her strategy. "I think if you tried to think you couldn't live. . . ." It was not the only way to survive, but it was Kitty's way. And so, for her, to go back was the final challenge: to compare memory with reality; to confront her evil spirits on their own ground.

Yet where Kitty and her fellow survivors from the *univers concentrationnaire* are different is that the demons which dwell in the recesses of their memories haunt the entire post-Auschwitz world.

There has been a remorseless inquest, the endless post-mortem of a civilization which destroyed its belief in itself. Yet paradoxically, together with a widespread rejection of the notions of reality and truth, there is a continuing search for the reality and truth about Auschwitz. It is as though having abandoned all hope of heaven, we compensate ourselves with hell. Who, or what, can tell us? Statistics too huge for sympathy or comprehension; a literature already so enormous that one person could not hope to read it all; or the survivors themselves? But Auschwitz was so efficient that the typical prisoner is no longer with us: The survivors are, by definition, exceptional. Individually, their stories can no more tell the truth about Auschwitz than a single fish can tell the truth about the ocean. To describe the most unutterable situations, their testimonies must be forced into the everyday conventions of narrative, history and art. Time and again they repeat the hopelessness of the task: "It is impossible to explain what it was like to anyone who wasn't there." Yet despite this the survivors have a unique position, some would say a unique responsibility. For whereas we look back at the horror and ask, How on earth could it have happened?, they look back and ask themselves, How on earth could it have happened to me?

Kitty was born in 1926 in the small, picturesque town of Bielsko (now Bielsko-Biala) in southwest Poland. It was a time when the nations of Europe were fast distancing themselves from the first Great War and did not know how soon the second would be upon them. In England the year was dominated by the general strike; France was torn by financial crisis; in Russia, Joseph Stalin won victory over his rival Leon Trotsky; while in neighbouring Poland political life was eclipsed by Marshal Pilsudski's coup d'état. It was still too early to see in the drift towards dictatorship, a drift towards war. But if the writing was not on the wall, it was already creeping into the bookshops. There the discerning reader could have found not only the newly published novel *The Castle,* by Franz Kafka, a prophetic analogy of the coming totalitarianism, but also the second installment of a treatise in which a little-known and till now luckless German politician stated baldly: "I hated the motley collection of Czechs, Poles, Hungarians, Ruthenians, Serbs, Croats, etc., and above all that ever present fungoid growth—Jews, and again Jews." The book *Mein Kampf* was not selling well. It was written by Adolf Hitler, who, it was noted later, had been about fifteen or sixteen before antisemitism held any special meaning for him. It is a measure of his success that by the time Kitty was that age, she would be in a concentration camp.

Although assimilated, German-speaking, and in no way different from their neighbours, Kitty's family was not only Jewish but manifested exactly those qualities of cosmopolitanism, wealth and business acumen which most excited the envy and suspicion of central Europe's burgeoning antisemitism. Kitty's father, Karl Felix, was a lawyer who ran the family's prosperous agricultural-supply business. Her uncles in a nearby village ran the local brewery. In Bielsko the Felixes were a family to be reckoned with, and Kitty and her elder brother, Robert, grew up in comfortable and privileged circumstances. The two children were very different from each other. Robert was gentle, good and studious; Kitty, competitive, tough and full of mischief. She played practical jokes on her mother, infuriated her teachers and wanted most of all to be canoeing or skiing in the nearby Tatra Mountains. It was, she remembers, a very happy childhood, and yet, looking back after forty years, Kitty recalls most vividly those qualities that helped most when her childhood came to an abrupt and untimely end. "I was a terrible child . . . I was terribly disobedient . . . very independent. I didn't allow my parents or people at school to take me over. As a person I always wanted to do my own thing and would rebel against everything that I was made to do. I never really obeyed any rule whatsoever. And this helped me to survive."

Childhood for Kitty was not so much a preparation for life as an apprenticeship for Auschwitz.

Two pieces of evidence help flesh out Kitty's picture of herself during this period. In 1938 she won a bronze medal swimming for the Polish national youth team against Hungary, and in the Convent of Notre Dame in Bielsko, which before the war ran a fashionable and expensive college for the daughters of Bielsko's more prosperous citizens, a school report confirms that Kitty's talent was more athletic than academic. It was written at the end of the summer term in 1939 and was the last report that Kitty would ever receive from the sisters of Notre Dame. It is also the only remaining documentary evidence that the Felix family ever lived in Bielsko.

If the young Kitty Felix, the pupil at a convent school, had reached the threshold of the war untroubled by the international situation and almost oblivious of her Jewish origins, the same cannot have been true for her father. Karl Felix was a shrewd and able man, and Bielsko was not a place in which a Jew could hide from the realities of life. Before 1919 the town had belonged to Austria, and after its incorporation in the newly re-created Polish state, it had retained a sizable German-speaking minority, whose confidence and arrogance swelled with Germany's growing power. Only thirty miles west of Germany and twenty miles north of the Czechoslovak border, Bielsko was well placed for a grandstand view of the fast-approaching catastrophe. Karl Felix, whose business often took him to Vienna, could hardly have failed to be aware of the fate of Austrian Jews after that country's annexation into the Reich in March 1938. Even in England it had been reported that over seven thousand Jews had committed suicide in the first few months of Hitler's rule. Events tumbled after each other indecorously. The march of history became a stampede. In September 1938, Czechoslovakia, abandoned at Munich, sacrificed the Sudetenland to the Nazis. In November, on *Kristalnacht*, the night of broken glass, Jews and Jewish property in Germany were attacked with unprecedented savagery. In March the following year, Hitler devoured what remained of Czechoslovakia. In London, where these events were officially described as a "quarrel in a faraway country between people of whom we know nothing," Chamberlain was asked in the House of Commons about the British guarantee to Czechoslovakia. How can we fulfil a guarantee, he responded, to a country which no longer exists? Such olympian detachment was impossible in Bielsko: The country which no longer existed was just half an hour's drive away. "If only we could kill these barbarians," Karl Felix wrote in a letter around this time. "And if only English politics became more honest than they are." He watched, powerless, as a nightmare turned to reality before his eyes. Since 1934, Poland had had a nonaggression treaty with Germany: "There can scarcely be any difference of opinion today among the true friends of peace with regard to the value of this agreement," Hitler had told the Reichstag as recently as January. But by the early summer the poisonous attacks of the German press, which in the previous year had been directed at Czechoslovakia, were now being aimed at Poland. In Bielsko and elsewhere the local Nazis became increasingly aggressive and impatient. The Polish authorities were accused of persecuting their German minorities, and even of aiming to exterminate them. "It is strange," wrote one contemporary of the Nazi campaign of hate, "how, when the circus man performs the same trick for the third and fourth time, some people are still taken in."*

There is no reason to suppose that Karl Felix was taken in, but throughout the summer of 1939, as Europe prepared for war, the Felixes remained in Bielsko. Their problem was that of German-speaking Jews everywhere. At what point did you say good-bye to homes, professions and businesses that had been the work of genera-

---

*Quoted in E. O. Lorrimer's *What Hitler Wants* (Penguin Books, 1939).

tions? Exactly when did you accept that the goal of assimilation within a liberal and civilized world had been delusive and that the attempt to distance yourself from the racial penalties of Judaism in a Christian world had ended, once and for all, in failure?

On August 23, 1939, Ribbentrop and Molotov signed the Nazi-Soviet pact in Moscow. The next day Kitty, her mother and her grandmother—the women of the Felix family—were on the first train out of Bielsko. It was a week before the war began, but already it was too late.

There was no longer anywhere safe to go. The sheer speed of the blitzkrieg confounded everyone's calculations. Bielsko fell to the Germans in the first days of fighting. Lublin, in central Poland, where the Felix family had taken refuge, was surrendered to the Germans a fortnight later. Within weeks the Nazis told the world that they intended to form a gigantic concentration of Jews in the Lublin region as a step towards the solution of the Jewish problem. It took Hitler less than a month to win his Polish war and by that time he had already begun his war against the Jews.

Over the next eighteen months the machinery of the Holocaust was gradually assembled: yellow stars, ghetto walls, "transports," "resettlement," "selection," "special treatment." In Berlin, Eichmann's bureau drew up railway schedules; in Poland, *Einsatzkommandos*—death squads—exhausted themselves with mass executions. Writing just before the war, the English author Philip Gibbs asked the question: "What can be done with these Jews? *One thing is certain,*" he asserted, *"they cannot be killed en masse* [emphasis added]. People would make a fuss about it. A nation might be considered uncivilised if it adopted such measures." How naïve this confidence seems now, but how widespread it was at precisely the moment the Nazis were seeking a new and more efficient method of killing the Jews en masse. In the summer of 1941 two civilians were dispatched from Hamburg to instruct the SS in Poland in the use of Zyklon B gas. One by one the death camps came on stream: in December 1941, Chelmno. Early in 1942, Belzec, Sobibor, Majdanek, Treblinka and Auschwitz. Slowly the outline of the Final Solution came into focus: "Beginning with Lublin," wrote Goebbels in his diary on March 27, 1942, "the Jews of the Gouvernement Général are now being evacuated eastwards. The procedure is pretty barbaric and not to be described here more definitely. Not much will remain of the Jews."*

The Felix family were trapped. They had fled from Bielsko only to find themselves at the very center of the biggest extermination program in history. Kitty was twelve years old. By the time it dawned on her that school was over forever, she was already learning other lessons very quickly.

"Well, I'd never seen Germans before, and I thought they looked absolutely splendid. They had these fantastic uniforms and black boots, and I remember them marching across the city with the sergeant-major waving his baton and conducting a military band. I was most fascinated. My father used to run after me and pull me home and not allow me out; and I couldn't understand why. I felt, Well, all these marvellous soldiers—why am I not allowed to go and see them? So I used to sneak out to watch the parades. . . .

"The fact that the Germans were out to kill people like me came very suddenly. Of course there were rules and regulations: People had to wear the yellow star; all Jews were made to live in a particular section of the city, and we had to move. But life was still bearable.

---

*Quoted from *The Goebbels Diaries*, ed. and trans. Louis P. Lochner (London: Hamish Hamilton, 1948).

"But there was one incident that brought it all home to me: I was walking along with a boy who was my age, and there were three soldiers from what was known as the *Einsatzgruppe*—the special regiment which was actually responsible for persecution, whose job it was to enforce the laws against Jews and Poles—and they walked along the pavement. However, there was one very important rule and this was that when soldiers walked around the town, everybody else had to get off the pavement. I instinctively got off the pavement, but my boyfriend didn't. And one of the soldiers pulled out his gun and shot him through the head—and there was this friend of mine just dropped dead. I ran home. And this was the very first moment I realized they were out to kill."

To beware of Germans was not the only lesson Kitty learned. With a mixture of fascination and repulsion she became gradually aware that her fate was awesomely linked with the curious and exotic throngs of Orthodox Jews who now passed before her in the Lublin ghetto. For the young Jewish girl from the Convent of Notre Dame in Bielsko it was her first realization that Jews were different. The Jews she saw now, parading with all the garb and marks of their ageless and esoteric custom, were those same Jews that even in the so-called liberal West constituted the "Jewish problem." For Professor W. J. Rose, writing in 1939, the only way forward for the Polish Jews was to break out of their centuries-old ghetto mentality which clearly, for him, placed them somewhere between sorcery and barbarism:

> Processes are at work which are doing much to *civilise* [emphasis added] the orthodox masses of Jews. They are going to school, and for the first time in history. They are beginning to play games—a revolutionary thing. This will transform their whole physical and mental make-up. Most of the younger generation

speak and think in Polish—again for the first time in history. Even some of their distinguishing racial characteristics begin to disappear.*

For Kitty, multilingual, a champion swimmer, and the pupil of a convent school, to be summarily associated with such a class of people was incomprehensible. To be doomed with them was not only unfair, it was unreal. Fortunately, her father had a better grasp of reality. When, at the start of the Occupation, the Germans had demanded all Jewish men to come forward, Karl Felix had refused.

"Why don't you go?" Kitty asked him.

"I don't think it will be for anything very good," he replied. It was Karl Felix's sense of realism that more than anything else kept the family going for the next two years.

In one of his essays, a sad and moving reflection on the story of Anne Frank, Bruno Bettelheim, a distinguished child psychologist and himself a survivor of Dachau and Buchenwald, discusses one of the key distinctions between those who lived and died among the millions of Jews in Nazi-occupied Europe. It hinged on the ability to see that everything had changed completely. "Those Jews," Bettelheim writes, "who submitted passively to Nazi persecution came to depend on primitive and infantile thought processes: wishful thinking and disregard of the possibility of death. Many persuaded themselves that they, out of all the others, would be spared."† But each compromise they made with the Germans diminished not only the will, but the very possibility for resistance and survival. Waiting and hoping were not enough. The old way of life had become a way of

---

*W. J. Rose, *Poland* (Penguin Books, 1939).

†Bruno Bettelheim, *Surviving and Other Essays* (London: Thames & Hudson, 1979).

death. What was needed above all was to realize that desperate situations called for desperate remedies. To survive was to choose to accept the implications of the New Order and act accordingly. Only after such a choice was it possible to know how to act at all. *The Diary of Anne Frank*, turned first into a play, and then a film by Twentieth Century–Fox, has been a phenomenal success, perhaps the most widely read firsthand account of a victim of the Holocaust. Its charm and appeal reside in the account of how the Frank family struggled to stay together and preserve their way of life in the most difficult circumstances. And yet, argues Bettelheim, it also conceals a deeper tragedy. For the truth is that Anne Frank would have had a better chance of hiding from the Gestapo if the family had broken up. By remaining together they increased enormously the chances of detection. In other ways too the Franks betrayed a lack of realism: They had no weapons and they made no contingency plans for escape if they were discovered. Bettelheim's intention is not to criticize the Franks so much as to point out the mistake of considering their efforts as a practical and adequate response to the situation they were confronted with. The desire to go on living as usual is understandable, touching, perhaps even noble . . . but if survival is the aim it is not realistic, or ruthless, enough. As with the Franks in Amsterdam, so with the Felixes in Poland: two families among millions struggling for survival. Yet from the time he left his business and his home in Bielsko, Karl Felix knew that he was fighting not for a way of life so much as for life itself. He was determined to keep one step ahead of the Nazis and never to allow the fate of his family to pass into their hands. He fought for the lives of his loved ones with an unblinkered sense of realism until the time came to say good-bye to them forever.

Before long, Kitty's elder brother, Robert, had split from the family and fled farther east, towards Russian-occupied Poland. Before the war Robert had gained admission to Nottingham University in England, but the Polish authorities had refused to allow him to go as he was of military age. He was now attempting to reach England through Russia.

The shrill communications, sent to his aunt in far-off Birmingham from this lonely and sensitive boy, fleeing for his life in the no-man's-land between Hitler's demonic panzers and Stalin's menacing divisions, testify to the pandemonium in those lethal months at the start of the war:

Stanislav
December 25, 1939

Dear Aunt,

I take this opportunity to give you a sign of life. I will tell you everything briefly. A week before war broke out, Mama, Grandmother and Kitty travelled to Lublin, taking a few things with them. On the second day of the war Papa and I followed as the Germans were before Bielsko. After a strenuous journey we arrived. We were there one week and then there was a terrible bombardment and the next day we heard that the Germans were before Lublin. So I packed all my things in a rucksack and went on alone. There were no trains as the railway lines were threatened, as were the roads. I travelled by night with map and compass. I saw and experienced things that would make your hair stand on end. After two weeks of travelling, incredible hardships, nothing to eat, with my life in danger a dozen times, I arrived in a little town. Finally we learned that the Russians had marched in. We *felt* as though we were saved. I am completely alone; no one to turn to; no news from parents; no money. Please try to arrange so that Lola's son [i.e., Robert himself] can come to you. It is most urgent as things are far from well with him. For the time being, greetings and kisses to you all,

Robert

A month later he writes again from Lemberg (Lvov):

> My dears,
> I have already written countless times but perhaps nothing has arrived. I am in Lemberg, making a precarious living with a job as washer-up in a restaurant where I have my keep. On your own it's not so hard to earn a living but the intense loneliness is terrible. I am very, very down and sometimes I lose all courage. It is very bitter—we are real refugees. It is like a fairy tale, what I went through to get here. By a miracle, and that indeed it was, I literally escaped death ten times. I still can't believe it myself. It's true that we are still alive—but I wonder whether it wouldn't have been better to have been caught then. It looks like it.
> Dear Aunt, dear Uncle, do please try: in the first place for my parents, for them it is vital to get to you. I learn indirectly they are well, including Grandmother—at least they are together.
> Please listen to my prayer. With fond kisses,
>
> > Yours,
> > *Robert*

After this the correspondence was broken for a long time. A last postcard arrived from Robert in October 1941. It was postmarked Samarkand. "I don't know whether this postcard will reach you," he writes. "I am alone here, so far from home, but I am healthy." Robert was killed fighting with the Red Army at the battle of Stalingrad.

The position of the rest of the family was no better, if anything even worse, than Robert's. In the ghetto life was hard. Karl Felix was not allowed to work and the family lived on the meager earnings of his wife, Lola, who gave English lessons, and by selling their depleting stock of valuables on the black market. Day by day the ghetto took on more and more the appearance of a death-trap: Already by Christmas 1939 the Felixes had attempted to cross the frontier into Russian-occupied Poland but were turned back under fire from Russian guards. They had returned to Lublin. Later they escaped again into the countryside and for almost a year kept in hiding in the small village of Zabi Wola to the south of Lublin. Once again they were forced back into the ghetto when troops ordered a roundup in the village. This time, though, they had to leave Kitty's grandmother behind. From a hill overlooking Zabi Wola, Kitty and her mother and father watched the *Einsatzkommando* surround the village and move in. All the Jews who had been left behind were either shot on the spot or loaded onto carts for deportation.

Reluctantly they once again returned to the ghetto in Lublin. The family had been on the run, living on their wits, for over two years. Kitty, a schoolgirl when the war began, had by now become ghetto-wise. She was expert in smuggling herself across the ghetto walls, dodging patrols, foraging for her food. She had developed a sharp instinct for self-preservation. But the system was daily becoming harder to beat. Random terror was being transformed into an industrial process.

The overlord of Lublin, the former *Gauleiter* of Vienna, SS *und Polizeiführer*, Odilo Globocnik, was a fanatical Jew-hater, obsessed by his own importance, who believed that in matters relating to the Final Solution (a phrase which he actually used) speed was of the essence "so that we don't get stuck in the middle of it one day." He had used his position to build himself a "vast kingdom of death" centered in Lublin. He talked of Sobibor, Belzec and Treblinka as "his" extermination camps. He would show visiting dignitaries from Berlin and elsewhere around the installations himself, taking every opportunity to exaggerate their capacity and efficiency. He is one of the very few men on record as having shocked

both Adolf Eichmann and Rudolf Hoess, the commandant of Auschwitz. The latter wrote of an evening spent
at Globocnik's house in Lublin: "He talked about all this
in his Viennese dialect in an easygoing way sitting in
front of his fire in the evening, as though it were a most
innocent adventure. I was rather shocked." It was about
the time when the first transports of Jews from Lublin
were arriving at Belzec. Now Karl Felix, driven against
his will back into the Lublin ghetto, made his last and
most desperate bid to keep his family alive. With the help
of a Roman Catholic priest, he arranged false papers and
new Aryan identities for his wife and daughter and then
succeeded in smuggling them on board a train taking
Poles to Germany for forced labour. It was the last time
he ever saw them.

For a year Kitty and her mother worked at the I.G.
Farben aluminum works at Bitterfeld, near Leipzig.
Their fluent German ensured that their tasks were ad-
ministrative rather than manual. Although they suspected that there were other Jewesses in their group
disguised, like themselves, as Polish workers, they did
not try to make contact. They feared denunciation by
their fellow Poles even more than detection by the Gestapo. With their German bosses their relations were
always respectful but not unfriendly. Given the alterna-
tives, life was not all that bad.

"There was just one man in charge, a Herr Meyer,
who was a German, and he was marvellous to me. He
brought me food and he taught me how to type. He was
just like my father and he felt terribly sorry for me. I
even learned to come into the office every morning and
say, 'Heil Hitler, Herr Meyer,' and I'd swear under my
breath. It was a fantastic experience at the time and I had
plenty of freedom really.

"It was intended that all Poles should wear not the
Star of David, but the *P*—Polish *P*—but still, speaking

German, I took it off and travelled around Germany. I visited many places I shouldn't have done. I was very carefree . . . I forgot about my previous life."

It did not last. After several months Kitty, her mother, and eleven other Jewish girls at the factory were arrested by the Gestapo. At first they were kept in solitary confinement. Later, after the Gestapo had discovered their true identity, they were herded together in a group cell.

"The Gestapo people came into the cell in civilian clothes—they were not in any uniform—and they said, 'Tomorrow we are having dancing . . . we're all going to have a dancing lesson.' And it's just the way he said it. We knew automatically we were going to die. There was something in the barking kind of voice that put it across. Oh, he did say, 'You might as well say good-bye to one another because tomorrow we are having a dancing lesson,' et cetera.

"And we were taken out at dawn and put up against a brick wall and all the machine guns were lined up, and the soldiers were there, ready to shoot—and shots were fired. My very first impression was that I had been missed because I was facing the wall—and there were screams—and then it was very quiet. All of a sudden there was a terrible laugh from beyond and we realized that they were not going to shoot us. It was just to frighten us. And of course many of us broke down and cried. I don't remember crying. I just felt a tremendous relief that I hadn't actually been struck. And we were taken back into the prison for further interrogations. . . ."

Kitty and her mother were sentenced to death on a charge of illegally entering the Reich on false papers, later commuted to hard labour for life. Some time afterwards they were led from Gestapo headquarters in Bitterfeld to a prison van. In the small crowd which had gathered outside, Kitty spotted her boss, Herr Meyer, waving a white handkerchief, tears running down his face. They went from prison to prison: Halle, Leipzig and finally Dresden. It was here that the prisoners' gossip and the jibes of the guards gave Kitty and her mother their first idea of what was in store. "Meet you in Auschwitz," earlier prisoners had scribbled on the walls. "See you in hell!" "No one who goes there ever comes back," the prison gossips assured them. "In the morning, it's off to Auschwitz," they were eventually told by an official.

On April 2, 1943, nearly four years of running came to an end almost where they began. Kitty and her mother arrived in the middle of the night at the small rail junction of Auschwitz. All their lives they had known it by its Polish name, Oswiecim. It was just fifteen miles down the road from Bielsko.

> *In Auschwitz, everything is possible.*
> —RUDOLF HOESS,
> *Commandant of Auschwitz*

November 1978. Kitty arrives at Auschwitz for the second time. The taxi pulls up, its engine purring before the entrance to the camp. It is cold. The tourist season is over. The visitors from America and Germany have gone away. The outside world has gone away. Kitty and her son are almost alone, hesitating before walking through the red-brick archway of the guardhouse. Above her in the watchtower, the lens of a camera follows every move she makes. Her first sighs, inaudible even to her son, David, standing at her side, are picked up and recorded by concealed spools of whirling tape. When Neil Armstrong first set foot on the moon, there at the end of a dream for mankind, he uttered a script that had been prepared, rehearsed and vetted by committees here on earth. When Kitty first sets foot back in Auschwitz, there is no one to help her. "Feeling slightly sick inside, that's all . . . I don't think I can . . . oh, God, I don't know where the bloody hell I am!"

Through the archway now. The camera high up behind Kitty watches as David puts his hand on her shoulder. The sound recordist listens in his headphones as Kitty sobs into the microphone hidden beneath her silk scarf. In front of them the Lagerstrasse, the main camp street, disappears into the trees and mist. Running parallel, the railway stops just short of the far western horizon of the camp, just before the gas chambers and crematoria.

"Just look at this terrible emptiness. Can you imagine this place full of people?" she says to David. Then as if remembering why she has come, and fighting back the tears, she goes on: "Just wait while I compose myself. . . . Perhaps I've come to speak for all those people who died here. I've had thirty good years, haven't I? Do you know why you're here? I mean, I'm not going to be here much longer, but you will be. You've got to tell your children about all this, haven't you?

"It's most important now. Do you know why? Because there are people in this world, they say, 'This has never happened!' They're writing about it, they're saying it's not true. Now you are here just to see that it is true. It was true. And so that when you have children you can bring them here and tell them about this.

"I owe this to all the people that have died. I'm sure I do. Thirty members of your family have died here. Your grandfather, your grandmother. My family. All my school friends. Everybody out of our hometown. All your father's family. Everybody's ashes are here. . . ."

Arrival at Auschwitz was always a moment of the most extreme danger for everyone. To this remote corner of Poland they came from all over Europe: from the

Aegean to the English Channel, from the Mediterranean to the Baltic, from the Dnieper to the Dordogne. Days and nights they had spent tossed together in the airless filth of the cattle trucks, wringing each drop of hope from the ambiguity behind the *Amtsprache*, the officialese, used by Eichmann's agents from Calais to Odessa. *Aussiedlung, Sonderbehandlung, Umsiedlung*, evacuation, special treatment, resettlement—such expressions could easily be made to yield some promise of life. This hope was all the millions of families shunted towards the middle of Europe had to cling on to. It disappeared as soon as their trains arrived at Auschwitz.

The shrieking, the whips, the dogs, the dumped bodies of those who had died of exhaustion and suffocation on the journey, the skeletal, hairless prisoners who looked and walked like zombies, the smoke and the stench of burning flesh: This first moment has been described by hundreds who went through it. But disoriented and desperate for air after the ordeal of the journey, the vast majority of those who came could have no idea that the next minutes and hours would decide their fate.

Three weeks before Kitty arrived, a transport came from Berlin bringing among a second detachment of Norwegian Jews, the three children that Sigrid Lund and her friends had failed to save. Vera and Tibor Tagelicht and their friend from Stavanger were given no chance. On arrival they had been selected to go immediately to the gas chambers. But Auschwitz needed slaves as well as victims. Kitty and her mother were more fortunate. Though Jewish, they had arrived on a transport of political prisoners from Germany. It was the stroke of good luck their years on the run had earned them. They were taken to a hut, shaved and tattooed with camp numbers: 39933 and 39934. They had been selected to work. For the time being, and to the smallest possible degree, the choice whether to live or die had been left in their own hands.

For many the choice was not an obvious one. Even if they survived the first selection and the impact of the first moments of the camp, what they saw during the days that followed comprehensively undermined their will to live. Some groups fared better than others. Poles and Russians, tougher perhaps, more accustomed to hard physical labour and less inclined to put their faith in any residual humanity in their captors, often produced stubborn survivors. But for girls from sunny Athens, or solidly respectable Dutch homes, Auschwitz was not only something beyond their experience, but something which they never could experience. They faded and died in their thousands, not from maltreatment but from shock. This was the intention, the outcome of Himmler's insistence on "Asiatic cruelties" for enemies of the Reich.

For the Nazis the extermination program had not only to be terrible, it had to be seen to be terrible. Its effectiveness was to be judged not only by how much it terrified its victims, but also by how much it terrified the Nazis themselves. The Germans were the *Herrenvolk*, a tougher, superior race. The SS, an elite among the *Herrenvolk*, had to be especially tough. The capacity to create and cope with the terrible on a scale never before contemplated and never to be spoken of reaffirmed their toughness in their own eyes. It was the cruelty of narcissism. With Himmler especially, a note of titillation is never far away. "I can tell you that it is hideous and frightful for a German to have to see such things. It is so, and if we had not felt it to be hideous and frightful, we should not have been Germans," he told a group of commanders during the war. And in another, infamous address to SS group leaders in Poznan in 1943, Himmler proclaimed:

> Most of you know what it means to see a hundred corpses lying together, five hundred, or a thousand.

> To have to go through this and yet—apart from a few
> exceptions, examples of human weakness—to have re-
> mained decent, this has made us hard.

It is commonplace to call Auschwitz hell; Kitty in her
prison was told she was being sent to hell. But it has even
been suggested that in their pursuit of "hardness," the
SS actually exploited every imaginative resource to be
found in the infernal visions of Dante, Hieronymus
Bosch and the long-accumulated anxieties of a collective
European unconscious, to build for their victims a hell
on earth; and that Auschwitz and the other camps were
"the deliberate enactment of a long precise imagining."
They succeeded only too well.

> I hardly looked. I could not; I could not. I had had
> enough. The shrieking, and . . . I was much too upset
> . . . then I saw the most horrible sight I had this far
> seen in my life. The truck was making for an open
> ditch, the doors were opened, and the corpses thrown
> out as though they were still alive, so smooth were
> their limbs. They were hurled into the ditch, and I can
> still see a civilian extracting teeth with tooth pliers.
> . . . There I got enough. I was finished.

The speaker was not a prisoner. Not someone straight
from home to whom such horrors were being revealed
for the first time. It was Adolf Eichmann, and as Hannah
Arendt rightly pointed out, "the fact is that Eichmann
did not see much. . . ."* Even Rudolf Hoess, the camp
commandant of Auschwitz, revealed in his testimony
written after the war that although he had always been
plagued with doubts about his work, he invariably told
others who had misgivings that "the iron determination
with which we must carry out Hitler's orders would
only be obtained by a stifling of all human emotions."

---

*Quoted in Hannah Arendt's *Eichmann in Jerusalem* (Viking
Press, 1963).

If this was the reaction of top-ranking Nazis, men who believed they were writing "a glorious page" in the history of Germany, how can we imagine the feelings of prisoners the Nazis had determined must be broken and exterminated? Can we blame those who, dumped in Auschwitz, on that immense field of horror and hopelessness, chose to "go on the wire," to commit suicide, or simply to give up the fight for life?

The will to live had first to overcome the devastating impact of the camp: the realization—infernal in itself—that the loves and comforts and certainties of the past had vanished without trace and that the terrors, pains and humiliations of the camp had replaced them for eternity. Kitty was determined to live, and in the fight for survival she had one great advantage over her fellow prisoners. For them arrival at Auschwitz was a disaster. For Kitty it was almost a deliverance.

"We had heard rumours in the prison cell of people who had been taken to Auschwitz: There were various rumours that whoever went there never came out. There were inscriptions on the walls: "I'm on my way to hell" —but I didn't relate this to any hell. To me hell was having been on the run for three years. This was the most desperate period of my life—to be on the run. I felt once I was in Auschwitz that there was the enemy, and I knew what I had to fight. As long as I was on the run, my enemy was invisible. Everywhere was the enemy. You really didn't know who your enemy was; you didn't know who you had to fight. I mean, you knew your German uniforms, but *everyone* was your enemy. In Auschwitz everyone was your enemy, but there it was concentrated in one place—you could fight it if you were prepared to make up your mind to live. It was purely a matter of whether you were going to live or whether you were going to allow everything to take you over. What kind of people were going to survive? It had nothing to do with whether they were physically strong: if they got a disease or if they were selected to die, they would die. But life was in your own hands—and you really had to fight for it."

Bruno Bettelheim, in explaining why the "vast majority of the thousands of prisoners who died at Buchenwald each year died soon," points to the "original trauma" of imprisonment in a concentration camp, the complete destruction of "one's social existence by depriving one of all previous support systems such as family, friends, position in life, while at the same time subjecting one to utter terrorisation, degradation, through the severest maltreatment and omnipresent, inescapable, immediate threat to one's very life." In short, they died of culture shock, not because there was a sudden transition of cultures, but because they had moved into an area where they could see no discernible culture at all.

This was recognized all too well by the SS. "The fact remains," wrote Camp Commandant Hoess, "that it is not physical hardships which make the prisoner's life so unbearable, but the incredible mental suffering caused by the tyranny and wretchedness and meanness of indifferent and malicious individuals among the guards and supervisors. The prisoner can cope with stern but impartial severity, however harsh it may be, but tyranny and manifestly unjust treatment affect his soul like a blow with a club."*

However, for Kitty the sudden fall into a state of nature, naked exposure to the *bellum omnium contra omnes,* the war of all against all, was neither sudden nor all that surprising. In her young life she had been to two schools: the Convent of Notre Dame, where she had been physically tough and temperamentally anarchic, mischievous

---

*Rudolf Hoess, *Commandant in Auschwitz* (Weidenfeld & Nicholson, 1959).

and wayward. Then from the age of twelve she had been propelled into the Academy of Total War, bombarded, starved, hunted and turned out of every refuge. Her home was gone, her family shattered, her grandmother dragged off before her eyes. In precisely those years when she should have been turning into a lady, every tomboy instinct was confirmed and reinforced. The entire adult world was tearing itself to bits. The only way to live was to lie, cheat, deceive, manipulate, not to fear risks, and to suspect everyone—Poles, Russians, Czechs as well as Germans. She had learned, in short, to regard as natural a world in which everyone was out to get her. Kitty had acquired a harrowing immunity to Auschwitz's most lethal challenge.

"I never felt inferior to anyone else in Auschwitz. I felt I was superior, rather than inferior, because I had come through the three years and I was still alive. This had given me a sort of spiritual strength. Whereas I felt people were inferior who came straight from home and couldn't adapt. I felt all these people were inferior, although some of them were very intelligent people and they came from wealthy families—but it meant absolutely nothing. I felt they were inferior because they couldn't cope with the bare necessities of life."

In Auschwitz, Kitty discovered a world that she knew. It was a rare and tremendous advantage. There is in her story an almost Darwinian dimension, the reverse side of that pseudo-Darwinism which the Nazis themselves used to justify their racial doctrines. In a place designed for killing, Kitty found herself preeminently adapted for life.

"I acted purely by instinct—by being young and not thinking. I think older people tended to be far more pessimistic because they understood the background. They understood the hopelessness of their position, which I didn't understand. All I knew was that I had to fight *like an animal.* . . . I never thought about my previous life. And the same on the run. I'd forgotten about my previous life. I couldn't remember anything about pre-war days. I only knew I had to stay alive and keep away from all people who tried to kill me. You developed a sixth sense . . . you got to know everything there was to know about people. You knew how they were going to behave. You knew what kind of people you were to associate with. You knew that if people were pessimists you must keep away from them at all costs. If they were trying to tell you there's no point in living, there's no point in fighting, well, those were the sort of people you never had to associate with. You had to be a sort of bystander and try and construct a life for yourself away from the camp. Although people were dying all around you, you had to pretend you were not seeing this.

"But people who were very intelligent—and perhaps even grown-ups—they couldn't play the make-believe and so for them it was very much more difficult to survive—and we found them very inferior. Because they couldn't adjust and couldn't play the game. . . ."

Every survivor found his or her own way to go on living. Kitty's is only one story among many. At times her outlook appears bleak and callous, but the laws surrounding the survival of the fittest were never for the fainthearted. She was sixteen. She found it easier than most to follow Goebbels's advice: "One must not be sentimental in these matters." Kitty was fighting like an animal; she had discovered her own way of "playing the Auschwitz game."

The Auschwitz game was getting dirtier. The plans to build a concentration camp had been drawn up only a few months after the invasion of Poland, despite the fact that the first Nazi commissioners who inspected the site rejected it as being too unhealthy and malaria-ridden for human habitation. The first Polish prisoners began to arrive in the summer of 1940. In March 1941, Heinrich Himmler visited Auschwitz for the first time and ordered a huge expansion of the camp at Birkenau to accommodate 100,000 Russian prisoners of war. Once again, the objections of German officials who claimed that the site was quite unsuitable were brushed aside. In September 600 Soviet POWs were gassed in Block 11. It was the first time that Zyklon B had been used at the camp. In October the order was given that Birkenau should be expanded once again, this time for 200,000 prisoners. By this time Himmler had summoned the camp commandant Rudolf Hoess to Berlin and acquainted him with the outline of the Final Solution. Adolf Eichmann had visited Hoess at Auschwitz to discuss the details. The camp authorities held sway over twenty-two subcamps spread over an area of fifteen square miles. The conditions for the prisoners were barbaric. Already tens of thousands had died—tortured, beaten, starved or worked to death. In the spring of 1942 transports began to arrive from Slovakia and France. "The fate of these people was terrible," records the Polish historian Jozef Garlinski. "They were murdered in such cruel ways that the plight of the other prisoners in the camp might even appear bearable by comparison. They were simply beaten to death, trodden into the mud." On May 12, 1942, a transport carrying 1,500 Jewish men, women and children was sent straight to the gas chambers. "This was," says Garlinski, himself an ex-prisoner of Auschwitz, "a turning point in the history of Auschwitz. . . . Up to then it had not been an extermination camp in the full sense of the word. . . . From 12th May 1942, the name *Vernichtungslager* (Death Camp) hung like an ominous cloud over the fenced-in marshes where a colony of human ants sought vainly for help."*

---

*Josef Garlinski, *Fighting Aushwitz* (Julian Friedman, 1975).

Strictly speaking, the thousands who arrived daily for extermination never actually entered the camp. They were not registered, they were not given numbers, they merely passed through on their way to the gas chambers and crematoria. Nevertheless, the influx left an indelible mark on the whole camp. With their arrival Auschwitz entered its mature period.

It was not the victims but their belongings that transformed the character of the camp. Gold, jewels, dollars, watches, silk, shoes, food, alcohol, tobacco: unheard-of luxuries, the worldly possessions of millions concentrated into suitcases, sewn into the linings of coats, and stuffed into pockets by people who had set out on a journey to a new life and ended up at Auschwitz. A whole section of the camp, known in Auschwitz slang as *Kanada*, was fenced off to sort out the mountains of loot. In theory it should all have been sent to Berlin. In practice it corrupted the camp from top to bottom. Not even the SS could resist the easy pickings. Inevitably much of the booty found its way into the camp. Garlinski reports astonishing sights: "The *Capos* and Block Chiefs began to wear the finest silk underwear, shaved with the most expensive soap, trampled in the mud with the most fashionable shoes. . . . The Block Chief of the Penal Company, a power in the camp, invited criminal prisoners to a birthday party with champagne and roast goose, smuggled from outside the camp for dollars." Before, the attitude of the SS to their victims was like that of a ratcatcher to vermin. There was no possible common interest between them. Now the Jewish loot formed a lurid nexus throughout the camp. It became a vast black market, flourishing under and upon the death factories. For the majority Auschwitz remained as harsh and murderous as before. But for insiders, wheeler-dealers, organizers, there was the chance to bend the system. Exchange became the key to survival. For the fortunate few with access to the goods, everything could be bought, everything was possible. This was Auschwitz at its zenith. This was Kitty's Auschwitz.

November 1978. For five cold and misty days Kitty struggles to convey the truth about her Auschwitz to her son. Since he was a child David has listened to fragments of his mother's story. Now, at last, in Auschwitz itself, he hears it all. Kitty, tense and alert, possessed once again by the demons of her past, speaks quickly with an exhausting intensity. Now in the camp her character has changed. Her answers to David's questions are full of aggression, sarcasm, and contempt. "Don't take any notice of the grass, because there was no grass. All this was mud. Just a sea of mud. Believe you me, if there was one blade of grass, you know what would have happened? You would have eaten it." When David asks about the toilet arrangements, Kitty snaps back, "Oh, paper! Boy! God! What sort of paper do you mean—toilet paper? You must be joking. You were lucky if you could go in there and do something and it didn't run down your legs!"

"What are you wearing?" she says to David at one point, pulling at his coat. "Five layers of clothes, eh? Right. Well, you imagine people in here working when it snows, when it rains, when the sun is hot, in the summer and winter in one layer of clothes—the same layer of clothes day in, day out—"

"Almost unimaginable," utters David.

"—and in the wet . . . in the wet . . . you couldn't take your clothes off," Kitty goes on. The camera records everything, sometimes close, sometimes far away, picking out the mother and her son as tiny specks in that vast rheumy landscape of barbed wire, barrack huts and watchtowers.

So Kitty continues, explaining everything. Her first night when she awoke next to a cold, dead Gypsy woman. The desperate struggles to get near a dripping tap, or a toilet, or even somewhere to sleep. The huts where a thousand starving, lousy and diseased women slept five or six to a bunk. The ruling prisoners who ran the camp for the SS, who held the power of life and death over the prisoners' lives and who beat them at the slightest provocation. The deadly early-morning roll calls, the *Zählappell*, which lasted for hours in all weathers and where the corpses were counted alongside the living. David, the boy from the comfortable middle-class suburbs of Birmingham, who earned his scholarship, who graduated at the university, who is becoming a doctor, watches as his mother shows him how to throw dead bodies on the back of a truck, how to sit three to a lavatory pan, how to wash in your own urine, and how the girls in the *Scheisskommando*, the shit squad, carried their pails of shit—in short, how to live in Auschwitz.

KITTY: You see, I realized one very important thing: that one of the best things to do in this camp was to do nothing. Just be invisible. Just hide, hide. I mean there were fifty thousand people here, so you could hide behind people if you were small, insignificant, invisible as I tried to be. But the other thing I found is that one of the best things to do was to carry bodies. Why? It was very hard work but (a) you worked inside the camp—you didn't do external work, and (b) the dead body had a ration of bread—a piece of bread. The dead body had . . . a change of clothes. And it wasn't any good to this dead body, was it? I mean, I don't have to feel guilty about it, do I?

DAVID: That's true.

KITTY: Well, this is what I thought. I'm not doing anybody any harm. I'm taking this piece of bread from this dead body, and I'm taking this one pair of boots, and I can sell it. And with this I can buy myself a place to live. I can buy myself a place to sleep.

They come to a long low shed with an iron trough running down the middle: the washhouse.

KITTY: Now the water was here, but you couldn't get in, because in charge of this was some ruling prisoner with a whip. Right? Now how do you get in? If you want to be beaten up you could have got in, you see. But if you could give her something, like your bread ration (which I got off my dead body that I loaded, you see)—I mean, there were dead bodies . . . three hundred, four hundred dead bodies . . .

DAVID: Then she let you in.

KITTY: . . . so I bought myself a little bit of access to go in there. . . .

The conditions in the women's camp were acknowledged to be the most dreadful in Auschwitz. The overcrowding, filth and squalor shocked even experienced prisoners. Rudolf Hoess wrote that "everything was much more difficult, harsher and more depressing for the women . . . living conditions in the women's camp were incomparably worse." Furthermore, the ruling prisoners, the *Blöckälteste* and the *Kapos*, in the women's section had been chosen from the worst of those at Ravensbrück, the women's concentration camp in the north of Germany. "They far surpassed their male equivalents in toughness, squalor, vindictiveness and depravity," writes Hoess. "Most were prostitutes with many convictions, and some were truly repulsive creatures. Needless to say, these dreadful women gave full vent to their evil desires on the prisoners under them. . . . They were soulless and had no feelings whatsoever." A chilling testimonial from the man who was, after all, camp commandant.

To survive in such a hostile environment even Kitty needed more than her well-developed self-sufficiency and fearlessness. She learned quickly to dodge the worst work commandos, and to trade the bread of the dead. She had that instinct or common sense (Kitty called it a "sixth sense") to avoid dangerous situations, essential in a place where disaster could strike so capriciously. But when she was hit by typhus, she could no longer fend for herself. Then it was her mother who saved her.

Lola Felix had been fortunate. Already in her early fifties, she was old by Auschwitz standards and she might easily have been selected for the gas chambers. Instead she had landed "a soft job" as a nurse in Block 12, one of the hospital barracks in the women's camp. It was an immense piece of luck.

When Kitty arrived at Block 12, prostrate with fever and bearing the telltale red spots of louse-borne typhus, death was almost certain. The Germans were terrified of typhus and made frequent selections in the hospital blocks to send victims of the disease to the gas chambers. When these took place, Kitty's mother hid her under the straw mattresses, or even on one occasion under a corpse. There were no antibiotics or medicines of any kind. The only hope was that the fever would subside and the patient recover enough strength to go out and endure the camp. That took time, and every day spent in the hospital block added to the risk.

As Kitty tells David on the site of the old typhus block: "The head camp doctor was Mengele. I went through a selection in front of Mengele. He stood there . . . wearing white gloves. I was after typhus and I had to strip naked and run. If you hadn't run, if you couldn't run, well, you were selected to go to the other side. But, of course, I was after typhus and I couldn't run at that time. I was still crawling. I was actually on my knees. And my mother said, 'Now—you've got to go! You've got to stand and you've got to run!' And I did. I ran in front of him and then he pointed that way. So I lived."

For the next few weeks Kitty hid on her mother's top bunk, regaining her strength, watching the sick, keeping well clear of *Kapos* organizing work parties. Eventually, she recovered and went to work as a *Putzer*, a cleaner, first in Block 29, the dysentery block, and then in the TB block. "At last," says Kitty, "I was on the staff."

With regaining health, a steady soft job, and her mother working nearby, Kitty's life in Auschwitz entered one of its quieter phases. Kitty's mother did much to restrain her daughter's wilder impulses and instruct her in the rudiments of camp morality, which consisted of two basic precepts: We do not steal from other prisoners (unless they are dead); and we will on no account join the ranks of the ruling prisoners and do the Nazis' dirty work for them. The work in the hospital blocks was hard and unpleasant. Cleaning was largely a matter of disposing of corpses by dragging them off their bunks and loading them onto a truck. The great privilege of the job lay in not having to attend the *Zählappell*. Kitty began to make friends. She re-met two sisters, Hanka and Genia, who had been with her in prison in Dresden. She began to open up. For the first time perhaps since Bielsko she was vulnerable.

It happened on December 1, 1943, Kitty's seventeenth birthday. Her mother gave her an onion as a present—an immense prize (Garlinski notes that an onion was worth a gold watch on the Auschwitz black market). Then, shortly afterwards, occurred the only incident in Auschwitz which broke her.

Thirty-five years afterwards, in the same spot, she weeps uncontrollably as she remembers it:

"I had two friends that we'd saved from a selection from prison—two girls, two sisters—and they had survived already eight months. And then one day Mengele came in and he said, 'The whole block's going to be emptied. Everybody out.' So all the staff—I was staff by then—we had to ring this area. I think it was this block over here. We all stood round here. We . . . we . . . we were standing around. They had brought all the people out, and we were standing holding hands, like this, so that they couldn't escape. And all the sick—even the convalescents . . . they were well, they were already well.

"[Mengele] wanted to clear the block because there were a lot of new sick ones coming in. So he cleared the whole block, and everybody had to be loaded on—and . . . I had to load my friends on . . . and . . . That finished me. That really finished me mentally, I think. That finished me. I'm sure it did. It was my mother that stopped me going on the fence that day. Everybody went. Everybody."

From a nearby hut another prisoner, a doctor from France, watched similar scenes enacted several times. Her name was Dr. Adelaide Hautval. She was a remarkable woman, a Protestant from France, who had been arrested because she had protested to the Gestapo about the way Jews were being treated. "Because you defend them you can share their lot," the Germans had told her, and then sent her to Auschwitz. In the camp, when she was asked to take part in the medical experiments on prisoners, she refused and told the SS doctor in charge that it was contrary to her conception of a doctor. Her story came to light at a libel trial in London in 1964 involving another prisoner doctor at Auschwitz. At the Old Bailey her courage made a deep impression. How did the SS doctors react to her refusal? she was asked. Dr. Hautval replied, "He asked me, 'Cannot you see these people are different from you?' and I answered him that there were several other people different from me, starting with him!"

A devastating reply, observed the judge, which "would live in the jury's memory for many years."

But that was many years after the event. In 1943, during the selections from the hospital blocks, as she and her fellow doctors remained indoors, "waiting for the dreadful moment to pass," what she saw from her window was that other prisoner nurses and orderlies were trying to save their own skins or ingratiate themselves with the SS by loading their patients onto the trucks for the gas chambers. In Auschwitz it was difficult not to think the worst.

Kitty did not want to live. She had tried to climb on the truck with her friends, but her mother had grabbed her just in time. Young and thoughtless though she was, she did realize that she had helped her friends to their deaths with her own hands. "I could not forget the pleading and terrified look in their eyes." She became overwhelmed by feelings of guilt and exhaustion. She lost the desire to live. "When the women had reached the bottom," wrote the camp commandant, "they would let themselves go completely. They would then stumble about like ghosts, without any will of their own, and had to be pushed everywhere by the others, until the day came when they quietly passed away. These stumbling corpses were a terrible sight."

In Auschwitz slang these stumbling corpses were called *Musselmänner*. They were a familiar and frightening sight. It could happen to both men and women. They gave up the fight for food. They showed no interest in where they were going to work or sleep. Their faces took on a blank expression and they began to shuffle instead of walk, at half pace around the camp. It was clear to everyone that they had given in to hopelessness. Demoralized themselves, they became demoralizing to others. "The tendency was that when you saw the beginning of disintegration, you automatically tried to shun these people and keep away, and not see them, and pretend that they didn't exist—because you were frightened that this was what was going to happen to you."

After the gassing of her friends, Kitty began the slow fatal drift downwards. The camp authorities estimated that the life-span of the obedient prisoner was about three months at most. Kitty had already survived three times as long. She had been, in her own words, "quite settled"; she had known "the tricks of the trade." But now she wandered aimlessly. A familiar look came into her face. "You mustn't give up. You mustn't give up," her mother told her. And gradually, once again, Lola Felix succeeded in pulling her daughter from the brink. The struggle continued.

For the first part of her captivity in Auschwitz, the object of the struggle was quite clear. It was a single, pressing and immediate need: "You always felt hungry. The only thing you really thought about was food. This occupied your whole twenty-four-hour way of thinking —you were just preoccupied with food. You could put up with cold, you could put up with wet, you'd put up with the beatings—but you couldn't put up with hunger. This was the thing you had to fight for—something to go down your mouth."

Kitty had been in the camp for nearly twelve months when something happened which changed this situation completely.

At the end of February 1944, Adolf Eichmann once again visited Auschwitz. Any visit by Eichmann was likely to have sinister consequences, and this was no exception. Soon afterwards, Crematorium V was mended. Big new trenches were dug to burn extra bodies, and a small, unused gas chamber was reopened. The camp was gearing up for the destruction of the Jews of Hungary. At the top there were changes in the camp command. And at the bottom of the scale there were also changes. Along with the expected increase in numbers for extermination, the Nazis anticipated even greater hauls of loot. Preparations were made for this too. Reinforcements were needed for the *Effektenkommando*, who sorted and packed the belongings of the Jews. As a result, one fine spring morning Kitty left the hospital blocks, passed through the gates of BIa, the women's camp, and turned for the first time towards the chimneys at the western edge of the camp. She knew that she was going to Kanada, that evil and mysterious part of the camp where, it was said, there was an abundance of everything.

November 1978. For an afternoon Kitty has left the killing ground at Birkenau and for the first time in her life she passes underneath the wrought-iron slogan which Commandant Hoess placed above the entrance to Auschwitz I: *Arbeit Macht Frei*, Work Brings Freedom. It is a fine day in late autumn. The dark red brick of the barrack blocks glows in the low sunlight. Leaves from the poplar trees which line the camp streets rustle underfoot. Auschwitz is mellow, pretty; outwardly there is something quaint, almost benign. Inside the blocks it is a different story.

There are twenty-eight barrack blocks in the central camp, several of them now converted to museums depicting in the most gruesome way what went on inside them during the war. In others, historical evidence has been gathered together from the entire Auschwitz-Birkenau complex, including what the Germans left behind them in Kanada when they evacuated the camp in January 1945: 348,820 men's suits; 836,525 women's dresses; 5,255 pairs of women's shoes; 38,000 pairs of men's shoes; "together," as the official guide book says, "with great quantities of toothbrushes, shaving brushes, articles of everyday use, artificial limbs, spectacles, etc." The blocks have become museums of genocide: great warehouses of history.

Kitty enters Block 6 with David, a tourist visiting her own past. Upstairs behind a long glass screen is displayed a mountain of suitcases, each with a name and a town painted unnaturally large on the side. Thousands of suitcases. But no, Kitty tells David, she did not see these. The people whose belongings she sorted were mainly from Hungary. These cases mostly came from Holland. Besides, she points out, by the time her work party came to their task, the clothes had already been tipped out of the cases. She does not remember the cases piled up like this. In the long museum gallery they turn to see another display case.

KITTY: Ah! Now that's more like it. All the . . .
DAVID: Shoes!
KITTY: . . . Oh, isn't that terrible. Children's shoes. All the children's shoes. [*Kitty begins to cry.*] I remember now. That I remember very well. Because, you see, the adults used to put their shoes together—bundled them up—but the kids didn't. They just threw them off, and they didn't bundle them up. That is why you see them jumbled up like that—because the adults always put their shoes together. Also when they went into the gas chambers—because they were told to put their shoes together. But not the kids. These are all children's shoes. Look. Tiny ones. Can you see? You get one or two bigger ones, but those are not adults' shoes . . .
DAVID: No. Those are children's shoes.
KITTY: . . . These are . . . these are all the children's shoes . . . those are all the kids that died. . . . [*She sobs.*] That I remember very well. There were heaps and heaps of these shoes; and we didn't sort the shoes. That . . . that was never sorted—never sent to Germany. Only the very good things were sent to Germany. The Germans didn't want this. . . .

The distance from the women's camp to Kanada was less than a mile. As the small gang of new recruits to the

Effektenkommando marched along the railway track, they passed one by one the wired-off compounds of the camp. Behind them to the right were the quarantine huts, where newcomers spent their first six weeks at Auschwitz. Then came the so-called families camp, BIIb, where families from Theresienstadt, the "model" ghetto in Czechoslovakia, still lived altogether. Within weeks they would all be gassed. Then came the Hungarian camp, the men's camp and the Gypsy camp. The huts stretched back as far as the eye could see, and behind them was Mexico, a farther, equally large section of the camp still under construction. As the girls approached the tall chimneys of Crematoria II and III, Kitty's eyes glanced over her shoulder, past the disappearing huts of the women's camp, over the barracks of the penal company, southwards towards her home in Bielsko, only fifteen miles away, and beyond to the Tatra Mountains —her mountains—where she had played as a girl. Each step she took brought her closer to the camp's last and most terrible secret.

"About all actions necessary in the evacuation of the Jews, I must keep absolutely silent even among my comrades" was the strict injunction of the special declaration signed by all SS men who took part in the Final Solution. A cloying secrecy surrounded everything that happened at the far end of the railway track in Birkenau. In the camp it was forbidden to speak of what went on there. Although the odour of burning flesh had spread wide across the countryside and the local Polish population spoke openly of the burning of the Jews, the news didn't seem to spread. Two years after the mass-extermination program began, the outside world knew nothing, or believed nothing, of what was really going on at Auschwitz. At great risk the camp underground smuggled out reports to Warsaw and London, but if they were received, nothing happened. Air reconnaissance experts, more interested in pictures of nearby factories, put to one side frames of film on which it was actually possible to see queues of prisoners entering the curious industrial installations at the western end of the camp. Month after month, thousands, then hundreds of thousands, and finally millions of Jews boarded trains bound for central Europe and simply vanished, never to be heard of again. It was as if a black hole had opened up in the middle of the Continent. When Kitty arrived in Kanada, she became an initiate of a new age. For what she saw there was not only the end of the line for the Jews, it was the end of the line for a certain view of civilization and human nature.

There had been many presentiments. In different ways this vision had been presaged in the literature and poetry of a generation. Perhaps some glimmer of it was what made Sigrid Lund shudder all those years before while taking tea at Wagner's house in Bayreuth; perhaps the young schoolgirl Hiltgunt Zassenhaus caught some hint of it at the Hitler rally in Hamburg. Now, no longer metaphor or premonition, it actually existed—the outcome of that illogical fanaticism and fanatical logic which had bent the twentieth century in two. Standing at the doorstep of her new hut, adjacent to Crematorium IV, the young Kitty Felix stared into the heart of darkness.

"I was very conscious of the fact that people were being brought in from all over Europe, because the belongings that I was sorting out—which I had to take out of people's pockets—showed that people were being brought in from Hungary, from Holland, from Belgium, from France, from Greece. And so it gradually dawned on me that the Germans were intent on disposing of the whole of Europe. But whether they were all Jews—that didn't actually occur to me. *I thought they were disposing of people as a whole.*"

"All Europe contributed to the making of Kurtz," wrote Joseph Conrad of the man at the center of his long short story *Heart of Darkness*. Kurtz was manager of an ivory trading post on the Congo, a genie standing at the confluence of African savagery and European greed. Slowly, irresistibly, the reader is pulled towards the vortex of evil which surrounds him, and yet at the last moment Kurtz has a vision which transcends even his sinister surroundings, and where we can no longer follow him. It is "a supreme moment of complete knowledge"—a vision not permitted to men. "The horror! The horror!" is the only clue to what he saw, and then he is dead. Kitty, on the brink of a vision no less terrible, chose not to look. "I think if my brain had taken it in, well, then I would have committed suicide, like many of my friends . . . because they lost all desire to live."

Once she was inside the Kanada enclosure, Kitty's life in Auschwitz was transformed. She had food, clothes, toilets and showers, even leisure. Her hut was "very luxurious" in comparison with the rest of the camp; she had windows and "proper bunks." Kitty had become one of the spoiled children of Auschwitz. She no longer had to fight to eat, to sleep and to shit, "the three basics of life," as she put it. All this was provided for. The fight now was to retain sanity in the face of everything that was going on around her.

"I was assigned to a night shift and I worked right through the night and I was supposed to sleep during the day. But in fact we had a very short sleep during the day because all around us were the screams of people, and you couldn't actually sleep. You had the stench coming out of the chimneys—great big dark smoke and the . . . peculiar smell of burning bodies.

"And you didn't really want to see all this, and you pretended that it didn't exist.

"All you were interested in was that there was the sun,

and there was this tiny bit of lawn, and all you wanted was to be able to eat and to enjoy this sun and live this one day. You pretended you didn't see what went on around you—although you saw it all the time—but your brain didn't take it in. So you pretended you didn't see it. People who—or friends of mine who . . . who continually said, 'Well, look. Can you see the smoke? They're burning, you know. They're screaming,' I used to say, 'Well, no. I'm afraid I can't hear this. I'm sure you're imagining it. It's not really happening'; or, 'Don't look at it. You must not look at it. You're here. You've been working right through the night. We've sorted all the clothes. But don't look at what you can see. You stay here and we're going to pretend we're on holiday.' "

It was, Kitty reminds us, the glorious summer of 1944. The girls of the Kanada commando knew they had no hope of getting out alive. They lived from day to day, sunbathing when they could on the little lawn outside their hut. They knew that the impression of well-fed, well-dressed girls relaxing in the sun would probably reassure the long queues waiting their turn for the gas chambers, that there was some sort of life for them. But they also knew that it was impossible to give a warning, or help them in any way. "Because everybody would have died. It would not have saved anyone, and people would have died a violent death, than perhaps a more peaceful one. I think it was better," said Kitty, "for them to have a feeling of calm."

It was a calm that was frequently shattered. Not all the transports went quietly to their deaths. From time to time someone in Kanada would spot a relation in the crowds outside the compound. There were heartrending scenes with mothers and children which upset all but the most hardened SS. "My pity was so great I longed to vanish from the scene," Hoess wrote of one such occasion, "yet I might not show the slightest emotion." Kitty's determination was just as great: "It took an enormous effort, constant effort, to drive this thing out of my mind. . . . You had to pretend that this didn't happen. You had to be completely detached . . . or you pretended that these people were not really people. *You tried to see it maybe as the guards themselves were seeing it: that these people were no longer people.*

"To keep up this wall of detachment, we pretended to live in a different world. I remember a group of us actually preparing a play. In this play most of the actors were playing SS and what we were going to do to them after the war.

"And also many of the plays were staged in beautiful surroundings. We were pretending, you know, that we were having a banquet, and there were these marvellous sardines and wines and sausages on the table which we, you know, pictured in our minds.

"And we pretended we were in a different world. Also I remember finding a mouth organ and one or two instruments. And we actually formed a little orchestra, and tried to compose some music, and pretended we were giving a concert. To nobody, you know, just to ourselves. Just pretending—and at the same time not looking at what was happening—not looking over the shoulder—and yet hearing the screams of people just behind us going into the gas chambers."

On May 17 the first transport of Jews reached Auschwitz from Hungary, four thousand people in forty sealed wagons. The next day four thousand more arrived. They were followed by another four thousand on each of the two succeeding days. Then, on May 21, three trains from Hungary came on the same day, in addition to two from Holland and one from Belgium. Twelve thousand people died in a single day. It was the largest number so far recorded at Auschwitz. Henceforth it became the standard. It was a fortnight before D Day. The camp's last and most ghastly summer had begun.

Throughout the summer Kitty worked in Kanada and

grew stronger. She made new friends, Isa, Jola and Ruda, who shared the work and the risks. The Kanada girls no longer wore the striped shifts of the other prisoners. Some whim of their SS supervisor to see them smarter had provided them with navy blue dresses with white polka dots. When washing their undergarments proved difficult they exchanged them "for fresher ones that had just arrived."

"Of course it was right for us to help ourselves. You had a conflict of conscience, but you had to get on with the practical way of living, and it was so important—each day was so important. You'd lived another day, and another day, and anyway you knew your days would have to finish, that you were doomed."

It was a cardinal belief, sanctioned by her mother, that the possessions of the dead were of use only to the living, and during this period, when Lola Felix herself contracted typhus, Kitty smuggled food and clothing back into the main camp at every opportunity.

Several times these trips almost ended in disaster, but Kitty escaped with little more than a beating. She stayed in Kanada and she stayed alive. Not all the Kanada girls were so lucky. All around, the frenzy of extermination continued. People were arriving in such numbers that the crematoria could not contain them and bodies were burned in open pits. After the Hungarian Jews it was the turn of the Jews from Lodz, the largest of the remaining ghettos, to "come in through the gates and out through the chimney," as the camp joke had it. On August 15, 16, 21, 22 and 24, a total of eight trains arrived at Auschwitz-Birkenau, bringing thirty thousand people to the gas chambers. On one of them Kitty's friend Ruda recognized her father. All night Kitty begged her to stop staring at the crematorium where her father had perished. But it was no use. Her mind had been unhinged and in the morning she threw herself onto the wire. Such episodes put extra strain on everyone. "When something like this happened, you simply had to distract yourself," says Kitty, "by doing something different."

The Germans began to evacuate prisoners from Auschwitz as early as July 1944 in response to urgent calls for more slave labour from war industries inside the Reich. Nevertheless, the killings went on throughout the autumn as transports from France, Belgium, northern Italy, Germany, Slovakia, Rhodes, Corfu, Silesia, Holland and Rumania still continued to arrive. Within the camp too, selections were still being made. Gradually, however, the extermination program was scaled down. In Kanada the girls worked slowly through the backlog of belongings that had built up during the summer, fearful of what would happen to them when the day came when there was no longer anything left to sort. No one believed that the SS would have much use for them then.

It was in October. Crematorium IV had been partially destroyed by a revolt of the *Sonderkommando*, the men whose ghastly job it had been to take the corpses out of the gas chambers and pile them up for burning. The SS were already beginning to dismantle the other gas chambers and crematoria for use in camps less threatened by the advancing Red Army. The end for Kanada was very near. One morning Kitty's number 39934 was called out at roll call. To be singled out at Auschwitz was always dangerous, but what she heard surpassed her wildest expectations: "You are to be returned to the women's camp" she was told. "You are to go on transport with your mother."

On transport. It meant she would be leaving Auschwitz. Once again her mother had intervened at a vital moment. In fact, as Kitty learned later, she had dared to approach Lagerführer Hössler to request a transfer for her daughter. Was it because of her perfect German and her formal style of address, or because he had responded to the courage of an old prisoner? It is impossible to tell. But something in this direct appeal momentarily cracked his SS indifference to the fate of this old woman; and at that moment Hössler, knowing he had within his hands the fate of both mother and daughter, had reacted by allowing his dangerous caprice to fall on the side of survival. As night fell on November 11, 1944, Kitty and her mother, together with one hundred other women, were once again pushed on board a goods train. This time, however, they were on their way out of Auschwitz.

It was six months to the end of the war. For the Nazis' prisoners all over Europe, they would be six of the worst months. For Germany the war was lost, but with a perverse tenacity the SS tightened their grip on their prisoners. From the time they left Auschwitz, Kitty and her mother were shunted from camp to camp through Hitler's shrinking Reich. And when there were no longer any cattle wagons to take them, the death marches began. Long columns of refugees trudged through Germany. Those who fell were shot. Those who could not rise in the morning were shot. It was winter, there were no rations, there was no cover. Kitty, who had left Auschwitz stronger than when she arrived, needed every ounce of her strength to survive. The Auschwitz girls stuck together, desperately trying to help one another. All of them were survivors. "We believed we were the toughest," says Kitty. Their solidarity was reinforced by the idea that they had been in the worst camp and they had suffered most. "Only people who had been to Auschwitz, and were prepared to risk their lives every moment in order to obtain some sort of food, could survive." Yet even for these girls the brutalities of the death marches were too great.

"Even I thought that I could not possibly live through these last six months, having seen many of the very tough girls who had been in Auschwitz two years, even three years, lag behind during the death march and be simply clobbered to death."

By the time they reached the final camp, Salzwedel, midway between Berlin and Hamburg, of the one hundred Auschwitz girls who had set out, only twelve were still alive. Among them, Kitty and her mother.

Friday, April 13, 1945. In Salzwedel the prisoners had had nothing to eat for days. They stared through the electrified wire fence at the bread piled up high in the SS stores. The SS had vanished. The guards had gone. The prisoners continued to look longingly at the bread, waiting for some signal that the electricity had been cut off. "I cannot remember how many hours we were just sitting and looking at the loaves. Everybody was watching, literally watching the bread, waiting for the signal that the electricity had been cut off."

There were rumours that strange soldiers were outside the camp, but Kitty took no notice. She continued to watch the bread. Finally the gate of the camp swung open. Men in strange uniforms approached. Five and a half years after the war began, the Americans arrived.

"A lot of people were very weak and could hardly walk, and they threw themselves at the soldiers. But I remember very clearly that at the point of liberation I made a dive for the bread."

It was the last triumphant moment of realism: "I ran immediately to my mother and we had something to eat after ten days. It was a most fantastic feeling. Perhaps the best feeling of all, being able to have some food."

In 1946, after a year of working as interpreters in a displaced persons camp in northern Germany, Kitty and her mother, travelling with new papers which still recorded their Auschwitz numbers, set out to create a new life in England. Of their old life in Poland nothing remained. In Bielsko everyone of the large and prosperous Felix family had been exterminated. Karl Felix himself had been discovered by the Germans hiding in the small village of Tarnow in southern Poland. He was shot at the top of a nearby hill and his body thrown into a ravine.

At first it was difficult to come to terms with everyday life. The social skills Kitty had acquired over the previous six years were of an entirely different order from those required in postwar England. After Auschwitz she found people superficial, with their trivial preoccupations and petty grumbling. In Birmingham they carped endlessly about the rationing and austerity, but they did not seem to want to know about what life had been like in the concentration camps. Well-wishers warned Kitty not to talk about it. She had jumped from the frying pan into the fridge, and for a time the transition demoralized her more than Auschwitz itself had.

An early attempt at nursing was abandoned because, characteristically, she could not put up with the restrictions of life in a nurses' hostel. However, in 1947, Kitty took up radiography in earnest at Birmingham's Royal Orthopaedic Hospital. In 1949 she married Ralph Hart, a Polish émigré who had arrived in Britain just before the war. Their two sons, David and Peter, were born in the fifties.

Lola Felix never saw Poland again. She lived with Kitty until her death in 1974. She had survived the years on the run and the years in Auschwitz. In Bielsko her family and friends had been swept away, but she had lived long enough to watch Kitty's family take root and prosper in Birmingham and her grandchildren take their places at English universities, an opportunity so tragically snatched from her own son, Robert, in 1939.

After her mother died, Kitty had the tattooed camp number removed from her arm and encased in a glass paperweight alongside her own. The two numbers, 39933 and 39934, a triangle etched under each of them, stand together on the mantelpiece of Kitty's bright and modern home. There is no souvenir in all Birmingham which has more meaning, or which has been bought at a greater price.

In the spring of 1979, three months after Kitty had returned from Poland, we returned to Birmingham to ask how she had felt being in Auschwitz a second time. "It was very confusing," she replied. "I knew I had only come on a visit, and yet it all seemed so unreal. At one stage I wasn't sure whether I had ever left. I felt I belonged to Auschwitz. . . .

Kitty has been settled in England now for many years. She speaks English with only the slightest hint of a central European accent. She has a job which she is good at and a home she is proud of. She works hard and plays hard, an attractive, cheerful, vigorous woman in her prime, and apart from those on the mantelpiece, the only numbers in her life—as in everybody else's—are those on tax returns and credit cards.

And yet Kitty remains the creature of Auschwitz. At the bottom of her garden there is a shed where every morning she undertakes physical exercise on a truly intimidating scale. She regularly attends a health center for more workouts. But it is not only this constant need to prove to herself that she still has the necessary self-discipline to survive that links her with the past. It goes deeper than that. In a very real sense, Auschwitz made her. "It was," she says, "a very good education and preparation for my future life. After Auschwitz, there was absolutely nothing you didn't know about people. . . .

"I had a sixth sense where people were concerned. I could see through the superficiality of people, all their artificial politeness, which I always dispensed with—and therefore I tend to be misunderstood by other people. But in one respect I was very tolerant—long-suffering—

putting up with inconveniences. On the other hand I found I was very intolerant because I couldn't bear fussy and . . . inconsiderate people, because I knew instinctively how these people were going to behave when the chips were down. *Automatically, every single person that I meet in the course of my life is classified somewhere in the society of Auschwitz.*"

For Kitty, Auschwitz teaches us about the world, because for Kitty the world is like Auschwitz. Among the brutal ruling prisoners were people from many nations, classes and religions. Not even the SS were all Germans. The humble *Häftling*, the ordinary prisoner, the *Zugang*, the newcomers, faced an international chorus of blows and abuse. Perhaps this is why, when Kitty had the chance to take revenge in the first few days of liberation, she let it pass by. "I came to the conclusion I'd have to hate everybody or no one. I couldn't find a group of people that I could particularly hate. It's very difficult to hate a whole nation. You have to find some people to focus your hate on. And that wasn't possible."

So it is not upon whole nations that Kitty's silent judgment falls. It is upon individuals. Today Kitty's eye makes the same vital calculation that she made in the camp: Are you a survivor? How would you survive? As an ordinary prisoner, or as a servant of the SS? Once, in Auschwitz, her judgment of character had been a matter of life and death. Now the answers to these unspoken questions place everybody that she meets "somewhere in the society of Auschwitz."

For Kitty, Auschwitz has become the standard to measure the world. But it is not a measure without hope. For strangely—and it is a paradox which touches the lives of many survivors—Auschwitz sets the very highest as well as the lowest standards. Kitty learned more there than simply how to claw her way out of the abyss. This is why at the heart of Kitty's harsh and unsentimental account of her sufferings there remains a kind of nostalgia.

"In the camps you had a feeling that people would make a sacrifice, sacrifice their lives, sacrifice everything for their nearest and their best friends without asking for anything in return. You learned to understand the meaning of friendship, which a lot of people don't understand: that friendship means total commitment.

"Auschwitz brought out the best in some people and the worst in some people. There was no politeness in Auschwitz, but there was far more humanity and, in some respects, more kindness than you find in society today.

"And this . . . this is what I've been searching for."

Epilogue

The use of history is to give value to
the present hour.

—R. W. Emerson

In the early days of March 1945, the House of Commons was in a self-congratulatory and end-of-term mood. Churchill, brimming with confidence, was "behaving like a schoolboy." Harold Nicolson, who five years before had sat in the House deeply moved as Winston had recounted the fall of France, was beginning to feel a long-forgotten tingle in his blood. He had lived through the darkest hour, and the finest hour, the "end of the beginning," and all the other turning points and crises of the long struggle, but now he was packing his bags and off to Paris in the morning. He knew at last that the Allies had won the war. He had felt sure when he read the headline on the *Evening News* tossed over the back of a leather armchair in the smoking room: Tanks Massing for Cologne. It was all over bar the shouting.

It was in this jubilant frame of mind that on March 6 Parliament heard for the first time that the Royal Air Force had dropped British women behind enemy lines in France to help in the secret work of the Resistance. It was a brief announcement, buried deep in the business of the day, giving no details of who or how many were involved. *Hansard*, the official record of Parlia-

275

ment, reported that MPs laughed as they heard the story of a WAAF officer whose parachute had failed to open until the very last minute and who was saved from serious injury only by the thick wads of paper francs that were packed around her body. It was as though, even after six years of total war, the idea of women at arms was still not entirely serious. Perhaps if they had been told more of the truth, MPs would have reacted differently. It was only a few weeks since several of the women agents had been shot at Ravensbrück. Others, Mary Lindell among them, were still clinging on to life in the nightmare world of the concentration camps.

But the object of this book has not been to prove that women can be brave as well as beautiful. Who in the 1980s would deny it? The strange thing is that it was not more widely accepted in 1940. Nor has the purpose been to demonstrate that women have the political nous and moral insight to make important decisions, although, once again, this was not an idea that could be taken for granted in 1940. For instance, in that year, in *The Psychology of Fear and Courage,* a popular handbook designed to boost morale, the author, Edward Glover, director of research at the Institute of Psychoanalysis in London, could write:

> There are many broad-minded women who feel that the immediate welfare of the family comes before any long distance war aim. Only when the husband himself is devoted to these aims is an effective solution possible, for the woman can devote herself to the ideal simply because it is her husband's. It is a solution that depends on the woman's indulgence of the man's ulterior devotions—which appear to her sometimes as rather boyish whimsies.*

---

*Edward Glover, *Psychology of Fear and Courage* (Penguin Books, 1940).

Tell that to Mary Lindell, or Hiltgunt Zassenhaus, or Maria Rutkiewicz, or Sigrid Lund, or Kitty Hart.

Five stories among the millions. Too few and yet too many for generalization. What conclusion can we draw from these remarkable wartime careers? The ideals from which their actions derived authority differed in almost every case: patriotism, communism, the sanctity of life, or sheer lust for life. Of the five perhaps Sigrid Lund and Hiltgunt Zassenhaus were closest in spirit. But what did Mary Lindell, whose world view had remained unchanged since the time when the definition of an island was a piece of land surrounded on all sides by the Royal Navy, have in common with Maria Rutkiewicz, a child of purge and revolution? What can be said about these five women except that they all had the courage of their convictions?

"Courage," said Winston Churchill, "is rightly esteemed the first of human qualities because . . . it is the quality which guarantees all others." But courage itself does not discriminate between right and wrong. At one time the "blond god" Reinhard Heydrich was the most admired and popular man in Germany, his courage a byword among a whole generation of Germans who would now regard him as a monster. "Evil has its heroes as well as good," wrote La Rochefoucauld. Virtue has no monopoly on loyalty, fortitude, patriotism, camaraderie, courage or conviction. They are qualities shared by the SS as well as the Knights of the Round Table, or for that matter the Boy Scouts. How can the Knight be certain as he rides from Camelot that he will not end up in the *Einsatzkommando?* If, as it has been said, history demands not only exemplary choices, but also efficacious attitudes,* courage may well be indispensable for the attitudes—but does it help with the choice? Who decides whether the quest is good?

---

*Albert Camus.

The two traditional ways of answering this question were summed up by the Italian general and historian Pietro Colletta: "The gods placed upon earth two judges of human actions—Conscience and History." But this does not help us now. Under a totalitarian state these judges, though perhaps appointed by God, are in the pay of the state. State theologians replace the promptings of conscience; state historians write only the official version of events. Colletta's contemporary Napoleon was probably nearer the truth when he remarked, "History is a set of lies agreed upon by historians." In Nazi Germany it was a set of lies agreed upon by Hitler. Recognizing his enormous and sinister power, we should not be surprised that his view of the world gained an extraordinary plausibility.

The Nazi state monopolized all powers of persuasion. It controlled all blandishment and punishment. It did not only threaten—it mesmerized even those it had promised to destroy. This is the memory of a young Jewish girl: "It was 1936, I was 13, travelling to Vienna from my boarding school in England. The train stopped at Nuremberg—it was the day of the rally and we were told we would be held up for several hours. 'Why don't you go and see it?' said the guard to me and another little girl. 'It's exciting.' We went. We stood way back on the very edge of what looked like a million people, all standing in perfect symmetry and brilliant light and darkness. It was the most beautiful thing I had ever seen. And when this man suddenly appeared, seemingly out of nowhere, and all alone, the sound of his steps echoing in the huge arena, and walked the long long distance to the platform, I felt and shared the vibrant silence of that mass of people, and then, when he arrived, and the shout began— 'Sieg Heil, Sieg Heil' . . . I suddenly felt myself shouting with them—and so did my English friend, who spoke no German."

"I knew, at 13, what Hitler was. I had listened to clever people; and I knew that dreadful things were going to happen in our lives. I never told anyone about my hour at the Nuremberg rally: it was then, and remains, a thing of shame."*

As theatre and as politics, it was incredibly successful. The show ran and ran. Within five years it had run all over Europe. Who, then, in 1941 or 1942, with the German Army in control from Moscow to the Mediterranean, could have doubted that Hitler and his eighty million Germans were providentially blessed, or that they stood at the very pinnacle of history? Who could have been sure, in the face of such manifest success, that one's scruples were not "bourgeois sentimentality" or "human weakness"? Now, with hindsight—and in safety—it is easy to recognize the enormities of the Nazi period. But then it was easier and often more tolerable to be deceived. Those who resisted at this time were either very desperate or very sure of themselves. Most people were neither.

"What impressed me in all this Nazi experience was how vulnerable human nature is," Adelaide Hautval, the brave French doctor from Auschwitz, told listeners on BBC radio in 1971. "We always thought in France that we were above certain practices, certain theories. But it is not true. You only have to be indoctrinated about something for months, for years, to end up believing it. And once you believe certain people inferior, it becomes perfectly natural to subject such people to experiments, and no reasoning can touch you."†

It did not help to try to keep apart, or to remain silent. Pastor Martin Niemöller, a German church leader, wrote in his memoirs published after the war:

---

*Gitta Sereny, *New Statesman*, May 19, 1978.
†Adelaide Hautval, *The Listener*, Vol. 86, No. 2221, 1971.

As soon as Hitler came to power, he arrested the leaders of the opposing parties, but I did not speak up, for it was not I. Then Hitler turned against the intellectuals in the universities, but I did not speak up, for it was not I; then he took the Jews, but I did not speak up, for it was not I. And when at last it was my turn, I could not speak up, for it was too late.

Silence was no answer. If you did not kill, you allowed others to kill for you. It was an important part of Adolf Eichmann's defense in Jerusalem that he heard no voices from the outside to make him think twice. "His conscience," wrote Hannah Arendt, "was indeed set at rest when he saw the zeal and eagerness with which 'good society' everywhere reacted as he did."

Not everyone in Germany was silent. By 1939 the concentration camps were full of those who had spoken up, Pastor Niemöller among them. But the opposition to Hitler in Germany was too little and too late. They put off stopping him until the price for stopping him grew too high. The European nations, in a similar fashion, missed their chances of containing him until it was no longer possible for them to do so. All Europe stood mesmerized like the little Jewish girl at Nuremberg.

Hitler was a wolf in wolf's clothing. Power was what mattered to him; power, and the appearance of power. If he had been in any doubt, it had proved its worth in the thirties when his enemies had backed away from any show of determination or force. In 1942, at the height of his conquests, when he held up the mirror of Europe, everything he saw told him his power was unassailable. What it did not tell him was that power was not everything.

Maria Zaborowska is now nearly sixty years old and lives in Warsaw. During the war she suffered more than her share of the horrors of Nazi Europe. In Paviak she worked in the laundry, washing the clothes of fellow prisoners the Gestapo had tortured; in Auschwitz she narrowly survived selections for the gas chambers; in Ravensbrück she was nearly starved to death. Today she looks back to the last moment of innocence. She was seventeen and still at school. It was the last day of the summer term at the end of the school year 1938–39. The headmistress entered the classroom and told the young girls, "I do not know in what circumstances we will meet again, but whatever they are, I hope you will never lose your humanity." From this moment Maria knew that something dreadful was going to happen. With this eerie warning, to guard the indefinable against the unimaginable, her childhood came to an end.

I met Maria Zaborowska in the autumn of 1978. I had travelled to Warsaw to find Polish women who had taken part in the Resistance, and for a week, in overheated coffee bars or sometimes at their homes, I listened as one by one they told me of their lives during the war. It was an overwhelming experience which I shall never forget. They are all getting old now, long entered upon a comfortable middle age. Yet from their handbags and bureaus they took out snapshots of a time when they were young girls and women living on the edge of existence. They spoke of extremes of cruelty and courage, and of events of horror and heroism as if they had happened only yesterday. Indeed, they spoke as if anyone could be a hero or heroine and that only by chance had it happened to them. The effect of these histories was at the same time exhilarating and difficult to bear. Often I would turn round to see that my interpreter, a young economics student, had begun to cry. *Gestapo, Auschwitz, roundup, transport, interrogation, concentration camp, execution* recurred so often that they seemed to denote everyday occurrences as natural as childbirths or weddings. During that brief week in Warsaw I learned from the faces of these ordinary women what it has cost in the twentieth century to be Polish and remain human. But more than that: In their way, they were a living definition of what humanity means. For they had seen humanity at its limits: when it was taken away, and when it was restored.

One of the women I spoke to was Ryszarda Hanin, a well-known actress in Poland. During the war she fought in a "rifle-girl" battalion of the First Division of the Polish Army, which had been created in the Soviet Union after the invasion of 1941. It was then that she first began to act, as a member of an army theatre group. But, as she insists, her main job was to be a soldier. "I took part in all the battles from Lenino to Berlin!" Ryszarda Hanin is a beautiful woman, with the countenance of a mature actress, sure of her powers. She told me her story in the bar of the National Theatre in Warsaw. Though she is a Communist, there was something almost regal about her as she spoke the long soliloquy of her history, interrupted from time to time only by young men who in the Polish way stopped to kiss her hand.

"I remember very well our first performance in Lublin. When we arrived there the city was silent and empty. The people, afraid of Germans, had hidden themselves in their houses. We saw the castle on the hill which had been used as a Gestapo jail during the war. We had to put it in order. When we entered, it seemed to be almost beyond our powers to look at the scenes we found. At the last moment, just before leaving the town, Germans shot all the prisoners in their cells. That summer was very hot and the corpses had to be buried quickly and the place disinfected with chemicals. The whole town smelled terrible. Later we would find out that almost on the outskirts had been the concentration camp Majdanek.

"We were busy with the castle until the afternoon and then we walked down to the city. It was still empty but we had a feeling of being observed carefully from behind the curtains. The poor, scared people did not believe our Polish uniforms, or the eagles on the caps. They thought that it was German provocation.

"Downtown we met the sappers who told us that the theatre had been cleared of mines. It was an old building, a Polish theatre changed by Germans into a cabaret. We moved our costumes over there. For the majority of us it was the first time on the stage. We wrote the announcements about the performance. As the town was blacked out, we decided to illuminate the theatre. It was the only bright building in the darkness. After an hour waiting, curtain down, somebody made the little hole and looked out. The auditorium was full of people sitting like dead bodies. Those scared people, at the verge of nervous breakdown, had come to the bright theatre like the moths to the lamp.

"We started with the performance. It was the new one, full of joy, happiness from our victory. The reaction of the soldiers for whom we had played before was spontaneous from the first minutes. But here in Lublin, after half an hour, was no reaction at all. We continued the performance, being watched with the dead eyes, until one girl presented the poem about Auschwitz camp. At one point in the poem an SS man shouts in German, '*Alle raus.*' [Everybody out!] The moment she spoke those words we witnessed a scene we had never seen before. The audience jumped out of the chairs and crowded towards the exits. The people panicked. They were scared to death, trampling over each other. We screamed at them hysterically. All of a sudden the idea came to us: Those people had not trusted us; they were sure that it had all been a trick. The Polish language meant nothing; Germans also could speak Polish. Those words *alle raus* had proved that they were right. For them it was one more German trap.

"But we were at a loss, none of us could stop them. Our director, Władysław Krasnowiecki, stepped onto the stage and tried to explain, speaking as if to children. His voice reached the first rows of the audience for whom there was no room at the exits. Gradually, those still crowding at the doors stopped since they were not pushed anymore. After some time we started the performance once again. This time all the people participated, singing the songs all together till three o'clock in the morning.

"I had never seriously thought about being a professional actress. I made up my mind after that performance. All the great words about the special mission of the theatre and the actors proved to be true. Today I think about my profession as a job, but that night I realized how it could be. It was not good theatre but we felt that we were needed badly.

"Next evening we wanted to stage one of Fredro's comedies. It was only twelve hours after our first performance in Lublin, but how different the audience was! The girls and women were wearing makeup and all of them put on their best clothes. They were chatting with friends as in a normal theatre. They hadn't seen anything like it for four years. Now they were glad to welcome us with the atmosphere of a great theatre and we did not want them to be disappointed. That was why our director's assistant came in front of the curtain and asked the audience to do the special favour for the actors. We already had made some costumes out of bandages and German uniforms, but our soldier boots were not suitable. We had played on the ground before and our boots had not been viewable from the audience.

"But in Lublin we played on a real stage, wearing shoes borrowed from the audience."

"Hell can endure only for a limited period and life will begin again one day," wrote Albert Camus. In such a way, with actors and actresses on a stage, the dead were reawakened in Lublin.

The women whose stories are told in this book fought for many reasons, but they did have one thing is common. For most people the true nature of the Nazi offense became apparent only after it was too late. They realized what they had lost only when they had lost almost everything. But these women knew what they were fighting for, before they knew what they were fighting against. Mary's patriotism, Maria's communism, the high principles which inspired Sigrid and Hiltgunt had all been at work in the world before Hitler appeared on the scene. This helps to explain why they were among the first to resist. It is difficult to imagine thinking of any of these women without at the same time thinking of what they stand for. So for them the threat of Nazism was only too clear from the start. Hitler wanted for Nazi Germany what he was not prepared to allow for others. Moreover, once he controlled everything outside peoples' heads, he was determined to control everything inside as well. This was only acceptable to those who did not value what was inside their heads. For Mary, Sigrid, Maria and Hiltgunt, it was an attack on their humanity. It had to be resisted as powerfully as Kitty resisted the attacks on her life.

There is a way in which, like Ryszarda Hanin, these five women were actors too. Hitler had no part for them or their ideas in his new Europe. They each decided to act nevertheless. The performance was necessarily lonely and secret, but even so there were always at least two in the audience. They were Pietro Colletta's old friends History and Conscience. Only this time they no longer represented the gods, nor were they in the pay of the state. This time they were working at the level of ordinary men and women, seeking no more than to build a world fit for ordinary men and women. And so, on the shaking, half-lit but magnificent stage of the Resistance, Mary, Sigrid, Maria, Hiltgunt and Kitty appeared for a short while, playing the parts of heroines but wearing the shoes of ordinary people.